20—
(296)

D1351489

COLLINS GUIDE TO
THE RUINED ABBEYS OF ENGLAND,
WALES AND SCOTLAND

COLLINS GUIDE TO THE RUINED ABBEYS OF ENGLAND, WALES AND SCOTLAND

Henry Thorold

with photographs by Peter Burton and Harland Walshaw
and a Foreword by A. L. Rowse

HarperCollins*Publishers*

HarperCollins*Publishers*
77–85 Fulham Palace Road,
Hammersmith, London W6 8JB

Published by HarperCollins*Publishers* 1993

1 3 5 7 9 8 6 4 2

Copyright © Henry Thorold 1993

Henry Thorold asserts the moral right to
be identified as the author of this work

A catalogue record for this book is
available from the British Library

ISBN 0 00 217716 1

Set in Linotron Ehrhardt by
Rowland Phototypesetting Ltd
Bury St Edmunds, Suffolk

Printed in Great Britain by
HarperCollinsManufacturing, Glasgow

CONTENTS

ENGLAND

LIST OF ILLUSTRATIONS

All photographs supplied by Peter Burton unless stated otherwise.

Between pages xxx–1

Guisborough Priory, Yorkshire
The late Norman Lady Chapel, Glastonbury, Somerset
The 14th-century abbot's kitchen, Glastonbury
The new refectory, Cleeve, Somerset
The monastic guesthouse, Coverham, Yorkshire
Carved panel of the Norman Cavatorium, Wenlock, Shropshire
The Lay Brothers' undercroft, Waverley, Surrey
Fragment of the western tower and transepts, Kelso, Scotland
Carthusian church, Mount Grace, Cleveland
The grand east end, Walsingham, Norfolk
The 14th-century monastic gatehouse, Alnwick, Northumberland
Fragments of the Gilbertine priory, Mattersey, Nottinghamshire

Between pages 32–33

Denny Abbey, Cambridgeshire
The mediaeval figure of St Christopher, Norton, Cheshire
The 12th-century nave arcade and crossing arches, Calder, Cumberland
Doorway with the head of Amicia, Countess of Devon, Buckland, Devon
Early 15th-century gatehouse, Cornworthy, Devon
St Nicolas Priory, Exeter
Frithelstock Priory, North Devon
Plymouth Friary, Devon
Forde Abbey, Dorset
The monastic chapter house, Forde
The entrance to Abbot Chard's tower, Forde
Flaxley, Gloucestershire
Blackfriars Dominican church, Gloucester

Between pages 64–65

Fragments of arcades and cloisters, Hailes, Gloucestershire
The roof bosses, Hailes
14th-century gatehouse, Kingswood, Gloucestershire
Fragment of the Hospitallers' Chapel, Godsfield, Hampshire
13th-century fragments, Mottisfont, Hampshire
Netley Abbey, Hampshire
Titchfield Abbey, Hampshire
Wigmore Abbey, Herefordshire
The first Franciscan building in England, Canterbury, Kent
Reculver Abbey, Kent
Cockersand chapter house, Lancashire

Between pages 96–97

The monastic precinct of the Augustinian priory, Ulverscroft, Leicestershire
Gatehouse, and chapter house, Thornton, Lincolnshire
West front of small 14th-century Norfolk priory, Beeston Regis
Burnham Abbey, Norfolk
Norman west front, Castle Acre, Norfolk
The ruined Coxford Priory, Tattersett, Norfolk
Wall paintings in the refectory, Horsham St Faith, Norfolk
Marham Abbey, Norfolk
Hulne Priory, Northumberland
The Norman west front, Lindisfarne, Northumberland
East end of Tynemouth Priory, Northumberland
The Percy Chapel, Tynemouth

Between pages 160–161

14th-century Carthusian church, Beauvale, Nottinghamshire
Buildwas Abbey, Shropshire
The late Norman entry into the chapter house, Haughmond, Shropshire
Lilleshall Abbey, Shropshire
Stavordale, Somerset
The long single lancets of the west front, Croxden, Staffordshire
The gatehouse, Butley, Suffolk
Newark Priory, Surrey
Battle Abbey, Sussex
The east wall, Bayham, Sussex

Between pages 256–257

ACKNOWLEDGEMENTS

Collins Guide to the Ruined Abbeys is, of course, a sequel to *Collins Guide to Cathedrals, Abbeys and Priories*, which was published in 1986. The first volume dealt only with England and Wales: it was Mr Ian Chapman, then Chairman of Collins, who suggested that this succeeding volume should include his native Scotland; what a pleasure and what hard work this addition has been! Melrose and Dryburgh, Inchcolm and Inchmahome – what marvels these are, and, above all, Oronsay, most elusive and inaccessible of all.

Once again I am extremely grateful to Mr Peter Burton for his photographs and his company, driving mile after endless mile from Aberdeenshire to Cornwall, from Flintshire to Kent, and to Mr Harland Walshaw for his photographs and his unfailing help. Dr A. L. Rowse's magnificent Foreword provides a wonderful boost for the book: great gratitude to him.

Great gratitude, too, to a host of friends who have entertained us and sent us on our way – friends at the four corners, such as Lady Victoria Wemyss at Wemyss, and Sir William and Lady Gladstone at Hawarden, Mr and Mrs Harold Hartley at Trenarren, and Mr and Mrs John Cooper at Waldron; and friends throughout the country – it is thanks to them that we can claim to have visited every ruin described in this book: Miss Dorothy Bartholomew at Norwich, Mr and Mrs John Bell at Lancing, Professor and Mrs Peter Branscombe at St Andrews, Mr and Mrs Mark Bence-Jones at Orwell Park, Mrs Croft-Murray at Croft, Canon and the late Mrs John Fitch at Monks Eleigh, Lady Harrod at Holt, Mr and Mrs John Holder at Ellesmere, the late Mr John Piper, C. H. and Mrs Piper at Fawley, Mr and Mrs Dennis Seaward at Sherborne, Professor and Mrs Arthur Terry at Colchester, and the Bishop of Winchester and Mrs James at Wolvesey. Besides all these, we are more than grateful to those who have accompanied us on numberless expeditions: Mr John Barratt, Dr Mervyn James, Mr Gordon Partington, Dr John Martin Robinson, Mr John Stevens-Guille and the Revd George Thomson. Mr Bryan Hall and Mr Norman Scarfe assisted us with valuable information concerning Norfolk and Suffolk, Mr Hubert Fenwick with the account of Pittenweem, Dr Arnold Taylor provided fascinating information concerning Evesham, Mr Anthony

New inspired us with his remarkable guidebooks to the abbeys of England and Scotland (published by Constable), Mr Robin Reeve lent me his copy of that invaluable work *Medieval Religious Houses* by Dom David Knowles and Mr Neville Hadcock, and Prebendary Gerard Irvine helped in his usual way.

Finally I must thank Mr Richard Ollard for befriending the book from the beginning, Mr Stuart Proffitt, most sympathetic and able of editors, and Miss Rebecca Wilson his assistant, and Miss Vera Brice for its accomplished and delightful design.

HENRY THOROLD
Marston Hall, Grantham
St Matthias the Apostle,
February 1993.

To the memory of

DAME EUGENIA THOROLD, OSB
Abbess of Pontoise
(died 1667)

DAME CHRISTINA	DAME ANNE CATHERINE
THOROLD, OSB	THOROLD, OSB
of Pontoise	*of Pontoise*
(died 1699)	*(died 1707)*

and

SISTER CATHERINE THOROLD, OSB
of Ghent
(died 1634)

Daughters of St Benedict

LAUS DEO

MAPS

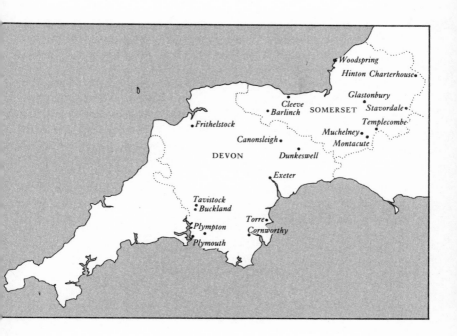

South West England

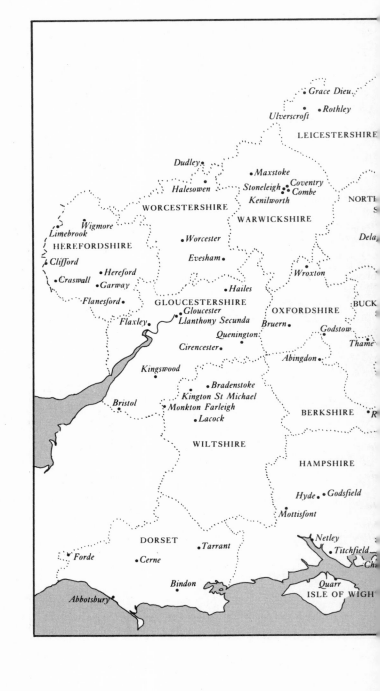

Grace Dieu
Rothley
Ulverscroft
LEICESTERSHIRE
Dudley
Maxstoke
Halesowen
Stoneleigh
Coventry
Combe
Kenilworth
NORTH
S
WORCESTERSHIRE
WARWICKSHIRE
Wigmore
Limebrook
Worcester
Dela
HEREFORDSHIRE
Evesham
Clifford
Wroxton
Hereford
Craswall
Garway
Hailes
Flanesford
GLOUCESTERSHIRE
OXFORDSHIRE
BUCK
Gloucester
Flaxley
Llanthony Secunda
Bruern
Godstow
Quenington
Thame
Cirencester
Abingdon
Kingswood
Bradenstoke
Bristol
Kington St Michael
Monkton Farleigh
BERKSHIRE
Lacock
R
WILTSHIRE
HAMPSHIRE
Hyde
Godsfield
Mottisfont
DORSET
Netley
Tarrant
Titchfield
Forde
Cerne
Chi
Bindon
Quarr
Abbotsbury
ISLE OF WIGH

Burnham Norton •
North Creake •
Coxford •
Walsingham •
Beeston Regis •
Broomholm •
Hickling •
King's Lynn • Pentney • Castle Acre • Ludham •
West Acre Yarmouth
Marham • Horsham St Faith • Carrow •• Norwich
NORFOLK Langley •
Herringfleet •
Thetford •
Isleham •
Dunwich •
Ixworth • Eye • Sibton •
Denny • Anglesey Little Welnetham Alnesbourne •
ushmead • Cambridge •• Barnwell Butley •
CAMBRIDGESHIRE SUFFOLK
Old Warden • Clare •
Chicksands Sudbury • Kersey •
OFORD-
SHIRE
Colchester •
ESSEX St Osyth's •
Latton •
Bicknacre • Beeleigh •
Tho'by •
Prittlewell •
Charterhouse • Barking •
LONDON Lesnes •
St John's Jerusalem •
Reculver •
ewark Boxley • Canterbury •
SURREY KENT
rley Moatenden •
Swingfield •
St Radegund's • Dover •
brede Bayham Horton •
SUSSEX Robertsbridge • Bilsington •
ourne Rye •
Hardham Battle • Winchelsea
Lewes •
Tortington Michelham •
Wilmington •
Langney •

Southern England

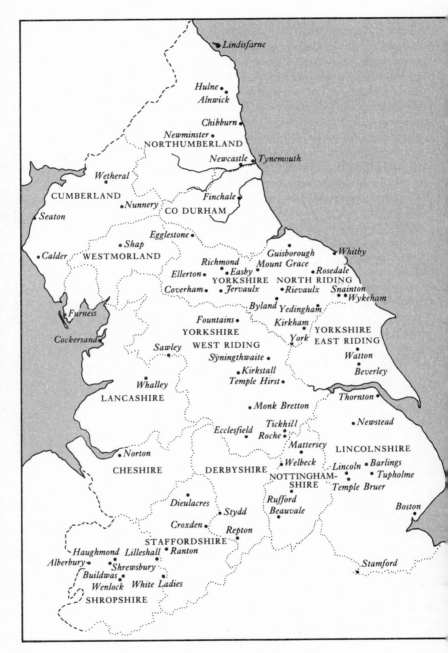

Northern England

Basingwerk

Valle Crucis

Cymmer

Strata Florida

Abbey Cwmhir

St Dogmaels

Talley

Llanthony

Neath

Tintern

Cardiff

Wales

Scotland

FOREWORD

Half the pleasure of living in an old country comes from the relics and evidences of its historic past. Of these among the most remarkable are the ruins of the abbeys, cathedrals and churches of the Middle Ages. They take us into the heart of that vanished age – if we would understand it, and its beliefs and values.

These works of love, of religion and art – with their soaring arches and gables, their piers and traceried windows, occasionally an image of the Virgin Mary or Saint left high up to tell us their dedication – add distinction to the landscapes where we encounter them. In later centuries they have been an inspiration to many artists for paintings or detailed drawings – Turner, Girtin, Cotman – so that Tintern, Fountains, Glastonbury are familiar to us even if we have not visited them. And there has been a cult of ruins from the eighteenth century, if not before, with the antiquarian Dugdale, the poet Gray and Horace Walpole leading the way.

Henry Thorold is of that select company. Here the pleasure is doubled if we visit these delectable scenes with someone who can tell us so much about them. And what an eye he has! Not only for the buildings, the architecture and the skills that went into their making, on which he is an expert, but their setting, the scene itself, the hills and vales (which the monks usually chose for their location), the streams and meadows and trees.

Goodness, how much I envy his sense of topography! He has travelled the country over years, penetrating into Scotland and to the far-off Hebrides, *terra incognita* to me. We may recognize famous Holyrood and Melrose, along with Walter Scott – another devotee of Henry's company. But he has managed to get to the lonely little isle of Oronsay, in pursuit of ruins, and I love his description of having to paddle back to Colonsay to get away again, unless he and his companion were to be marooned for days. For this book is as human as it is scholarly – he knows about Arbroath smokies as well as Craster kippers.

The knowledge that we can pick up as we go along with him, the expertise we can admire, the sheer virtuosity so lightly worn! Who among us had ever heard of the Valliscaulian Order (from the Val des Choux)? I hadn't. Apparently there were three of their houses in Scotland, of which one has been valiantly revived today, at Pluscarden up on the beautiful Moray Firth. Henry, of course, has visited this rarity.

We need not go into the historic issues. I suppose the Reformation was inevitable, but it was a pity that it was so drastic. As an historian I never forgive artistic losses, the boat-loads of treasures – books, manuscripts, vestments, alabasters, sculptures – that went abroad. Henry VIII should have saved more of the abbeys for cathedrals – I lament the loss of Bury St Edmunds, as splendid as Ely, or Reading; Kirkstall would have made a good cathedral for Leeds, as Osney for Oxford – its fine tower remained to decorate the skyline right up into the eighteenth century. Actually it was intended to retain a dozen – and then the bellicose old monster got involved in the frightful expense of his third French war.

Henry Thorold shares the faith that inspired those marvellous, so much regretted, fanes. But even a secular person like myself can share his enthusiasm, and be grateful for all that he brings alive for us again.

A. L. ROWSE

INTRODUCTION

There it stands, like a great piece of stage scenery, across the fields, across the hedges, a tree here or there, chimneys or rooftops of the little town to the right, a copse to the left, the long line of the Cleveland Hills in the distance behind. It is an enormous Gothic gable end all by itself, a huge empty window bereft of its tracery – only the little window above with some tracery left – solid pointed pinnacles on either side, solid pointed pinnacles to terminate the lower walls below. This is Guisborough Priory, founded for Augustinian canons *c.* 1120.

It is a tremendous piece of scenery – all that we possess to tell us all that we can ever know of a great foundation. The first church was destroyed by fire in 1289 – and this is all that survives of the rebuilding, which started, as usual, from the east – a grand new east end of perhaps 1300. We can see the magnificent outline, the one little traceried window, and visualize the tracery, the geometrical tracery, which filled the others, admire the buttresses, the crocketed pinnacles – and imagine the rest: the cruciform plan, the transepts, the nave, the two western towers which, as at York or Beverley, completed the west end.

But all is over now; the play is done, the players departed, the audience gone. It must have been a great performance – the rebuilding perhaps completed by the end of the century, life going on, the quire filled with its canons, the music, the plainsong, the prayers – a great performance indeed, day in, day out, night in, night out, the canons fulfilling their obligations according to the Rule of St Augustine, in their church and in their monastery, going out from here to minister in the churches and parishes around. The priory was their powerhouse and their home, and so continued until the end, when the final act was performed, the concluding prayers recited, the last candle put out.

This is a book about the ruined abbeys and priories and other religious houses of England, Wales and Scotland. It is a sequel to *Collins Guide to Cathedrals, Abbeys and Priories of England and Wales* (published in 1986), which dealt with the abbeys and priories still in use for worship.

That was a very different task to which author and photographer set themselves: the former book took them all over England and Wales to see such monastic churches as are still in use: great churches like Westminster or Bath, Tewkesbury or Sherborne – and many a smaller church, or part of one, like Croyland or Boxgrove, Blanchland or Stogursey. It was an orderly procession of churches, all in orderly state.

But this has been a very different task, not merely visiting the great ruins like Glastonbury and Tintern, Fountains and Cleeve – but those incredible smaller fragments, like Coverham and Latton, Beauvale and Cerne. Some, moreover, were well concealed, embedded in later buildings, or stranded and put to unexpected uses: farms, or old people's clubs, or girls' schools or stately homes, or public bars; or even one abandoned in a car breaker's yard. They took us from Aberdeenshire to Cornwall, from North Wales to Kent.

The Religious Orders

Something must be said about the Religious Orders which built these fabulous churches, now torn down. St Benedict was the founder of Western Monasticism: in 529 he established his first monastery at Monte Cassino, and formulated his rule, based on the vows of poverty, obedience and chastity. The monks' day was divided between the worship of God in the celebration of the Mass and the recitation of the Canonical Offices, the work of the cloister in meditation, and the copying, translating and illuminating of manuscripts, and the work of the fields to provide the necessary food and clothing. St Augustine (of Canterbury) brought this noble rule to England, and founded the first Benedictine abbey in England, in Canterbury in 598. Most of the monastic cathedrals in England were Benedictine, and many of the most famous abbeys. Many of these are still in use, but Glastonbury, Whitby and Battle are among the celebrated Benedictine ruins.

During the eleventh century, the Benedictine Order seeming insufficiently austere, a Reformed Benedictine Order was founded at Cluny under the Abbot Hugh, which spread rapidly. The Cluniac houses were all completely dependent on Cluny, and were therefore only priories, all real power being in the hands of the Abbot of Cluny. Lewes was the first Cluniac house in England, founded in 1078; Much Wenlock followed in 1080, and Castle Acre, daughter to Lewes, in 1089. Very little remains of Lewes, but there is a good deal to see at Much Wenlock and Castle Acre.

Towards the end of the eleventh century a still stricter Order was founded at Cîteaux, and its rule, again based on St Benedict's, was drawn up by St Stephen Harding, an Englishman from Sherborne in Dorset. He and his disciple St Bernard of Clairvaux were the founders of the Order – and it spread like wildfire through Europe, and in England. The Cistercians (who took their name from Cîteaux) insisted that their houses should be built in desolate, wild places, far from towns and civilization, and forbade in their churches all unnecessary ornament and decoration. It was the spiritual ideals of the movement, the intellectual prowess of their leaders, and the calm beauty and simplicity of its buildings reflecting the peace and serenity of its life, which were its powerful influences. Waverley, in 1128, was the first Cistercian foundation in England; then Tintern in 1131, and Rievaulx and Fountains in 1132, followed very soon; and the movement spread throughout the country. As their houses were in such remote places, little use could be found for them after the Dissolution, and it is the Cistercian ruins – Fountains, Rievaulx, Tintern especially – which are the most magnificent anywhere.

Mention must be made of the 'family' of Savigny, who were almost identical in their aims to the Cistercians, and merged with them in 1147; also of the Benedictine Order of Tiron, with its houses at Kelso and St Dogmaels, and of the Grandmontines, who are represented by what appears to be a farmhouse at Alberbury in Shropshire, and that exceedingly remote priory at Craswall in Herefordshire; both were small ascetic orders, owing much to Cîteaux as well as to St Benedict.

The most austere Order of all was the Carthusian, which was founded by St Bruno at La Chartreuse in 1084 – a name which was anglicized into 'Charterhouse'. St Bruno's rule was based on the hermit ideal of each monk living almost entirely on his own, in his own little house, or 'cell'. All these were grouped around a spacious cloister, and each cell had its own little garden: here each monk could live an almost completely isolated life, meeting his own brethren only in church, or occasionally in chapter house or refectory. There were only nine Carthusian houses in England. Mount Grace in Yorkshire is remarkably well preserved; the chapter house at Hinton Charterhouse in Somerset is a building of the greatest charm; fragments of the church and prior's house now incorporated in part of a farm still stand at Beauvale in Nottinghamshire.

The Augustinian Canons, or Black Canons, so named because of the colour of their habits, first appeared in England c. 1100: they were quite different from the other Orders, an altogether more comfortable lot. They were an order of preachers, who, though living under rule, and in communities, worked in the world. Their rule was based on the rule of St Augustine of Hippo, and their more liberal ideals and more sociable way of life commended them to the people at large. Never as rich as the Benedictines, they had their smaller houses all over England – little priories like Bicknacre and Thoby, Bushmead and Shulbrede and Bilsington. In addition, they had their larger houses like Walsingham and Thornton, and St Botolph's at Colchester, their first foundation in England. So there is plenty of theirs to see, everywhere. Under the term 'Augustinian' we include those canons who followed the observance of Arrouais or of St Victor; common links and common culture gave the Black Canons unity under the rule of St Augustine.

The Premonstratensians, or White Canons because of their white habits, were an offshoot of the Black Canons, but more austere; they were far less prolific, and owed much to the Cistercians. They took their name from Prémontré, where they were founded by St Norbert in 1123. Bayham and Torre, Alnwick and Easby and Shap are all evocative ruins, and reminders of the White Canons.

The Gilbertines were the one English Order, named after St Gilbert of Sempringham, their founder. Theirs was a double Order, of monks and nuns, who occupied adjacent houses, and had separate cloisters, but worshipped in the same church, which was divided by a high wall so that they could hear each others' voices, praising God, and all share in the celebration of the Mass, but could not see each other. The men followed the rule of St Augustine, the women that of St Benedict. The Order was founded c. 1130 at Sempringham in Lincolnshire, and it spread rapidly in Lincolnshire and neighbouring counties, twenty-six houses being founded in all – but few ruins survive. Chicksands Priory in Bedfordshire now stands within an important RAF and USAF base – converted into a grand quadrangular country house after the Dissolution; at Watton in the East Riding of Yorkshire the imposing prior's house survives, still a private house; the only Gilbertine ruin is the small romantic fragment at Mattersey in willowy flat countryside by the River Idle in Nottinghamshire. Nothing whatever survives at Sempringham itself, in the low undulating country on the edge of the fens north of Bourne, where the saint was born in (probably) 1083 – only a few bumps in the grass, and the lonely church across the fields from the road, the Norman church built by the saint's father, where the Order was founded – the village church, except that there is no village. Here was the mother house of the only English Order, here was the saint's shrine; it is a place of beauty and romance, which, in the words of Dom David Knowles, 'makes in its own way as striking an appeal to the imagination as . . . Fountains or Glastonbury.'

There were, besides, the two military orders, the Knights Hospitallers, and the Knights Templars. The Hospitallers were founded in 1092 with the building of a hospital in Jerusalem, for the benefit of pilgrims to the holy places, and to provide hospitality for them on their way to Jerusalem. They were essentially an international and military order, and in the twelfth century established some fifty houses in England, their headquarters being at St John's Priory, Clerkenwell. They were the Knights of the Order of St John of Jerusalem, followed the rule of St Augustine, and wore a distinctive uniform, a white cross emblazoned on their black tunics.

The Templars were founded in 1118 to guard the Holy Sepulchre in Jerusalem, and to build and guard the roads leading to the Holy Land. They built round churches after the plan of the Holy Sepulchre, and their headquarters in England, the celebrated Temple Church in London, survives as the church of the Inns of Court. They became rich and very powerful, and therefore suspect, and, accused of many crimes (never wholly explained), were suppressed by the Pope between 1308 and 1312, many of their houses being transferred to the Hospitallers. Few of their houses survive, even as ruins: there is the hall of the preceptory at Snainton in Yorkshire, for centuries embedded in a later farmhouse, a fragment at Templecombe in Somerset, much more at Temple Bruer in Lincolnshire, and the important preceptory at Torphichen in Midlothian (part used as the parish kirk).

Early in the thirteenth century there appeared in England the friars – a new type of religious order, their name derived from *frère* (the French) or *frater* (the Latin) for brother; they came as mendicant brethren, relying solely on alms for their sustenance. St Francis was born in 1181 or 1182, and 'his coming was like the coming of a fresh spring breeze to a tired world'. He was such an attractive character, and his influence so infectious that he rapidly gathered around him a great company of disciples; so was the Franciscan movement born. The first Franciscans reached Canterbury in 1224: some moved on to London, Oxford and Cambridge, and soon the movement reached Norwich and Bristol and York. The Franciscans were the Grey Friars, from the colour of their habits; the Black Friars, the Dominicans, were the disciples of St Dominic – the '*Domini canes*,' the dogs of the Lord – who reached this country a year or two before; the Carmelites, the White Friars, *c.* 1241, the Austin Friars a few years later. They all had much in common, and worked on much the same lines, making at once for the towns and cities – and especially the universities – as preachers and missioners, to minister to the people both spiritually and physically, and, particularly the Dominicans, intellectually. The monks had shut themselves up in their community houses, away from the world; the friars were in the world, if not of the world: their influence was far-reaching and enormous. They held no property, and their churches or houses were held for them in trust – so they have left no great buildings, no great ruins, behind them. The ruin of the Greyfriars church in Gloucester is of great interest, as are the towers of their churches in King's Lynn and Richmond in Yorkshire; the friary of the Austin Friars at Clare is a rare survival, as is the Carmelites' gatehouse at Burnham Norton; the friary at Canterbury makes a special appeal, the first Franciscan house in England. So many of their houses survive as small mediaeval buildings in back streets, hard to find; but in so many ancient towns in England there is likely to be a street called Friargate, or Blackfriars, and even an Underground station in London of that name – reminding us that the friars were there.

The Dissolution

The whole story of the Dissolution is, of course, disgraceful and distressing. We know that the Templars were suppressed by the Pope between 1308 and 1312 – at least there were charges against them, and their property was mostly handed on to the Hospitallers; we know that a number of alien priories were dissolved in the fifteenth century during the French wars – at least a plea could be made on account of the 'national emergency'; in the next century Wolsey dissolved a few smaller monasteries in order to endow his college at Oxford (later Christ Church), and Bishop Alcock suppressed St Radegunda's at Cambridge, where numbers were down to two, in order to found Jesus College. All this seems questionable. But the wholesale destruction of monasteries, great and small, was a disgrace, and performed in a most dishonourable and dishonest way. To begin with, the smaller houses were destroyed, on some specious charges – and at the same time fulsome and insincere compliments were paid to the greater foundations, to assure them that no designs were being planned against them. Then the axe fell. One or two holy abbots were murdered – the Abbot of Glastonbury, the Abbot of Kirkstead, and some of their brethren with them. The rest were 'pensioned off' or given bishoprics or deaneries – as though any man can 'pay off' a religious vocation, or life vows, like that. The nobility, the landowners of England, were bribed with the spoils of the monasteries, and so silenced: thus were the desires of a greedy king satisfied. Many may have been closed because of the shortcomings of a number of monastic houses in the sixteenth century; even members of religious orders are human, and fallible, prone to sin, victims of the Devil. But time and again we cannot but be struck by the obviously healthy state of many of the monasteries – and the way numbers kept up, especially in the smaller houses. But in an age of faltering faith and cooling piety, life must have been depressing at times. It was in some of the great houses that numbers were so reduced – at Rievaulx, for instance, where three hundred years before there had been 150 monks and 500 lay brothers, there were but 22 monks.

But despite the actions of a cruel king, religious faith – and the call of the cloister – ultimately survived. Meantime, the abbeys and priories of England became but 'bare ruined choirs', to become objects of curiosity and romance as time went on. So darkness descended.

There were, however, a few flickers of light: one was that little Anglican community at Little Gidding, founded by Nicholas Ferrar in 1625, mainly for a few members of his family, and one or two close friends. The saintly King, Charles I, visited it twice – but all was abandoned and destroyed in the Civil War; that other Cromwell was, after all, a near neighbour. Even now the adorable little seventeenth-century church survives, in the green fields of Huntingdonshire, and in our own time a new Anglican community has been founded here, the Community of Christ the Sower, once again on informal, family lines, and flourishes.

And the light flickered, too, across the water, where English exiles, members of faithful religious families, established themselves – especially the women – in Benedictine houses in France or Flanders. This book is dedicated to four such holy women, members of the author's family, who forsook England in order to help keep the Benedictine flame alight among English people in the seventeenth century. It was an act of self-sacrifice, and faith.

Then the tide turned: a few English exiles crept back to England, monks from Douai arrived in Shropshire in 1795, and settled at Downside in 1814. So that great Benedictine house was established, great house, great school. At much the same time that other exiled Benedictine community, descendants of the Benedictine community of Westminster, driven out of France by the Revolution, returned to England, and, thanks to Lady Anne Fairfax, settled at Ampleforth in 1793: hence that distinguished community, hence that famous school.

Dawn was at hand. The year is 1835, the site is Charnwood Forest.

Here, not far from the ruins of Ulverscroft, not far from the ruins of Grace Dieu – in a setting solitary, exposed and rocky, Ambrose Phillips de Lisle founded the first Cistercian monastery since the Reformation. This is Mount St Bernard's, in communion with the Church of Rome. Others followed. The Church of England followed – Cowley (1866), Mirfield (1892), Kelham (1894), the Oratory of the Good Shepherd (1913), the Society of St Francis (1921) – besides all the women's Orders: Ascot, Wantage, Clewer, East Grinstead, famous names indeed; contemplative nuns have since 1916 reoccupied the mediaeval priory buildings at Burnham – the Augustinian Society of the Precious Blood; and Burnham was originally founded in 1266 for Augustinian nuns. That deep religious impulse, that strong sense of vocation, that thirst for God, that call to the cloister, cannot be suppressed for ever by civil power or ecclesiastical legislation.

So here, in all these places, the praises of God are sung, sung again, still sung. Here the play is not over, the players not departed, and the worshippers once again stand or sit or kneel around, and the age-old refrain is taken up: *Gloria Patri et Filio, et Spiritui Sancto – sicut erat in principio, et nunc, et semper, et in saecula saeculorum. Amen.*

Guisborough: the east end of the church makes a most magnificent piece of stage scenery.

Cleeve: the new refectory, occupying the south walk of the cloister and as grand as a college hall at Oxford or Cambridge.

Opposite above: Glastonbury: the 14th-century abbot's kitchen from a corner of the late Norman Lady Chapel.
Below: Looking up into the vault of the abbot's kitchen.

Coverham: part of the nave arcade comes striding across the garden of the former monastic guesthouse.

Opposite above: Wenlock: a carved panel of the Norman Lavatorium, representing Christ walking on the water.

Below: Waverley: the Lay Brothers' undercroft is the best preserved fragment of the first English Cistercian house, near the River Wey in Surrey.

Kelso: the gaunt fragment of its western tower and transepts.

Opposite above: Mount Grace: the little Carthusian church against the background of the tree-hung Cleveland hills.

Below: Walsingham: the grand east end of the priory church is supported by buttresses decorated with flint flushwork.

Right: Alnwick: the awe-inspiring 14th-century monastic gatehouse looks down on the site of the Abbey in the park.

Below: Mattersey: fragments of the Gilbertine priory in Nottinghamshire, beside the River Idle, with views across the lonely meadows and stumpy willows.

ENGLAND

Bedfordshire

BUSHMEAD PRIORY

Augustinian

An unassuming iron gate in a leafy Bedfordshire lane in that quiet countryside on the borders of Huntingdonshire, and a long mysterious drive, little oak trees on one side, older chestnuts on the other, leads to another iron gate marked 'Private'; but on its left the drive goes on, and round another corner to reveal the mediaeval remains of Bushmead Priory.

Bushmead was founded by Hugh Beauchamp of Eaton Socon *c.* 1185 for Augustinian Canons. What remains is the thirteenth-century refectory, which must have formed the south range of the cloister, with the kitchen adjoining. After the Dissolution this was divided horizontally; a beautiful trefoiled doorway leads into the building, where later, sixteenth-century windows were inserted upstairs, with some old glass; the monastic range continues as a charming smaller eighteenth-century brick house. Nothing survives of the church, or other monastic buildings. It was always a small Augustinian house, with a prior and perhaps three or four canons.

In 1562 the property was acquired by William Gery, and the Wade-Gerys in course of time built an imposing eighteenth-century house, at right angles to the monastic range; but this has been pulled down. Grand garden walls, ancient trees, the surrounding woodlands, and at a short distance a pretty farmhouse, all combine to make this a delectable, evocative spot.

CHICKSANDS PRIORY

Gilbertine

ROYAL AIR FORCE
CHICKSANDS

proclaims the notice at the gate: in fact Chicksands is one of the principal US Air Force bases in Britain – the British HQ of the

USAF Security Services, commanding international communications worldwide. On the hill behind is the amazing erection, 110 feet high and 400 yards in diameter, officially termed the 'Flare 7 Antenna', unofficially nicknamed 'the Elephant Cage'. It is American airmen that we see everywhere, an American patrol car which sweeps up and down the drive, an American who is on duty at the gate. It is possible, by special arrangement, to visit the priory, but security is tight. This is Chicksands today.

But the Gilbertine priory was founded here in 1154, and was one of the largest of such houses, with some 55 canons and 120 nuns. The south cloister, the larger, was the nuns', the north, the smaller, the canons', with the church in between. Church and north cloister have disappeared, but the south cloister survives, reclothed maybe in eighteenth- or early nineteenth-century dress, converted into a family seat after the Dissolution. But the mediaeval bones are there all right, and it is the mediaeval timber roof which still encloses this great quadrangular building.

After the Dissolution, Chicksands was purchased in 1576 by Peter Osborne, Keeper of the Privy Purse to Edward VI, and remained in the possession of his descendants till 1936. The first Peter Osborne's grandson, Sir Peter, was Governor of Guernsey, and Guernsey was the last Royalist stronghold to survive in the Civil War. His son was created a baronet in 1661 in recognition of his father's services to the King, and the family remained prominent in national and local life.

Perhaps the most interesting member of the family was Dorothy Osborne, the daughter of the Governor of Guernsey, who married Sir William Temple, ambassador and statesman. Both their families were against their marrying, and her letters to him during the long years up to their marriage have survived and have become a classic. Dorothy herself is the subject of one of the portraits in Lord David Cecil's *Two Quiet Lives*. It was Sir William Temple who negotiated the marriage between William III and Mary II.

The only known picture of Chicksands at this time is the Buck print of 1730, which shows the monastic building still looking decidedly monastic, with Gothic windows, gabled ends to the west and south ranges, and great chimney breasts on both east and south sides; an outside staircase ascends to the first floor at the southeast corner, and a lower north wing extends at the side. A formal garden with topiary and flowers lies beneath the south front.

'Last night I was in the garden till Eleven a clock,' wrote Dorothy to William Temple on 16 July 1653. 'It was the sweetest night that ere I saw, the Garden looked soe well, and the Jessomin smelt beyond all perfumes, and yet I was not pleased. The place had all the Charmes it used to have when I was most sattisfied with it, and had you bin there I should have liked it much more then ever I did, but that not being it was noe more to mee then the next feilde . . .'

In about 1740 Isaac Ware was brought in to improve the place; he removed all the chimneys, which stood out like great warts along the two main fronts (east and south), and formed two even façades with long rows of Gothick windows, above and below, and pinnacled buttresses at the corners. On the east front he left the two mediaeval doorways, and the tiny oriel window near the south corner upstairs – a puzzling little mediaeval feature. The choice of Isaac Ware is puzzling, too: he was a strict Palladian, and protegé of Lord Burlington. He is said to have dismissed Gothic with the words: 'We will not descend to call it architecture' – yet here, although his interiors are Classical, his façades are Gothick, and very early Gothick at that, earlier than Strawberry Hill, or Lacock or Arbury.

In 1813 James Wyatt was called in to make further improvements: it was he who made the east front the entrance front, and built the charming little pinnacled porch, and tidied up the brick north wing – which, with its stone quoins and mullioned windows, forms a colourful gabled foil for the grey, orderly, rendered façades of the main house.

We enter by Wyatt's porch into his new entrance hall: this is low, wide and spacious, with an elegant ribbed plaster vault. It is one of Wyatt's happiest creations. To the left we enter the long mediaeval undercroft, now divided into various rooms, long, low and vaulted; or by Wyatt's staircase we can ascend to the grand eighteenth- or early nineteenth-century rooms of the *piano nobile*. To think that the nuns' dorter or frater could be so transformed! In the music room is the little mediaeval oriel window which we noticed outside: it is filled with fascinating stained glass of various periods collected by the 4th Baronet, and all most colourful; one panel portrays a lifelike fly, making its way across a sundial – '*Hinc humana leguntur tempora*' runs the inscription. All these eighteenth-century rooms are very handsome, and extraordinarily little known.

One room should be mentioned in particular, and in the north wing: the King James Room – formed to take the King James bed, which was presented to the family, the 'warming-pan bed', into which the Old Pretender was said to have been smuggled as a baby. It is a remarkable octagonal room, vaulted in plaster, and decorated in trompe d'oeil, if not by Wyatt by another hand working for him. It is a triumph, and again completely unknown to literature.

Chicksands was sold to the Commissioners for Crown Lands by Sir Algernon, the 7th Baronet, in 1936. It soon after became an RAF Signal Station, the USAF taking over in 1950. The future of this great house is uncertain and problematical, standing as it does empty and unused in the middle of this top-security site. Mercifully now there is a greater awareness of its importance, historically and architecturally. A few years ago a local society, The Friends of Chicksands Priory, was formed to care for the building – which remains RAF property. On Sunday afternoons – usually twice a month – the Friends show visitors round the priory, and refreshments are served. Opening times are advertised, and these are rare opportunities to visit a rare and very special house. But, as has been said, security is tight.

OLD WARDEN ABBEY

Cistercian

Warden Abbey was founded for Cistercian monks *c.* 1150. After the Dissolution the Gostwick family, who acquired the place, seem to have demolished everything, building a new Elizabethan brick house close to the east range of the cloister. Of this a very small fragment remains – battlemented, with a prominent chimney stack, mullioned windows, and ogival door (a very pretty piece). None of this appears to be monastic – except on the west side, part of a mediaeval buttress. But its purpose seems inexplicable. Excavations have revealed the layout of the cloisters, and of the chancel of the church, the rest being under the adjacent farmhouse. The little house now belongs to Sir John Smith's Landmark Trust, and of course is available for holiday letting. Monastic or not, it is an endearing little landmark.

Berkshire

ABINGDON ABBEY

Benedictine

The only photograph that anybody sees of Abingdon Abbey is of that familiar chimney: tall and solid, probably of the thirteenth century, it terminates in a gabled top, and under each gable there are three lancet-like openings for the smoke. But imagine the grand church, of which not one stone stands upon another, but which in its day was crowned with those three great towers. All that Abingdon Abbey can now boast is a chimney.

There is the tradition of a very early foundation (seventh century); the Abbey was refounded *c.* 954 by King Edred, under St Ethelwold, a pupil of St Dunstan; the town grew up at its gate.

The fifteenth-century gatehouse faces the town, and is attached to St Nicholas' Church; within the public gardens here is the site of the church; but there are not even foundations to see – only two re-erected arcades of low Perpendicular arches; but it is not known exactly where these came from. There are no cloisters or claustral buildings: there has been a clean sweep.

Only by the millstream are there what were the administrative buildings – first, the Granary Barn, then the checker hall ('checker' meaning exchequer), now used as the Unicorn Theatre; then the checker itself, then the so-called Long Gallery. This in its day formed various rooms, with the open gallery alongside, with its long unglazed window. This is undoubtedly the best, and least-altered surviving part of the Abbey, an important mediaeval building, if not in itself particularly monastic. Underneath are interesting undercrofts – and above the checker the celebrated chimney.

BISHAM ABBEY

Templar : Augustinian : Benedictine

That beautiful, mellow, country house, of many dates and many textures – stone, chalk, flint and brick – surrounded by smooth and

7

spacious lawns on the very bank of the Thames is always called Bisham Abbey, which indeed very briefly it was, but only very briefly. It has certainly had three monastic incarnations. The first was as a preceptory of the Templars, founded here *c.* 1139. On the suppression of that Order, the property did not pass (as so often) to the Hospitallers, but to the Augustinians (*c.* 1337). Almost certainly they built a church and cloister to the northeast: they may have made use of the preceptory for some purposes, but all this is uncertain. When the Augustinian priory was dissolved in 1536, it was – oddest twist of all – refounded by Henry VIII as a Benedictine abbey to pray for the soul of Jane Seymour; the community came from the dissolved abbey at Chertsey. But Henry soon changed his mind, and the abbey was again dissolved, in 1539.

Bisham was then granted to Sir Philip Hoby, and to him and his family we owe the house as it appears today. The vaulted thirteenth-century porch must be the Templars', with the original oak door leading into the screens passage and Great Hall. All this the Hobys transformed; indeed they wrapped the mediaeval preceptory round with an Elizabethan house. Most of what we see outside, and much of what there is inside is theirs, and their successors'. It became the perfect country house, in the perfect setting.

It is now the headquarters of the Central Council for Physical Education.

READING ABBEY

Cluniac : Benedictine

How many of those arriving here from Paddington realize that the site of a once-great abbey lies close to the railway line? Looking out of the window of the train there may be thoughts of Huntley and Palmers, of Oscar Wilde and *The Ballad of Reading Gaol* – there is a view of the gaol itself, and the crowded streets and buildings of the busy town – but thoughts of a great mediaeval abbey? Not likely. But wedged between the gaol, and the Roman Catholic church, and the railway, are indeed the scanty remains of Reading Abbey, founded by Henry I in 1121 – and where he was buried.

Reading Abbey was founded for Cluniac monks: Henry I had a special interest in the Cluniac Order and great were the endowments which he bestowed upon it. The church building was sufficiently far advanced for the King to be buried in front of the high altar; the church was finally consecrated by Archbishop Thomas à Becket in the presence of Henry II in 1164. Reading was the only Cluniac abbey in England, a sign of Royal favour (all the other Cluniac houses were priories). For reasons which are not known it became Benedictine in the thirteenth century.

The abbey gatehouse is the only building to survive complete: it is thirteenth century, but much restored by Sir G. G. Scott in 1879, and is now an interesting museum. Not far to the east stood the west front of the church, but of the church only fragments of the crossing remain, together with parts of the apsidal transept chapels. The chancel was apsidal, with a square-ended Lady Chapel added in the fourteenth century.

Much of the cloister is now used as a car park for the local offices: all the same, it is just possible to get some impression of the claustral buildings. The slype adjoins the south transept and the chapter house adjoins that: it was an enormous, lofty, vaulted building, where Parliament sat once or twice during the middle ages – still impressive in its roofless state. Otherwise it is a case of a wall here, a lump of masonry there. Little idea of architectural features can be grasped: there is nothing but cliffs, great or small, of flint rubble.

After the Dissolution Henry VIII formed some kind of royal palace from the claustral buildings, and the stone from the church seems to have been taken away and used elsewhere – for instance at Windsor. Henry I's tomb was broken up, and his bones scattered.

There was a great library at Reading Abbey, and some volumes survive. The most famous is one in the British Museum, which contains that very early and much-loved poem, 'Cuckoo Song' (c. 1226): 'Sumer is icumen in . . .'

Buckinghamshire

NOTLEY ABBEY

Augustinian

Gentle undulating Buckinghamshire countryside, of copses, and
hedges, and water meadows by the River Thame: Notley was founded
c. 1160 for Augustinian Canons, and was one of their larger houses,
with twenty or more canons in its heyday, and still about fifteen just
before the end. What survives is, as so often, the western range of the
cloister, together with the abbot's house, which adjoins it at the north
end. This makes a grand L-shaped house, with the abbot's hall, parlour and solar, built in the early sixteenth century by the last abbot,
Richard Rydge. However, to see some of his panelling it is necessary
to go to Weston Manor (Hotel), not far away at Weston-on-the-Green
in Oxfordshire: it is sophisticated work, adorned with Renaissance
motifs, and bears the name of Abbot Rydge. It was removed to Weston
at the end of the eighteenth century, when that house was one of the
seats of the Berties, Earls of Abingdon, and Notley had descended to
farmhouse status. Nothing much else is left of the cloister: there is a
little thirteenth-century arcading in the refectory (as it was) on the
south side – but this has otherwise been replaced by a large barn. The
bases exist of two or three piers in the church, which lay on the north
side, but it has otherwise completely vanished. From excavations
it appears to have been a large church, originally built in the twelfth
century, but considerably enlarged in the thirteenth, with a still later
central tower. The fourteenth-century monastic dovecote still graces
the hill behind the church: it would have held between 4,000 and
5,000 nests.

Notley is a private house, and not open to the public, but there is
a delightful view of it from the Aylesbury road, across its smiling valley.

Cambridgeshire

ANGLESEY ABBEY

Augustinian

The great interest of Anglesey is not monastic, but horticultural. There is indeed a delightful fragment of the Augustinian Priory of Anglesey within the house which is called Anglesey Abbey – but it is the garden and the landscape which everybody comes to see. This is all the creation of one man, the first Lord Fairhaven, who came to live here in 1926. An achievement of this magnitude – and it is a very large garden – is of great interest; it is also fascinating for us, accustomed to the enjoyment of gardens and landscapes planned in the eighteenth century, to see this, planned on the most generous scale, and all planted in our own time. What is more, Lord Fairhaven started with open fields, and a fen landscape which possessed few features or landmarks. So great avenues have been planted, grand rides formed, splendid vistas made. Nearer the house there are herbaceous borders or dahlia beds against long beech hedges, a rose garden in a setting of stone walls, a magnificent display everywhere of eighteenth-century garden ornaments: sphinxes, or gods, or goddesses, warriors, urns or obelisks, all rescued from lost gardens or landscapes elsewhere. And, befitting a fen garden, there is water.

To turn from the twentieth century to the thirteenth, Anglesey Priory was founded for Augustinian Canons *c.* 1212. It was not a large house: there were usually about ten canons in residence, with the prior; in 1534, on the even of the Dissolution there were actually two novices. Despite all the work in the gardens, the site has never been excavated, so there is some uncertainty about the plan. It is thought that what remains represents the prior's lodging, and that church and cloister lay to the south; it is not even clear whether the prior's lodging was part of the cloister (as so often) or a freestanding building, as it sometimes was. In any case this rump of the monastic building was converted into a house in the late sixteenth or early seventeenth century. There is a very pleasant Elizabethan front facing the Great Glade, which from the house appears to go on for ever: it is partly formed of older trees, partly Lord Fairhaven's planting. On this side the house has the mien of a smaller Elizabethan manor house, but in the wing behind is the vaulted undercroft of the prior's house, standing unaltered and beautiful, with octagonal piers of Purbeck marble carrying the elegant vault: this can be dated *c.* 1240. The rest of the house has been over-restored, 'opulent and pile-carpeted', James Lees-Milne remarks, describing his visit on behalf of the National Trust in 1943 (*Ancestral Voices*, Chatto & Windus, 1975); but he admired Lord Fairhaven's grand new library, which is in the wing which he built to the west of the house. This contains a very fine collection of books: these, together with the wonderful watercolours and everything else, he generously bequeathed to the National Trust in 1966.

BARNWELL PRIORY

Augustinian

The Newmarket Road in Cambridge may not seem a likely place in which to search for monastic ruins, but there are clues. There is the Abbey Stadium, and there is the Abbey Tyre Company; moreover nearby will be found Abbey Road and Priory Road, and at the corner of Priory Road and Beche Road stands a small, square, stone mediaeval building, undoubtedly of monastic origin. Barnwell Priory (it was never an abbey) was founded in 1092 for Augustinian Canons – at Cambridge – and was transferred to Barnwell in 1112. This odd little building, with springers for a vault along the outside wall, must have been at a corner of the cloister, and was probably the kitchen or storeroom. On Newmarket Road itself is a small thirteenth-century towerless church, optimistically called Abbey Church – which it never was; it may have been the *capella ante portas* to the priory. In Abbey Road is a picturesque late seventeenth-century house, called The Abbey House, of brick and timber, with a big Dutch gable dated 1678. It is (obviously) postmonastic, but may in origin have been connected with the priory, and its impressive garden wall may be part of the precinct wall. A short distance to the north is a beautiful bend of the Cam, inappropriately dominated by the Gas Works.

CAMBRIDGE – BLACKFRIARS
(Emmanuel College)

Dominican

St Andrew's Street in Cambridge was once called Preachers' Street, after the Dominicans' (or Preachers') house which it contained. This was the site on which Sir Walter Mildmay built Emmanuel College in 1584, incorporating some of the monastic fabric, as a 'seed plot of learned men for the supply of the church', and to prepare them for 'preaching the Word'. 'I hear, Sir Walter, that you have erected a Puritan Foundation,' said Queen Elizabeth to her Chancellor of the Exchequer. 'No, madam,' Mildmay replied. 'Far be it from me to countenance anything contrary to your established Laws, but I have set an acorn which, when it becomes an oak, God alone knows what will be the fruit thereof.' The fruit was a college which became a great source of Puritan influence in the early seventeenth century, and which spread the Word far and wide, providing twenty-one of the Pilgrim Fathers, and the founder of Harvard University.

The Dominicans came to Cambridge in 1238; Mildmay used the site of their church for his hall, and the buttresses in the north wall are the buttresses of that church. The monks' refectory became the chapel, defiantly running north–south, until it was superseded by Wren's chapel in the late seventeenth century. Known now as the Old Library, it still has evidence of mediaeval masonry, both inside and out. Monastic masonry can still be seen, too, on three sides of New Court, which was in fact the original college court, and which now encloses a famous and appropriate herb garden.

The other monastic survival needs a little imagination. At the centre of the wonderful gardens in which 'Emma' is set is an ornamental pond, enlarged in the nineteenth century, and given its present shape in 1964; but this in origin was the monks' fishpond.

DENNY ABBEY

Benedictine : Templar : Franciscan Nuns

Six miles or so out of Cambridge on the road to Ely (A10) are what appear to be elegant eighteenth-century Gothick stone gatepiers – at first hard to comprehend, leading as they do only to the farm road to Denny Abbey, itself only a farmhouse. The farm road leads up to the farm – a pleasant enough stone farmhouse, it seems, with sash windows, rather oddly patched perhaps here and there, with old blocked windows or doorways. The drive leads on, past the west side of the house to the south – more sash windows, more odd patchings – into the car park. And so, walking round to the entrance on the west side, we can absorb a few details of the south: a blocked doorway or two, a blocked window, and, high up in the gable, two tiny windows, one over the other, which could only denote a mediaeval spiral staircase. And so, going round to the west, we are perhaps prepared for a shock; and such it is, for here, unnoticed maybe as we drove round, is what is plainly the Norman west doorway of a church. If, overcome with curiosity, we go on round to the east side, we shall find the final shock: embedded in the wall is what can only be the crossing arch of a Norman church. What is the explanation of all this? Thanks to recent investigation by archaeologists, nearly everything can be explained.

Denny began life as a Benedictine priory, founded *c.* 1159, and dependent on Ely; for some reason it did not flourish, and in 1170 the few brethren there returned to Ely, and the buildings at Denny were taken over by the Knights Templars. These earliest buildings comprised a small Norman cruciform church: crossing and transepts are still here under later accretions, as is the nave to which the Templars added; it is their west door which we have just seen.

In 1308 the Templars were suppressed, and in 1342 the property was acquired by Mary de St Pol, Countess of Pembroke (foundress of Pembroke College, Cambridge) for her Franciscan nunnery, which had been originally founded in 1293 at Waterbeach nearby – an inhospitable spot, prone to flooding.

Denny is thus unusual in having been at different times occupied by three different monastic Orders, and is a very rare survival of a nunnery of Franciscan Minoresses or Poor Clares. They promptly demolished the Benedictine chancel, and built an entirely new church to the east of the crossing; the Norman nave and transepts they adapted for living accommodation. The crossing became the lodging for the Countess herself; here she could look down from her window (now blocked up, but visible outside) into the new church grafted onto the crossing of the Norman church.

Entering by the west door, we are able to investigate the interior of this astonishing building, now largely gutted to reveal the bones of the Benedictine and Templar church – nave, south aisle and transepts. It is fascinating to see Norman windows or doorways, later blocked (or sometimes pierced by later openings), or perhaps a farmhouse kitchen fireplace, and ascend by means of the recent wooden staircase into the new wooden galleries in the upper part of the crossing where the Countess lived, devoting the years of her widowhood to the Franciscan nuns; indeed, she may herself have become a tertiary of the Order. After her death in 1377 these became the abbess's quarters. The nuns occupied cells formed in the nave, and the night stairs descended into the church from the north transept; guests were accommodated in the south. We can descend, and go out again by the east door and stand on the site of the nuns' church, which has completely disappeared. To the northeast stands their splendid refectory, which has survived as a barn; the nuns' cloisters connected this with the church – but all this has to be imagined. The original Benedictine cloister – much smaller – nestled in the corner of the nave and north transept.

A remarkable feature of the English Franciscan Minoresses is that they were drawn from well-connected families. The last Abbess of Denny was the redoubtable Elizabeth Throckmorton, who at the time of the Dissolution (1538) retired to her family home at Coughton in Warwickshire – still the home of the family – where with two or three of her nuns she continued to live an enclosed life in a wing of that wonderful (then) moated house.

Denny then passed through various hands – until in 1929 it was acquired by Pembroke College, Cambridge; an act of *pietas* since their foundress was buried here before the high altar in 1377. In 1952 they transferred the abbey to the Ministry of Works – but in the summer of 1984 the college held a great garden party here, *in piam memoriam*. The college flag flew, and some of the college silver was displayed; tea was served, preceded by champagne. The place had to remain open to the great British public, some of whom helped themselves to champagne.

As has been said, nothing survives of the nuns' church – except for one thing: the solitary shafting of the clustered column of the north nave arcade, close to the Norman crossing arch already noted. Its southern counterpart has gone: in fact, however, it was this, adapted, that became the gatepiers which greeted us on the Ely road on our arrival. So, equally unexpectedly, what appeared to be Georgian Gothick, turns out to be the genuine thing, a charming touch from some unknown eighteenth-century antiquarian.

ISLEHAM PRIORY

Benedictine

The long straight road from Prickwillow and Ely finally bears right in the village of Isleham, then left, passing this very rare and precious little building – a small Norman chapel, with apsidal east end. Both its existence and its survival here seem equally puzzling. Founded in the eleventh century as an alien priory, its monks left it in 1254 for the sister cell at Linton, a few miles away. This was suppressed, with other alien priories, in 1414, and both were granted to Pembroke College, Cambridge. Isleham has survived as a barn. Here it is, seven hundred years and more since its monks left, with its remarkable herringbone masonry, its tiny windows, its sturdy buttresses, all almost unaltered.

Cheshire

NORTON PRIORY

Augustinian

Many priories were (as we have noted) unofficially raised to the rank of an abbey by eighteenth-century owners: 'abbey', after all, sounds better. Here it is the other way round: Norton, which was founded as an Augustinian priory *c.* 1115 (first at Runcorn, moving here in 1134), was actually raised to the rank of an abbey in 1422. Somehow, since the Dissolution, it has always been called Norton Priory.

Norton is not far from Runcorn, indeed is overlooked by new housing at a comfortable distance, and the priory is approached rather oddly through a part of the demesne of the former mansion now used for industrial development: modern factories stand in a spacious tree-lined setting. Suddenly the road leads us to some unexpected elaborate gilded iron gates (of recent fabrication), and a notice proclaims that this is Norton Priory Museum, owned and administered by Cheshire County Council. At first sight it all appears like yet another new factory. The factory building turns out to be an excellent museum of the history and life of the priory. Through it doorways open on to the nineteenth-century Classical porch of the mansion, of which nothing else survives. The porch leads into a spacious hall, with two spectacular Norman doorways facing us – one the genuine thing, though moved at some time to its present position; the other is a magnificent nineteenth-century copy. These both lead into the grand twelfth-century vaulted undercroft of the west range, with ribbed vaults growing from squat round columns with scalloped capitals. At one end are eighteenth-century brick wine bins, where the Brooke family stored their wine; indeed this undercroft made a wonderful cellar for the eighteenth-century mansion which stood above it till 1928.

The great surprise of Norton is to go into the partially reconstructed chamber at the north end, to find the colossal mediaeval carved stone figure of St Christopher – some 11 feet high. Where this could have stood in mediaeval times seems unknown; equally mysteriously, it was not destroyed at the Dissolution, but became a sensational garden ornament in the formal garden on the south side of the house. Briefly it was housed in Liverpool Museum, but recently has been returned to Norton.

The undercroft opens out into the cloister court: the site was excavated in the 1970s, and it is possible to explore all the foundations of church and claustral buildings, although no other building still stands.

After the Dissolution the place was bought in 1545 by Richard Brooke, member of an old-established Cheshire family, whose great-grandson was created a baronet in 1662. The claustral buildings were converted into a house, and an engraving by Buck exists of this charming place. But later in the eighteenth century this was all replaced by a somewhat ponderous mansion, ascribed (perhaps incorrectly) to James Wyatt. As has been said, this survived until 1928. The Irish branch of the family descends from Richard Brooke's brother, represented in our own day by Viscount Brookeborough, Prime Minister of Northern Ireland (1943–63), and his brother FM Viscount Alanbrooke, CIGS 1942–46.

Cumberland

CALDER ABBEY

Cistercian

Calder is one of the most mysterious and inaccessible of all the ruined abbeys of England. It stands in a remote valley, up a long track, off a byroad, northeast of the village of Calder Bridge. On the coast, not far away, is the intimidating conglomeration of the Calder Hall Nuclear Power Station, built in 1956, and the first nuclear power station in the world.

Calder was originally a Savigniac house, founded in 1135; refounded from Furness in 1142, it became (like its parent) Cistercian in 1148. The long track leads up and on; there is a notice marked 'Private', and then another – 'No Visitors'; the gate is padlocked, the adjoining fence barbed-wired. But from this point a good view of the buildings may be obtained.

First there is the church, of which a surprising amount survives – the late twelfth-century north nave arcade, the tall crossing arches carrying the base of the tower, a considerable part of the transepts, and the beautiful blank arcading of the south transept triforium. Beyond this is the east walk of the cloister, with the triple-arched entrance to the chapter house, and the long lancets of the dorter above. At the west end will be seen the twelfth-century Norman west doorway.

In his *Guide to the Country Houses of the North West* (Constable, 1991), John Martin Robinson speaks of the abbey ruins 'forming a poignant Gothic contrast to the plain, somewhat unlettered, Classicism of the façade of the house.' This is the melancholy Georgian house, which stands to the right, and has swallowed up much of the claustral buildings round the cloisters: the refectory and other rooms on the south side have all been absorbed into the basement of this large, curious, silent house. The visitor may wonder if the house is lived in – shuttered windows suggest that it may not be. But little windows at the top are open. The gardens appear completely unkempt. All around is the beautiful park, but fallen trees suggest decay. Calder Abbey is indeed mysterious and sad.

NUNNERY near KIRKOSWALD

Benedictine

There is little more than the name left: there are no records of the foundation, no records of the Dissolution, there is no mention of it in Knowles and Hadcock's *Mediaeval Religious Houses: England and Wales*, and but a few little mediaeval fragments survive in the kitchen quarters of the house. But the house – always called Nunnery – is superb. It was built in 1715 by Henry Aglionby, MP for Carlisle, and has a long distinguished stone front, two storeys high, nine bays wide, with a balustraded parapet. The three centre bays break forward, the front door with Doric pilasters supporting a segmental pediment. It is an austere composition, perfectly proportioned, and very beautiful. Moreover, it is in a glorious position, standing on a steep bank of the River Eden, with wonderful wooded walks along the river banks. A blocked thirteenth-century arch, little mediaeval fragments, hard to interpret, down the kitchen passage, and the name Nunnery perpetuated by Henry Aglionby, alone speak of a monastic past.

SEATON PRIORY

Benedictine Nuns

This is the least known part of Cumberland – the coastal strip in the southwest of the county. Yet a glance at the map will show wonderful things close at hand: Windermere, Coniston Water, Wastwater, Eskdale, the Furness Fells, the Old Man of Coniston. The hills come down to within a few miles of the sea; the main road which makes its way north from Broughton-in-Furness along the coast rounds Black Combe – as does the railway – and soon reaches the village of Bootle. And a mile on is Seaton. This is more pastoral country, with woods forming a backdrop, woods which embrace the foothills of the fells.

Seaton Priory was founded for Benedictine nuns towards the end of the twelfth century. It was a very small house, and originally a cell of Nunburnholme (in the East Riding); it never seems to have numbered more than five or six nuns; at the time of the Dissolution there were but two, and one novice. In 1542 it was granted to Sir Hugh Askew, who out of the stone of the monastery built the house called Seaton Hall – or Nunnery: old names cling, as at Kirkoswald (qv) – which occupies much of the site. The house was much Victorianized, but is obviously in origin old. And quite unexpectedly the east end of the nuns' church survives, three Early English lancets, and little more. Sir Hugh died in 1562, and there is a brass to him in Bootle Church.

WETHERAL PRIORY

Benedictine

Wetheral is in a dramatic position, overlooking a long tree-hung stretch of the River Eden. The parish church commands the view – the priory is hard by. If only a fragment of an ancient religious house is to survive, there is everything to be said for its being the gatehouse. Here is the gatehouse of Wetheral, tall and conspicuous: a tunnel-vaulted archway, and two floors above, each lit by a Perpendicular two-light window. It is a handsome tower, and now leads into a farmyard. This is partly walled – a monastic wall, no doubt, now enclosing cows and chickens, not Black Monks. Wetheral was founded *c.* 1106, for perhaps eight or ten Benedictines, and their prior.

Derbyshire

REPTON PRIORY

Augustinian

Repton has always been a place of importance, and in the seventh century was the capital of Mercia. St Guthlac was a member of the Mercian royal house, who, tired of soldiering, became a member of that very early religious community here, and after two years of study resolved to become a hermit – and on St Bartholomew's Day in 669 reached the remote swamps of Croyland, where he established his hermitage. Everything at Repton was swept away by the Danes in 875, but in the tenth century a new church was built, and of this the precious crypt survives, with a short chancel above, one of the most complete Saxon buildings left in England.

The Augustinian Priory of Repton was founded *c.* 1153, from the Priory of Calke, nearby; by 1172 the transfer to Repton was complete, Calke being relegated to a mere cell. A great cruciform church was built, to the east of the parish church, and of this some of the foundations survive, together with the priory arch, and the west wing of the cloister buildings – all now part of Repton School. In its day Repton became a large community, with twenty-five or more canons, and fifteen at the time of the Dissolution.

In 1539 the monastic buildings were sold to Thomas Thacker, whose son Gilbert pulled nearly everything down, saying that he would destroy the nest, for fear the birds should build there again. Sir John Port of Etwall left money to found a school at Etwall or Repton, and his executors bought what remained of the monastic buildings in which to establish this school. The school flourished, and in the nineteenth century, under the headmastership of Dr Pears, grew enormously (like other old foundations) – indeed, became a nursery of archbishops: William Temple and Geoffrey Fisher both being head masters, Michael Ramsey a boy in the school.

The mediaeval monastic gateway makes a delightful entry to the school; the west cloister wing was probably the monastic guesthouse, and the upper part, which is early sixteenth century, with its gables might almost pass for a Tudor manor house. It makes an ideal school library. The undercroft is Norman, and must date from the foundation. It is now the museum – while to the north stands Prior Overton's Tower (fifteenth century), adjoining the Hall, the head master's house, overlooking the meadows of the Trent.

STYDD PRECEPTORY

Hospitaller

A mile from the village of Yeaveley, not far from the border of Derbyshire and Staffordshire, and deeply hidden in a remote and beautiful valley, approached by a private road, stand the remains of the Preceptory of Stydd, founded for the Hospitallers *c.* 1190. One wall of the chapel still stands which must go back to the time of the foundation, a charming fragment with narrow lancet windows – enough to give us a little idea of what a perfect little Early English building this was. Alongside is a tall, square, brick Tudor house, now a farmhouse, but embellished, perhaps in the late eighteenth century, with Strawberry Hill Gothick bay windows. It is a secluded and altogether mysterious place.

Devon

BUCKLAND ABBEY

Cistercian

Of the numerous Bucklands in Devon this is Buckland Monachorum, a few miles south of Tavistock: at the hamlet of Milton Combe, very close to the abbey, there is a delightfully named public house: the 'Who'd Have Thought It?'

There is something unlikely about Buckland Abbey, too: here is the monastic church, knocked about and filled in, serving as a house, its claustral buildings gone, whereas it is usually the church that has gone, and the buildings which have been converted into a house. Buckland is ungainly, too, in its pseudo-domestic dress, and looks uncomfortable, shorn of its transepts, but with odd additions, arches blocked up, windows filled in, roof lines still marking where transepts have been.

Buckland was founded in 1278, more or less the last Cistercian house to be founded in England, and certainly the most westerly. The church was straightforward, cruciform and aisleless, with a central squat tower. After the Dissolution the place was soon acquired by Sir Richard Grenville, and in 1581 was bought by Sir Francis Drake. It remained with his descendants until after the Second World War, and was acquired by the National Trust in 1949. Much of the house is now used by the Plymouth Museum and Art Gallery.

Inside, the house seems as ungainly as it does outside. Why did the Grenvilles convert this unpromising building into a house, filling it with floors at unlikely and unequal levels? Why did they pull down the transepts, and then build a kitchen wing on the south side, attached to the chancel? Why did they throw out a new staircase extension to the west of the former south transept – and all this in the architecturally conscious Elizabethan age, when the leading families were competing with each other in their building aspirations? The former crossing of the church has become the Great Hall. It has good plasterwork and panelling, but it is a low one-storey room, hardly to be compared with the great halls then being built. And it is the only grand room in the house.

Staircases lead up and down, and at the top seem curiously entwined with the arches of the crossing: such rooms as there are appear small, and the larger galleries in the upper part of the nave are filled with exhibitions and exhibits of a suitably naval character. Drake's drum is in the Great Hall.

In a way, the grand monastic barn – close to the east end of the house – is the finest building here. With its long buttressed sides and magnificent roof, it is a building of some distinction. Along the west side is a charming small garden between the barn and the house, which has been laid out as a knot garden, with miniature box hedges forming the long shapely knots. And the setting in its enclosed valley, watered by a stream, is superb.

CANONSLEIGH ABBEY

Augustinian Nuns

A wide empty valley between Burlescombe and Westleigh – remote and sequestered for all the proximity of the Great Western line to Exeter – and a commodious, busy farm called Canonsleigh Barton. A closer look at the buildings reveals among the cows and tractors an imposing mediaeval gatehouse, the gatehouse of an abbey of Augustinian Nuns, founded in 1285. But there was an earlier foundation here, for Augustinian Canons, established in 1161 – which in 1282 was transferred to the Canonesses. Little else survives, but for some high walls to the east, perhaps remains of the monastic mill. A lovely spot – but it is not easy among all the glorious farmyard mud to envisage the holy women in their spotless habits and starched linen.

CORNWORTHY PRIORY

Augustinian Nuns

Driving down narrow Devon lanes between Totnes and Dartmouth, suddenly a great mediaeval gatehouse appears across the tall hedge: it is the gatehouse to Cornworthy Priory, founded here for Augustinian nuns in the early thirteenth century. Fortunately the farmer has provided a stile across the hedge, so access is easy, and there before us is the gatehouse, built in the early fifteenth century, with two entrances, one for carriages, one for pedestrians, and both vaulted. It is built of local stone, but the quoins and arches of Dartmoor granite provided an attractive contrast, and catch the sunlight. A stairway rises to the room above, but this is open to the sky. Through the main archway there is a delightful view of the village of Cornworthy on its hillside, with the church tower rising over all.

Despite this grand gateway, Cornworthy was only a small house, with a prioress and nine or ten nuns. What little is left of the priory itself is in a corner of the field, lost in the undergrowth.

DUNKESWELL ABBEY

Cistercian

A very odd, and very small, monastic site – but charming. There is a pretty hamlet called Dunkeswell Abbey, a mile or two north of the village of Dunkeswell, in that delectable 'lost' countryside, north of Honiton. 'Dunkeswell Abbey. Ruins' – so it is marked on the map. There is a green, and a pump, and a thatched cottage, and a sign to announce 'Dunkeswell Abbey', close to a garden gate; and there, in the cottage garden, is a fragment of the mediaeval monastic gatehouse. Here the garden gate opens onto a path, bordered by box, which leads through a long and beautiful garden to a church. This is a surprise – a building of 1842, standing apparently on part of the site of the monastic church. It is an extremely simple building, lofty, with a plain north arcade, and long lancet windows; there are two mediaeval tombs, and some beautiful mediaeval tiles. Outside, there is a large, overgrown lump of masonry, which could be the northwest corner of the cloister buildings. Much has to be imagined. But it is a holy place, and the early Victorian builders did well to raise a new chapel, where the Divine Praises might be sung again. The abbey was founded in 1201 for Cistercian monks by William de Briwere. It is certainly a Cistercian setting – remote, secluded and watery.

EXETER – ST KATHERINE'S PRIORY, POLSLOE

Benedictine Nuns

St Katherine's is so well concealed, surrounded by suburban roads to the east of the city, that it is very difficult to find. Do not be put off – nor misled by a road called Priory Road, which is nowhere near St Katherine's. Very few people even know of its existence; indeed author and photographer, engaging a taxi, were taken first to a mad house; then, after persistent searching, they arrived at an old people's club. Right this time, as it turned out: St Katherine's now is masquerading as an Old People's Club.

It is a fascinating thirteenth-century building. St Katherine's was founded *c.* 1150 by William de Briwere for aristocratic Benedictine nuns: this was their great hall, and contains an important original oak screen, and other mediaeval features. Polsloe is a mile or so east of the city, north of the (Southern) railway line to London.

EXETER – ST NICOLAS' PRIORY

Benedictine

St Nicolas' Priory is tucked way in a tiny alleyway, leading off Fore Street, in the heart of the city, not far from the cathedral: the delicious smell of food from a local pub, adjacent to the priory, at lunch time will cheer and encourage the modern pilgrim. What survives of this priory is the guesthouse, which formed the west side of the cloister; the church lay to the south, but has disappeared. There is an impressive Norman undercroft, with a groined vault resting on short circular columns, a great kitchen, and a so-called Tudor Room (because of its plaster ceiling), formed after the Dissolution, when this became a private house. Above is the very grand guest hall, and the prior's room next door, both with magnificent open timber roofs. There are other small rooms, besides.

St Nicolas' was founded *c.* 1080, and was a daughter house of Battle.

FRITHELSTOCK PRIORY

Augustinian

The high, sweeping landscape of North Devon: woods, steep valleys, small, pretty villages, tall church towers; such a one is Frithelstock (pronounced Fristock), a very worthwhile church in its own right, and in a delectable setting, high up with grand views everywhere. And then, unexpectedly, just behind it, there is on its north side the ruined church of the Augustinian priory, founded here by Robert Beauchamp in 1220. It is an extraordinary surprise to find it here, only a few yards away from the church of the parish.

The west front, with its lofty gable and long lancet windows is memorable: there was a tower on its south side, to compete with, or complement, the parish church tower, and a Lady Chapel at the east end. All this seems to be thirteenth-century work. It was not a large house, but contained usually six or eight canons, and the prior. The cloisters must have been on the north side – no room on the south – but nothing remains. However, the farmhouse to the north probably incorporates monastic work: it is tempting to think that the little square garden represents the cloisters, and that the house is really the prior's house, dressed up in later clothes.

PLYMOUTH FRIARY

Dominican

There are some attractive small streets in the old town of Plymouth – among them Southside Street. A little way down, on the right-hand side, is a spruce, white-painted, plastered house with sash windows and a lofty, arched entrance, and over the arch, in big lettering, the words 'The Distillery'. This is Coates' Distillery, established in 1793. Alongside is a lower, much older, arched entrance, with a four-centred arch, perhaps of fifteenth-century date. Over this is a plaque recording that this was the entrance to the Dominican friary, founded in 1383.

In fact there is some uncertainty whether this was a house of Black Friars or Grey Friars. Dom David Knowles, OSB, in his *Medieval Religious Houses of England and Wales*, regards the evidence for the

28

Black Friars as 'not conclusive or even persuasive'. But he lists a house of Grey Friars here, founded for twelve friars in 1383.

But all who appreciate Plymouth gin will recall the splendid label – of a Black Friar, and note that Messrs Coates produce it at the 'Blackfriars Distillery, Plymouth, England'.

PLYMPTON PRIORY

Augustinian

Plympton in its day was more important than Plymouth. This was due to its castle and its priory; moreover, the priory owned Sutton Prior, the nucleus of Plymouth. So the priory was, in a sense, the mother of Plymouth. Plympton St Maurice was the birthplace of Sir Joshua Reynolds: 'Those who have a special feeling for the small, ancient and decayed boroughs of England,' wrote W. G. Hoskins 'will be delighted with Plympton, left on one side in the past two hundred years . . .' Plympton St Mary was monastic, and the grand church, with its handsome Perpendicular pinnacled tower, was originally only a chapel of ease to St Maurice, and attached to the priory.

The Augustinian priory was founded in 1121, and next to Tavistock became the most powerful monastic establishment in Devon; in its day it vied with Cirencester as the largest Augustinian house in the country. Now there are but the scattered fragments in St Mary's churchyard, to remind us of all this.

TAVISTOCK ABBEY

Benedictine

Driving or walking into the centre of Tavistock and surveying the ancient parish church and Bedford Square, the busy Plymouth Road, and Tavy Bridge, the Guildhall and post office and Bedford Hotel, it is hard to conceive that we are here trampling on the very site, if not the actual foundations of what was once Devon's greatest monastic house.

In the Middle Ages Tavistock had flourished on tin; as tin mining declined, the cloth trade took over, and as the cloth trade declined, copper mining developed and took its place. From the early eighteenth century until the early twentieth, copper mining dominated the town, and the Dukes of Bedford dominated the industry: it was the 7th Duke of Bedford who completely redeveloped the site of the abbey, and created the centre of the town we see today. He formed Bedford Square on the site of the chancel of the abbey church, drove the Plymouth Road through the site of the cloisters, widened the Tavy Bridge, built the Guildhall in the Gothic style (1848), and gothicized the Bedford Hotel.

Tavistock Abbey was founded for Benedictine monks in 971, and at the Dissolution was granted to John Russell, 1st Earl of Bedford. What remains? There is a little walling on the south side of the parish church, a tiny fragment of the monastic church. Opposite, the Bedford Hotel occupies the site of the refectory, and possibly incorporates a little of its masonry. Behind the hotel there still stands part of the precinct wall, with the west gatehouse (or Betsy Grimbal's tower) near the Plymouth Road, and another little tower (the still house) close to the river. Farther to the east the approach to the Tavy Bridge has swept all away, but next to the post office is the little Unitarian Chapel, which is in origin monastic, probably the misericord, attached to the infirmary; next to the Guildhall is the mediaeval Town Gate to the abbey, now the public library. All else has gone: progress.

TORRE ABBEY

Premonstratensian

Torre Abbey stands now in the middle of Torquay, surrounded by the grand Victorian villas, the residential roads, the hotels and churches, and all the trappings of a popular seaside resort. It is hard to visualize the scene here in 1196, when the Premonstratensian house was founded by William de Briwere, and the first monks arrived, all the way from Welbeck in Nottinghamshire. This site was unusual, anyway, so close to the sea.

After the Dissolution, as so often happened, the south and west ranges of the cloisters were adapted for residential use. Sir George Cary bought the place in 1662, and the family remained here till 1930: it was they who converted the south range into the Georgian house we see today, looking out to Torbay; the house now used as the Art Gallery for Torquay, the gardens now municipal gardens.

But approaching from the west there is still plenty monastic to see.

The west range of the cloisters was the abbot's house: here stands the early sixteenth-century Abbot's Tower, and above the undercroft the Carys' Chapel (the family were Roman Catholic). To the south stands the gatehouse, and beyond that the thirteenth-century tithe barn.

The cloister garth may be entered through the house. The grand Norman doorway of the chapter house is impressive – but nothing survives inside. Nor does much of the church, beyond – merely a few walls of the chancel or south transept, and piles of fallen masonry. But the cruciform plan can be observed.

As he writes these lines, the author is being overlooked, behind his shoulder, by the marble bust (by Rouw) of Mary Anne Cary of Torre Abbey, who in 1830 married Sir John Hayford Thorold, 10th Bart. She was his second wife, and none of our family descend from her; but her bust in the room here often brings to mind Torre Abbey – mediaeval monastic house, Georgian family home.

Dorset

ABBOTSBURY ABBEY

Benedictine

Abbotsbury is delectable: a village street with seventeenth-century houses of golden stone, a parish church with a seventeenth-century plaster ceiling, an eighteenth-century reredos, monuments and other notable furnishings – and the lane leads down to the monastic barn, and on to the shore and Chesil Bank, the gardens, the celebrated swannery (of mediaeval and perhaps monastic origin), and St Catherine's Chapel, standing on its little grassy hill. There is very little left of the Benedictine abbey, founded *c.* 1026. In the churchyard to the south of the church are some foundations of the abbey church, but they are very fragmentary and tell us very little: it was so close to the parish church that it must have dominated it completely. Down the lane to the shore there are remains of the two gatehouses – but again these are fragmentary, and one is built into a house. Finally there is the abbey barn. This is of great magnificence, and more than half of it remains intact. It was built *c.* 1400, and is 272 feet in length, and its wonderful thatched roof is supported on strongly buttressed stone walls. This is one of the most splendid mediaeval barns in England.

After the Dissolution the place was purchased by Sir Giles Strangways of Melbury. He built a house out of the monastic buildings, but this was destroyed in the Civil War. However, the family (later Fox-Strangways, Earls of Ilchester) still own the place, and still live at Melbury – which is not far from the Somerset border. To them is due the preservation of this uniquely beautiful spot.

BINDON ABBEY

Cistercian

Bindon Abbey lies close to Wool, close to the River Frome, which at Woolbridge is crossed by that rare sixteenth-century bridge, beside which stands the enchanting sixteenth-century house, Woolbridge

Above: Denny: blocked Norman doorways or openings, blocked mediaeval windows, Georgian sashes and low walls all have their story to tell.

Right: Norton: the enormous mediaeval figure of St Christopher adorned the monastic church; after temporary banishment, it is now back at Norton.

Calder: the 12th-century nave arcade and crossing arches survive here at this remote and mysterious church in distant Cumberland.

Left: Buckland: over a small doorway in the post-Dissolution kitchen wing is set the head of the foundress, Amicia Countess of Devon (1278).

Below: Cornworthy: through the early 15th-century gatehouse there is a delightful view of the village and Devon countryside.

Opposite above: Frithelstock: in North Devon, where the long,
narrow lancets make a most elegant west front for the monastic church.
Below: Plymouth: the erstwhile Dominican house, in the old town of Plymouth,
is now the distillery of Coates' Plymouth gin.

Exeter: solid Norman pillars, sturdy Norman vaulting in the undercroft of
St Nicolas Priory.

Above: Forde: angels provide corbels for the entrance to Abbot Chard's tower, built in the 16th century, just before the Dissolution.
Right: the garden in autumn, at all times a perfect foil for the south front of the abbey.
Below: the monastic chapter house has become a sumptuously furnished 17th-century chapel for the great house.

Above: Flaxley: in the Forest of Dean, where mediaeval Gothic and Georgian Gothick combine to make a delightful seat for an 18th-century Baronet.

Right: Gloucester: Blackfriars – Georgian windows with Gothick sash bars fill the space left by a large medi-aeval window in the Dominican church.

Manor, immortalized in Thomas Hardy's *Tess of the D'Urbervilles*. The ruins of the abbey are surrounded by trees, invisible, inaccessible.

Bindon was founded *c.* 1149 at Bindon Hill near Lulworth and transferred to Wool in 1172; it was a Cistercian house. After the Dissolution it was granted to Sir Thomas Poynings (afterwards Lord Poynings) and so to his nephew Thomas Howard, second son of the 3rd Duke of Norfolk, who was created Viscount Howard of Bindon in 1559. Much stone went for Henry VIII's castles at Portland and Sandsfoot, and Lord Howard made a house for himself out of the claustral buildings. The third Lord Howard built Lulworth Castle, that glorious 'folly castle', which was described as being 'mounted on high . . . well seated for Prospect and Pleasure; but of little other use.' It was, alas, gutted by fire in 1929. The Howards of Bindon died out, and both Bindon and Lulworth were purchased by the Weld family in 1641 – who were of much importance in the future history of Bindon and Lulworth.

The Welds were an important and devout Catholic family – not only founding Stonyhurst College (1794), but also in the person of Thomas Weld (1829) providing the first English Cardinal since the pontificate of Clement IX. It was the father of the Cardinal, another Thomas Weld, who in 1786 persuaded George III, over a particularly good bottle of port (it is said), to allow him to build the first post-Reformation Roman Catholic church in England. The King agreed – on condition that it did not look like a church. With its sash windows and dome it did not, and two hundred years later still does not, standing across wide, smooth lawns facing the castle, with a wonderful view of the sea below.

Thomas Weld interested himself in Bindon, too. Not much of the monastic building is there for us to see – just the foundations, or in a few places a little more of the walls of the church, which followed the standard Cistercian plan. It is the same with the cloisters and the claustral buildings – just low walls or foundations everywhere. But what Thomas Weld did was to build here also. In 1794 and following years he built what is called Bindon Abbey House, a little 'summer retreat' for himself and his family. As a prelude to this he also built a gatehouse. Both are Gothick – quite different from the demure Classical church at Lulworth – fanciful, pretty and romantic. Upstairs, in the house, and indeed the only large room in the house, he formed a chapel, serenely beautiful with its plaster vault glistening white, and rising from clustered columns at the sides, the prettiest of arched windows to light the place.

Bindon is a most evocative spot: to the east of the ruined church are the long monastic fishponds, looking, as Michael Pitt-Rivers writes in the *Shell Guide to Dorset*, 'like black canals beneath brown and melancholy trees'. The Abbey House is now used as a retreat house by Downside Abbey, and the place is not open to the public. Permission to visit it should be obtained from the Estate Office at Lulworth Castle.

CERNE ABBEY

Benedictine

Cerne was a very early establishment, ninth century, refounded in the tenth. But very little survives: no church, no cloister – not even a foundation. The site of the church, it is thought, is under the parochial churchyard.

Cerne Abbas is a beautiful village in a glorious setting of chalk hills, the Giant presiding. Abbey Street leads up towards the site of the abbey, past the Perpendicular tower of the parish church, lined with charming houses of all periods, mediaeval and later. At the end, and aligned on the street – it seems – is the Abbey House, which must have been the gatehouse, converted after a fire in the eighteenth century into its present domestic form; but its outline is mediaeval. There are two other monastic fragments – first, a longish two-storeyed oblong building, on the right just past the gatehouse, usually called the guesthouse; it has a charming oriel window on its north side. Second, and farther up, stands the very grand three-storeyed porch to the abbot's house. The house has disappeared, but this porch with its fan-vaulted entrance, and two-storeyed oriel window above, is so splendid that it must have led into something important.

There is nothing else but St Augustine's Well, in the angle of the churchyard wall (which might perhaps be part of the wall of the monastic church), associated by legend with St Augustine, and certainly a Christian wishing-well. Here, with our back to the wicked giant, we should make a cup of a laurel leaf, and facing the church make our wish.

FORDE ABBEY

Cistercian

The very borders of Dorset and Somerset, and the green valley of the River Axe: the old South-Western Railway line from Waterloo to Exeter runs behind the abbey, and from the carriage window there is an intriguing glimpse of the back of this long, spreading, monastic house; but the trains chug by at rare intervals: all else is silence.

The drive to Forde Abbey leads off a quiet lane to the east: from here the north wing looks monastic enough, with its line of small mediaeval windows; at its south end a taller block, with Perpendicular traceried windows and an eighteenth-century cupola must undoubtedly be the chapel, and, turning the corner, the south front of the house unfolds itself before us, in all its tremendous length. This amazing front is at first difficult to comprehend; it is difficult, too, as we stroll across these smooth, spreading lawns, to realize that the monastic church once stood where we are standing now, that what is now the chapel of the house was once the monastic chapter house, opening out of the eastern range of the cloisters, as usual.

Forde Abbey was founded for Cistercian monks in 1141 – it had originally been founded a few miles farther west five years previously. It had in its time a succession of able and energetic abbots, not least its last, Thomas Chard, whose great building works were still in progress at the time of the Dissolution. After the Dissolution Forde passed through various hands, until in 1649 it was purchased by Edmund Prideaux, Attorney-General to Cromwell, and a member of an old-established West Country family. It is to these two men, Chard and Prideaux, that we owe the south front which we see today.

Standing as we were on the great lawn before this front, we can admire Chard's late Perpendicular porch-tower, tall and dramatic, with its two-storeyed oriel window above the entrance arch, all elaborately decorated. To its left is Chard's Great Hall, with its long Perpendicular windows. But to its right Prideaux built a new centrepiece, broader than Chard's tower, but lower, and with its later eighteenth-century loggia projecting several feet from the front and its grand seventeenth-century windows lighting Prideaux's first-floor saloon, this forms an important frontispiece. To the right stands the north range of Chard's cloister, incomplete (as we shall see) at the Dissolution. Above this Prideaux added a series of seventeenth-century rooms on the first floor. On the far right is the Norman chapter house, dressed up externally in seventeenth-century style. To this Prideaux added an upper storey, so that it could balance the tall block which he contrived at the other end out of Chard's new abbot's lodging. The whole façade is battlemented – thus making a remarkable unity out of all these disparate parts. Nothing is known about the church, nor is it even known when it disappeared.

Entering the house by Chard's porch, we are in the Great Hall, a really splendid and delightful room – for all the loss of its two western bays, which Prideaux took to form his drawing room and dining room beyond, two splendid seventeenth-century rooms with panelling and lavish plaster ceilings. Prideaux completed the Great Hall also – and formed the magnificent staircase, which is built out on the north side of the hall. Three grand flights, balustrades with carved acanthus foliage, newel posts topped with baskets of fruit, make the perfect approach to Prideaux's ceiling and Mortlake tapestries – but from its windows there is a glorious view of the gardens, which are one of the special pleasures of Forde.

The north walk of Chard's cloister is approached through a vestibule from the Great Hall; uncompleted at the time of the Dissolution, it has a charming and delicate late eighteenth-century plaster vault, and always seems to be filled with a wonderful array of plants. And so to the chapel – the Norman chapter house, turned into a delightful chapel by Prideaux, with an elaborate late seventeenth-century carved screen, and other attractive furnishings, not least a very pretty small Gothick organ.

Beyond the chapel, the long north range which we saw from the drive is thirteenth century; above was the dorter, now divided into smaller rooms, and below is the vaulted undercroft. After the Dissolution these no doubt formed useful quarters, and so survived. They were obviously of no interest otherwise to Prideaux. Farther to the west is the refectory, actually in the conventional position for a Cistercian house, although no longer opening out of the north cloister walk. The upper part is now the library, but it still retains the recess for its monastic pulpit. Next door was the kitchen.

Forde is now a great house, but its monastic character is still strong. Prideaux died in 1658, and Forde eventually descended to a granddaughter and her husband, Francis Gwyn, and remained with their descendants till 1846. Since 1864 it has belonged to the Roper family, who still live here, and have done so much for the wonderful gardens.

Forde is a very special 'ruined abbey'; although very little survives of the twelfth century, and not much more of the thirteenth, the legacy of a really grand and ambitious abbot who reigned on the eve of the Reformation, is extremely valuable. It is equally important as a most beautiful and unusual seventeenth-century family home.

The gardens are a delight: to the west the Long Canal with its superb herbaceous borders is watered by cascades which descend from the Mermaid Pond and the Great Pond (perhaps in origin the monks' fishponds). There is also an enormous walled garden, filled with fruit and flowers and vegetables – and everywhere there are long walks, with borders and hedges, avenues and vistas, grand trees, and gracious, spreading lawns.

TARRANT ABBEY

Cistercian Nuns

The Tarrants are a string of tiny villages which adorn the valley of the Tarrant, the chalk stream which descends from Cranborne Chase to join the Stour at Spettisbury. Tarrant Crawford is the tiniest of them all. Here in 1199 a little nunnery was formed, of three ladies and their servants, not formally attached to any Order. In 1228 they became Cistercian, and the house grew. By the end of the century there were forty nuns and an abbess – hard to conceive now. Here today there is a good-looking farmhouse with its attendant buildings, called Tarrant Abbey Farm; this may be on the site of the abbey. Mediaeval buttresses support the cowshed, and there is talk of foundations nearer the stream. The little church has a Norman doorway and a thirteenth-century tower: inside there are remarkable fourteenth-century wall paintings, faded and beautiful. The odd thing about the building is that there are no windows on the south side of the nave, as though a monastic building once adjoined. But all remains mysterious.

Tarrant Crawford was the birthplace of Richard Poore, Bishop of Salisbury, founder of New Sarum, and builder of the Cathedral. He died in 1237, and is buried here at Tarrant; part of his tomb survives in the church, where the wall paintings are part of his memorial.

Co. Durham

FINCHALE PRIORY

Benedictine

Finchale – pronounced 'Finkle' – stands in a romantic, beautiful, solitary spot on the south bank of the River Wear, at a point where the river makes one of its customary sharp bends. There is a minor road from Durham itself which leads straight to Finchale, but the best means of approach is on foot, from the road which leads from the A690 to the A167; here a wicket gate, marked 'Finchale Priory' opens into a footpath through the woods and down to the river, and a footbridge takes us across the river to the priory itself. The view of the ruins opens up only by degrees: from the bridge the prospect of the river, up and downstream, and of the priory buildings ahead, is unforgettable. This is the perfect way to come, if we have time.

Near the priory there is an unsophisticated little café, selling ice-cream and postcards – otherwise it is all farmland. Although the city is only a mile or two away, a motorway and the main railway line even nearer, colliery villages all around, it is still possible to appreciate the loneliness of the spot when St Godric first established his little hermitage here in the earliest years of the twelfth century. St Godric died in 1170 (*aet.* 105): in 1196 the Benedictine priory was founded, and building proceeded all through the first half of the thirteenth century.

Finchale was never a large establishment: there were fifteen monks towards the end of the century, and from the fourteenth century until the Dissolution the priory was used as a rest-house for the monks of Durham. A prior and four monks formed the regular establishment, and every three weeks a group of four monks would come out to Finchale. This must have been delightful, both for the residents, and for their guests, seeking refreshment in this delectable spot.

For so small a community the buildings seem spacious enough. The church itself is long and narrow – the quire longer than the nave; in the fourteenth century the aisles were pulled down, and the arcades were filled in, probably at the time when the priory was re-established as a rest-house. But the circular piers, with capitals with stiff-leaf carving (including most unusual pineapples and flowers) are still visible; and windows with Decorated tracery were inserted, or probably reinserted, within the arches; the south aisle of the nave became the north walk of the cloisters. Chapter house and dorter were in their usual places in the east range, the frater on its undercroft (still vaulted) in the south. The prior's house and other offices stood to the south of the quire. At the crossing there was a tower crowned by a low spire, still standing in the early seventeenth century, as shown in the engraving in Dugdale's *Monasticon* (1665): it had fallen by the time Buck made his drawing in 1728. There was also a later (fourteenth-century) tower southwest of the west front.

The ruins are all beautifully maintained by the Monuments Commission; walking across the soft grass there are views everywhere – through gaping windows or broken walls – to the hillside hung with woods, the River Wear running swiftly below.

Essex

BARKING ABBEY

Benedictine Nuns

The middle of Barking: the mediaeval parish church, a great church-yard, swirling traffic – and then, at the east end of the church, the unexpected sight of a mediaeval gatehouse. It is not large, but it is attractive, two-storeyed, battlemented, with a stair turret in the south-west corner, a three-light window above the arch, fifteenth century in date. This important Benedictine Nunnery was founded by St Erkenwald, Bishop of London, *c.* 666, and refounded, after being sacked by the Danes, *c.* 965, by St Dunstan and King Edgar. It was a very important nunnery, and became for a while William I's seat of government (1066). There was a church of great size, of which the north wall stands to the height of a few feet, and the claustral buildings surrounded the cloisters, which were on the north side of the church. All this has been excavated, and the foundations marked out. But the gatehouse – the Fire Bell Gate, as it was rather charmingly called – alone stands upright to remind us of a once-important site.

BEELEIGH ABBEY

Premonstratensian

A byroad from Maldon leads down to a narrow leafy lane, and to the gate of Beeleigh Abbey, a beautiful, secret place. It is private property, and not open to the public, but it is possible, from the gate, to get a glimpse of a gabled Tudor house, surrounded by a lovely garden.

Beeleigh, a Premonstratensian house, was founded *c.* 1172 at Great Parndon (Essex), and moved to Beeleigh *c.* 1180; it was a daughter house of Newsham (Lincolnshire), the first house of the Order to be established in England. Nothing survives of the church, but the long range of claustral buildings to the south, originally the east side of the cloister, was made into a house after the Dissolution, and to this, at the south end was added a three-storeyed timber-framed wing in the sixteenth century. Next to the site of the church is the chapter house, with it slender octagonal Purbeck marble columns to support the vault, and next to this a smaller room, the parlour, also vaulted, and then the long rectangular undercroft to the dorter. This was the warming room – and with its mediaeval fireplace, and round Purbeck marble columns supporting the vault, is a room of great charm and beauty. Above is the dorter, with its timber wagon roof, containing the library of the late Mr W. A. Foyle, who made his home here between the wars, and whose family live here today. With its mediaeval rooms and romantic garden it makes a wonderful house.

To the north of the house there is a large rectangular pond, formed by Mr Foyle. Miss Foyle tells an entertaining story of this. When the pond was being dug, the site was found to be full of bones: it was the monks' burial ground. The bones were carefully packed for removal by the dustmen. But the Council refused, saying that they were not empowered to dispose of human remains. Mr Foyle had an idea: when he opened the garden to the public, and visitors' cars were parked in the car park, he would go round and fill the boots of the cars with bags of bones. Thus were the remains of the monks of Beeleigh disposed of.

BICKNACRE PRIORY

Augustinian

This is well-wooded countryside between Danbury and Woodham Ferrers: suddenly and unexpectedly there appears through the trees that border the road a tall mediaeval arch, standing all by itself in the middle of the field. It is all that remains of Bicknacre Priory, founded here in 1175 for Augustinian Canons. It is only accessible by turning at the crossroads, and going through the farmyard near the corner. But there it stands, the thirteenth-century arch of the crossing of the church, stately and solitary. It was a small priory, for four canons and a prior, and when the last prior died in 1507 there were no canons left. A sad end. The modern pilgrim should be warned that it is a very boggy field; but there is a useful stream nearby, for washing shoes or socks or trousers.

COLCHESTER ABBEY (St John's)

Benedictine

The Benedictine abbey of Colchester was founded in 1096, but nothing remains of it – and very little is known about it. In 1648 a Royalist army, 3,000 strong, under Sir Charles Lucas, whose family had acquired the abbey after the Dissolution and built a house there, was besieged in the town for ten weeks by a Roundhead army. Little of house or monastic remains survived, and Sir Charles Lucas was condemned to death by court martial (1648). His niece Margaret was wife of William Cavendish, the 'loyal' Duke of Newcastle, and herself a poet and playwright, the original 'blue stocking'.

Only one thing is left: the very imposing fifteenth-century gatehouse. This stands facing St John's Green, a magnificent example of flint flushwork. Long, elegant, traceried canopies of stone frame ten thousand knapped flints, all glistening and sparkling on a sunny day. There is a lofty central arch, with a small pedestrian doorway at its side; three crocketed, pinnacled niches above, and a pair of Perpendicular two-light windows, support a parapet adorned with more flushwork. Tall crocketed pinnacles of flint and stone at the angles complete the splendid composition.

COLCHESTER PRIORY (St Botolph's)

Augustinian

This was the first Augustinian priory in England (*c.* 1100) – and a particularly splendid ruin it makes. Only the west front and the nave survive; but what could be more eloquent of the Norman spirit than these? The west front is a great work of art, all rough and jagged as it is in its ruined state. There are three portals, then two tiers of interlaced arcading, with three little windows to pierce the upper one, and then what is always said to be the earliest round window in England, between a pair of bigger single-light windows. What came above all this we cannot tell, but it seems that there was a tower on either side.

The nave is also a work of art, also all rough and jagged. The arcades are magnificently austere, with a triforium almost as big as the arcade itself – and so many arches of that have fallen. The enormous piers are some 5 feet 8 inches in diameter, and stand here, like the west front, in naked state with no stone facing, no flint, to dress or adorn them. Yet even so they tell us so much of Norman building methods, the rubble, the Roman tiles and brick, still sound as ever after eight centuries. The aisles were groin-vaulted: what can the whole grand ensemble have been, when the building stood entire?

LATTON PRIORY

Augustinian

The village of Latton is now very much part of Harlow New Town, and new towns are intimidating, soulless places. But the site of Latton Priory is two miles farther south, and very much in the country, and the Essex countryside is warm-hearted and pleasing. A farm road leads across the fields to Latton Priory Farm; here, in addition to farmhouse and accessory buildings, is a barn of commanding size – and inside the barn is an astonishing sight: the crossing arches of a mediaeval church. This is all that remains of Latton Priory, founded here for Augustinian Canons in the twelfth century. Not only is the presence of this grand monastic fragment a great surprise: it appears that this was a very small house, with a prior and only two canons, and before the place was given up in 1534 there had for some time been only one canon, who was called the prior. Yet these lofty arches, supported by tall shafted columns, all of fourteenth-century date, represent the crossing of quite a large church. What can life have been like, with this great echoing church, and, no doubt, capacious claustral buildings, too?

PRITTLEWELL PRIORY

Cluniac

The grand late fourteenth-century Perpendicular tower of the parish church stands high above acres of suburban housing proclaiming the antiquity of the place, now submerged in Southend. Priory Crescent borders the municipal Priory Park, and a path runs across to the remains of the Cluniac priory founded here from Lewes *c.* 1121. Nothing remains of the church, but following excavations in 1954 the outline of nave, transepts and apsidal chancel are now marked out. There is still a strong feeling of the cloister court on the south side of the church, with the impressive refectory still standing on the south side, and the prior's chamber on the west. The choir of the church was twelfth century, and the nave and transepts thirteenth; the refectory was in origin coeval with the choir (there is one narrow lancet), but the big traceried windows are, of course, Perpendicular, as is the splendid roof with its tie beams and king posts. The prior's chamber is stone below, half-timbered above; storehouses occupied the ground floor.

After the Dissolution the church was pulled down, and the claustral buildings were converted into a house: there were various changes of ownership, until the Scratton family acquired the place in the late seventeenth century, and held it for two hundred years, adding a Georgian façade and wing to the west front. After the First World War the house and park were presented to the Corporation of Southend, and the house now contains the Borough Museum.

ST OSYTH'S ABBEY

Augustinian

The old Essex pronunciation is 'Toosey'. Toosey herself, daughter of the first King of the East Angles, founded a nunnery here in the seventh century, and was martyred here by the Danes in 653. The house was refounded in 1121 for Augustinian Canons – but little is left of the Norman and Early English period. However, the house flourished, and became powerful and rich, raised to the rank of an abbey in the thirteenth century. In the fifteenth century the magnificent gatehouse was built – with Thornton in Lincolnshire the grandest monastic gatehouse in England.

We can stand before it, and absorb the spectacular display of flint flushwork. On a sunny day the flints gleam and glisten, tied together by the stones that frame them into a thousand canopied and pinnacled panels flush with the walls, the embattled parapet adorned with flint and stone chequerwork, Perpendicular mullioned windows above the gateway itself and in the broad polygonal towers to right and left. St Michael and the dragon adorn the spandrels of the gateway, canopied niches above the two pedestrian doorways, and a still more splendid niche above the central archway, its canopy reaching the parapet itself. To left and right are lower ranges, all adorned with brilliant flushwork, and the gateway itself is vaulted, and adorned with carved stone bosses.

All this made a magnificent entrance to the mansion contrived within the monastic enclosure by the first Lord Darcy, who bought the property in 1553. The monks' church was in the way: he demolished it, and built a Tudor mansion on the north side of the cloister (which was on the north side of the church) using the refectory as his Great Hall. Much of this has gone, but his Tudor tower, standing at the east end of this range, survives, a very fine ornament in its own right.

Spreading lawns, a rose garden, a topiary garden, on the site of the church, make it hard for us today to envisage church and claustral buildings which once stood here. What is now the thirteenth-century vaulted Early English chapel was part of the undercroft of the frater – on the north side of the cloister. Lord Darcy built the attractive gabled range above the cellarer's range, which had occupied the west side; to it he added another tower, now crowned with an attractive eighteenth-century cupola for clock and bell.

To the west of this stand what are always called the Bishop's Lodgings – in fact the abbot's lodging – built c. 1525 by Abbot Vintoner, with its own arched gateway, surmounted by a wide oriel window, rather unfortunately rebuilt in the nineteenth century. In the eighteenth century the place descended to Lord Rochford, who built a new domestic range adjoining the abbot's lodging – again rather unfortunately refaced and embellished in the nineteenth century. These rooms are open to the public, and contain some of the glorious pictures from Wentworth Woodhouse – the present owner's wife being the daughter of the 8th Earl Fitzwilliam. Here in a low and otherwise undistinguished room, filling an entire wall, dominating the entire room if not the entire house, hangs Stubbs' *Whistlejacket*, which once adorned the Grand Saloon at Wentworth. Inappropriate here, perhaps, and unhappily wedged in between floor and low ceiling, Stubbs' great masterpiece is nonetheless a final and unexpected pleasure.

THOBY PRIORY

Augustinian

This sounds an amusing name for a religious house: Thoby is apparently so named after its first prior, Tobias – obviously a highly esteemed character. It was founded *c.* 1150 for Augustinian Canons. It was never a large priory and only numbered four or five canons; it was one of the small houses suppressed by Wolsey in 1525 to endow his college at Oxford (now Christ Church).

Thoby is hard to find in the outskirts of Mountnessing: there is suburban growth along the main road, and a drive turns off with a notice to say that this is a car breakers' yard. Can this be Thoby Priory? It is. Accustomed as we are to finding monastic buildings put to all kinds of uses – farms, or old people's clubs, or girls' schools, or public bars, or stately homes, or museums, or tourist attractions – this seems to be something entirely new. There they stand, two fourteenth-century arches of the chancel of the canons' church, all overgrown, pathetic – and around them old Morris Minors, Ford Consuls and Rovers, wrecked and rusting, awaiting their end.

Gloucestershire

BRISTOL – BLACKFRIARS

Dominican

Quaker Friars – no, not a new splinter group of the Society of Friends, but a Bristol place name, commemorating the building of a Quaker meeting house on the site of the mediaeval friary. The Dominicans settled in the Bristol outskirts *c.* 1230, an area which the nonconformists developed in the eighteenth century. The Quaker meeting house dates from 1747–8, and perhaps was inspired by Wesley's New Room. Of the friary three ranges remain, two with mediaeval roofs; and there is a dormitory with lancet windows on an upper floor. Part of the building is now a registry office, so at least one of the friars' duties is still performed – the joining of man and woman in matrimony.

CIRENCESTER ABBEY

Augustinian

The great Augustinian Abbey of Cirencester was founded in 1117, on the site of a Saxon church (perhaps monastic): it stood just north of the present parish church. After the Dissolution the site was acquired by the Master family, and Richard Master, late in the sixteenth century, built a house on the site of the claustral buildings. The Master family (later Chester-Master) rebuilt the house in the eighteenth century, and remained in possession until 1963. Thereupon the house was pulled down, and the site excavated. This was afterwards covered over, and the grounds have become a public park. The only surviving monastic fragment is the Spital Gate, close to the bypass (to the northeast), at the other end of the park. It is an imposing Norman archway, with a smaller pedestrian arch alongside, and Cotswold stone roof, composing, with its little attached cottages, a delightful relic.

FLAXLEY ABBEY

Cistercian

That mysterious and beautiful part of Gloucestershire: the Forest of Dean; Flaxley is the typical remote setting for a Cistercian house – and, since the seventeenth century, for a 'gentleman's seat'.

Flaxley was founded for Cistercian monks in 1157, and enjoyed special favours from the Crown, being long used as a royal hunting lodge, with the lay brothers' refectory being turned into a guest hall; indeed, Edward III had the abbot's guest chamber reserved permanently for his own use.

After the Dissolution the south and west ranges of the cloister were adapted for domestic use; the Crawley-Boevey family, baronets, were established here from the seventeenth century until the twentieth, and to them is due the appearance of this romantic house – a delightful marriage of the mediaeval and the Georgian, of Gothic and Gothick. The centre of the west front is what was the lay brothers' range and later the guest hall, with its vaulted undercroft below. The high gable on the right, with its big Decorated traceried window, was the abbot's hall, the gable to the left is eighteenth century. The south front is entirely Georgian, designed by Anthony Keck of Gloucester in 1771, built in front of whatever survived of the monastic south cloister range – a very pretty façade, with Gothick battlements and pinnacles, and Georgian sash windows. The church lay to the north, but of this there are few traces, and none of the other claustral buildings.

Flaxley Abbey is a private house, and not open to the public, but from the lane, past the parish church, it can be seen in its enchanting setting of gardens and parkland.

GLOUCESTER – BLACKFRIARS

Dominican

Apart from Gloucester, only at Norwich (qv) and (much more fragmentary) at Newcastle does anything of importance survive of the Dominicans or Black Friars. What survives here is of great interest and importance, close to Southgate Street. The Dominicans came here *c.* 1239, and their church was consecrated in 1284, with a north transept added in the fourteenth century. Although much altered and adapted, this church survives. After the Dissolution the place was granted to Thomas Bell, clothmaker, who turned the church into a house, and the monastic buildings into a cloth manufactory. To an experienced eye all that has happened will be obvious – for instance, in the transept three floors have been inserted (with later Gothick sash windows). But the general plan – with cloisters, chapter house, frater and so on – can still be made out, despite many alterations. Much work was done by the Ministry of Works in the 1950s, and it is fascinating to see what has been done, and undone, to reveal the original Dominican house.

GLOUCESTER – GREYFRIARS

Franciscan

It is an extraordinary experience to discover down a narrow alleyway, close to new shops and supermarkets (the Eastgate Market) the old church of the Grey Friars, a ruined fragment maybe, but an unexpected pleasure. The Grey Friars first came here *c.* 1230, but this new church and house are early sixteenth century, the benefaction of the Berkeley family (indeed their original patrons). The church comprises nave and north aisle, both of almost equal size – so it was a double-naved church, no doubt an excellent arrangement for preaching, and that was the great speciality of the friars. All is latest Perpendicular, with lozenge-shaped pillars for the arcade, and Perpendicular traceried windows. Nothing is left of any of their buildings, but the survival of so much of their church here is of exceptional interest – so few have survived.

GLOUCESTER – ST OSWALD'S PRIORY
(St Catharine's Church)

Augustinian

There was another Augustinian priory in Gloucester (in addition to Llanthony Secunda) – of which one wall still stands. It is a wall which contains two Norman arches, and two (blocked) Gothic ones. This is all that survives of St Oswald's Priory, originally a college of secular canons, which became Augustinian in 1153. This fragment is apparently the wall of the north aisle, used after the Dissolution as a parish church, dedicated to St Catharine. A new St Catharine's was built in the nineteenth century: somehow this one monastic wall survived.

HAILES ABBEY

Cistercian

The great pleasure of Hailes is its idyllic setting. Although only a mile off the main road from Broadway to Winchcombe, there are few signposts, and indeed on some maps Hailes does not even appear. Long may it so continue, hidden from the world. The lane which leads there seems inconsequential – but it leads to the little church (a jewel), and to the abbey itself, which in the Middle Ages was the goal of princes and many lesser pilgrims, possessing as it did a relic of the Holy Blood.

Hailes Abbey was founded for Cistercian monks in 1240 by Richard, Earl of Cornwall, a younger son of King John: it was the founder's son who presented the precious relic to the abbey in 1270: the east end of the church was rebuilt in the form of a chevet – very rare in England. Very little survives of the church – only foundations marked out in the grass, but the plan is clear; the cloisters retain the entrance to the chapter house, and some arches of the west range. In accordance with the Cistercian plan, the refectory stood at right angles to the south range.

After the Dissolution the property came into the hands of the Tracy family, who adapted the west claustral range as a house, and added greatly to it. Prints exist showing the splendid mansion – but all has disappeared. The Tracys (later Hanbury-Tracys, Lords Sudeley) built a grander house not far away, and their house here went to ruin, partly used as a farm. In course of time, nature took over completely, and Hailes was forgotten – to be rescued only at the end of the nineteenth century.

There is a particularly attractive museum at the entrance gate, containing beautiful fragments delightfully displayed, and some of the quite exceptional carved bosses in which the place seems to abound. The most celebrated is the one which depicts Christ rending the jaws of Satan (thirteenth century). Many of these, it seems, as the buildings went to ruin, just dropped to the ground, and were later discovered in the deep vegetation. There are also many very beautiful mediaeval tiles. The little church should be visited, too, for its wall paintings, ancient glass, and sixteenth- and seventeenth-century furnishings. As we have observed elsewhere, some of the best things have survived by being forgotten and neglected.

In one of the arched recesses of the north cloister wall are these words of St Bernard:

> *Bonum est hic nos esse*
> *Quia homo vivit purius,*
> *Cadit rarius, surgit velocius, accedit cautius,*
> *Quiescit securius, oritur felicius,*
> *Purgatur citius,*
> *Praemiatur copiosius.*

> *It is good for us to be here*
> *Because a man lives a better life,*
> *Falls more rarely,*
> *rises more quickly,*
> *continues more carefully,*
> *Goes to his rest more carefree,*
> *rises a happier man,*
> *Is cleansed the sooner,*
> *Rewarded the more abundantly.*

KINGSWOOD ABBEY

Cistercian

Below the Cotswolds, and close to Wotton-under-Edge, there stands at the end of the village street here at Kingswood the remarkable sixteenth-century gatehouse to the Cistercian abbey, founded in 1139. At first sight this looks a normal mediaeval gatehouse, gabled, with a wide arch, and two-light window above, pinnacled buttresses on either side; but on closer inspection it will be seen that the central mullion of the window is in the form of a most delicate madonna lily standing in a tall vase with leaves and flowers realistically carved. The tracery rises behind, and the window itself is elaborately crocketed, so is the gable, so are the pinnacles. In all, it is exceedingly pretty. The finial on the gable is in the form of a tiny rood, with figures still intact, and over the pedestrian entrance is an ornate niche, and above the canopy here is a dove descending: the niche must have contained a carving of the Annunciation. Nothing survives of church or claustral buildings, but this gatehouse is a monastic building of rare and special beauty.

LLANTHONY SECUNDA

Augustinian

This is Llantonia Secunda, founded *c.* 1134 as a daughter house of Llantonia Prima (qv) – as more than a daughter indeed, for it was a refuge for the brethren from the raids of the wild Welsh. Secunda indeed grew in numbers and importance as Prima fell. But its site is now in a squalid part of Gloucester, on the edge of the Gloucester–Berkeley Canal.

Some of the precinct wall survives, bordering a main road with its heavy, thundering traffic, as does the mediaeval gatehouse. Within there are a few monastic relics – first, a house of some size, of stone and timber, which could have been the guesthouse; second, a barn (to the south); and, third, another barn (to the north) – both of which must be mediaeval; indeed, the latter has a very unusual arched and buttressed porch. Nothing survives of cloister or its buildings, and the site of the church was where the canal now runs; when this was being dug (*c.* 1816) the foundations were discovered.

One last legacy of Llantonia Secunda is its library, saved through the tenacity and good sense of the last prior. The books are now in the library of Lambeth Palace.

QUENINGTON PRECEPTORY

Hospitaller

That wonderful Cotswold triangle: Cirencester, Fairford, Bibury – that is where Quenington is, and here the Hospitallers founded their preceptory at the very end of the twelfth century. All that survives is the dovecote, perhaps fourteenth century in date, containing its original potence (revolving ladder), and the gatehouse, which stands where the lane makes a gentle bend in this delightful village. The lower part, with its postern doorway, is thirteenth century, and the main entrance with its wider arch has a room above it, and must be fourteenth century. The little niche for a saint with its ogee canopy is charming.

Hampshire

GODSFIELD

Hospitaller

In quiet lanes between Alton and Winchester: the quietest lane of all leads to Godsfield, a cul-de-sac. Here stand farm buildings, an eighteenth-century house, and attached to that a tiny fourteenth-century chapel. This was a house of the Knights Hospitaller, founded *c.* 1171, comprising the Preceptor, the Chaplain, and half a dozen others. The community moved to North Baddesley (near Romsey) in the middle of the fourteenth century, leaving only a chaplain and bailiff here; indeed the west part of the chapel was the priest's house.

Nothing survives at North Baddesley, but this precious relic survives here. It is enchanting – God's field indeed.

MOTTISFONT ABBEY

Augustinian

'Mottisfont Abbey' sounds grander than 'Mottisfont Priory'. Of course. But it was only an eighteenth-century owner, Sir Richard Mill, 5th Baronet, who raised Mottisfont to the status of an abbey. Mottisfont was founded *c.* 1200 as a priory for Augustinian Canons by William de Briwere. Today the house, set in a landscape of spreading lawns adorned with glorious trees, cedars of Lebanon, beeches, planes and chestnuts, with the River Test flowing swiftly by, appears to be an eighteenth-century creation: indeed, standing before the south front with its pedimented centre, its short wings with canted bay windows and sashes everywhere, it appears a Georgian house; only the discerning eye will detect that it is really a Tudor mansion, formed from the nave of a monastic church; beneath the terrace near the front door is still the early thirteenth-century monks' cellarium – and, walking round the east end, the sudden appearance of a monastic pillar here, an unexpected mediaeval archway there, will reveal more. Indeed the north front reveals all. Here is the long, buttressed, aisleless nave of the church, a fragment of the tall archway which led into the vanished north transept, with the truncated tower above, and the long line of Tudor mullioned windows below, and Georgian sash windows above. It is an exceedingly attractive composition.

The priory was dissolved in 1536, and granted to William, 1st Lord Sandys, of the Vyne, Henry VIII's Lord Chamberlain, who formed a Tudor mansion out of the nave of the church, and some of the monastic buildings round the cloister court. The place passed by descent to the Mill family, who transformed the Tudor mansion into a Georgian house, and with whom it remained until 1934. In that year it was purchased by Mr and Mrs Gilbert Russell. To them is due the creation, or the recreation, of the beautiful garden; it was they who commissioned Rex Whistler to decorate the drawing room in 1939, his last major work, and a glorious trompe l'oeil fantasy. Mrs Russell presented Mottisfont to the National Trust in 1957: the gardens, the Rex Whistler Room, and the cellarium are now open regularly to the public.

NETLEY ABBEY

Cistercian

'But how shall I describe Netley to you? I can only do so by telling you that it is the spot in the world for which Mr Chute and I wish. The ruins are vast, and retain fragments of beautiful fretted roofs pendant in the air, with all the variety of Gothic patterns of windows, wrapped round and round with ivy – many trees are sprouted up against the walls, and only want to be increased with cypresses . . . In fact they are not the ruins of Netley, but of Paradise . . .' So wrote Horace Walpole in 1755 to his friend Richard Bentley, and Mr Chute was John Chute (of the Vyne), who shared with him to the full the romance of the Gothic. Indeed, engravings exist of Netley in this state, overgrown and romantic.

Now all is changed: the ivy is gone, and the trees no longer sprout against the walls, the grass is all neatly mown and manicured. Yet Netley is still very beautiful, set in its wooded valley, with Southampton water near at hand.

Netley Abbey was founded in 1239 by Peter des Roches, Bishop of Winchester, and (after his death) by Henry III. After its suppression in 1536 it was granted to Sir William Paulet, afterwards 1st Marquis of Winchester, who actually converted it into a mansion. This explains the puzzling domestic appearance of the building as we approach.

We are facing the south side of the cloister: here in Cistercian fashion the refectory would have stood, at right angles to the cloister: here instead is Sir William's front door, which leads into the cloister court – a grass courtyard in which a fountain once played. The former monastic quarters here he converted for domestic use, and the nave of the church became a magnificent Great Hall.

Sir William inserted a Tudor doorway from the cloister into his Great Hall; above and high up are the triple-lancet aisle windows – high up to clear the cloister roof. We enter the church: the arcades are gone, and the north transept is missing, but much remains of the south transept, including its eastern arcade with its chapels, still vaulted. Everywhere there were lancet windows, whether in pairs or in triplets: it is all elegant Early English, or early Decorated, of the thirteenth or very early fourteenth century. The aisles were narrow, and their east ends, each with a single lancet window, must have been of great beauty, as is the east window of the quire, with its (albeit fragmentary) tracery.

Sacristy, chapter house, parlour, dorter with its undercroft are in their usual positions, but here or there later brickwork or Tudor fireplaces denote Sir William's conversion of monastic rooms. The building at the south end, set, oddly, not at right angles to the main range, was probably the infirmary.

It is perhaps not surprising that in the early eighteenth century – before the days of the 'nostalgia boom' – this kind of house, with its immense Great Hall and draughty corridors, ceased to be popular. Its then owner, Sir Berkeley Lucy, sold the place to a Southampton builder, for the building materials. He duly set to work on the west front of the church; the tracery fell from the west window, and killed him. Thus were the ruins of Netley Abbey preserved for posterity.

Those who wish to see the north transept will have to go to Cranbury Park near Winchester, where it was re-erected *as a ruin* in the eighteenth century.

TITCHFIELD ABBEY

Premonstratensian

Of all the ruined abbeys of England, this is one of the most extraordinary. We stand before it – before what appears to be a great Tudor mansion, with a gatehouse like Cowdray or one of the great college gates at Cambridge; there are large castellated turrets (complete with arrow slits), oriel windows above the archway, and symmetrical wings, also castellated, on either side, with straight-headed mullioned windows, terminating in octagonal turrets, with an ample sprinkling of ornamental chimneys here and there. And what do we discover? That this was the nave of the monastic church. Sir Thomas Wriothesley, later 1st Earl of Southampton and Lord Chancellor of England, was granted the remains of Titchfield Abbey at the Dissolution (in 1536) and proceeded, most successfully, to convert the ruins into a mansion. The nave of the church was aisleless and lent itself to conversion like this; crossing, transepts, quire, chapels, were simply demolished. The new gatehouse led into a charming courtyard, the refectory opposite became the Great Hall. Chapter house and buildings of the east side of the cloister court, and other buildings on the west, were converted for domestic use. What could be simpler? And what better?

Titchfield Abbey was founded for Premonstratensian Canons by Peter des Roches, Bishop of Winchester, in 1232. The wholesale conversion of the remains for domestic use has obliterated almost every vestige of their former ecclesiastical use, only a few clues surviving by which to identify the chapter house, and little else. Houses like this ceased to be attractive in the eighteenth century: Titchfield became a roofless, ruinous, though impressive, shell.

A visit should be paid to the parish church, to see the great tomb of the Wriothesleys, where they lie in alabaster splendour – the work of Gerard Johnson of Southwark (1594).

WINCHESTER – HYDE ABBEY

Benedictine

Only the gatehouse survives of what was once an important Benedictine house – whose church was the burial place of King Alfred. Originally founded immediately to the north of the cathedral in 901 by Edward the Elder, son of King Alfred, it became Benedictine in 963, and moved to its present site in 1110.

The gatehouse is not easy to find in the streets of small houses north of the High Street in Winchester, but the name of Hyde Street provides a clue, and King Alfred's Place (turn right here) brings us to the gatehouse, opposite St Bartholomew's Church. It is a simple fifteenth-century one-storeyed building with a hipped roof, and a small thatched barn alongside. All else was ruthlessly pulled down at the Dissolution, and the tomb of King Alfred destroyed.

Isle of Wight

QUARR ABBEY

Cistercian

The Abbey of Our Lady of the Quarry: the quarry was at Binstead nearby, and its stones not only built this Cistercian abbey, but also the Cathedrals of Winchester and Chichester, and Winchester College. Not many of the stones which built this abbey stand above ground today; approaching the site down the lane we are greeted by a charming early nineteenth-century farmhouse (with some mediaeval features built in), behind which is what appears to be a mediaeval barn of prodigious size and grandeur; in fact it is the west cloister range, all that stands upright of the monastery. So, here was the cloister, with its garth to the east and the church to its south; the claustral buildings were in their usual places – and a little can be made out of the kitchen, very little of the refectory, a little of the dorter undercroft, and a little of the infirmary. The church (for once) was on the south side of the cloister, but the farm lane runs right across it, lengthwise.

Quarr was founded as a Savigniac house in 1132, but with the rest of its Order became Cistercian in 1147. At the Dissolution there were ten monks here, with the abbot; great attempts were made to save the abbey, on account of its goodness to the poor of the district, and to local seamen. But to no avail: the monks departed.

But four hundred years later they are back. Early this century a community of French Benedictines came to the Isle of Wight, settling first at Appuldurcombe, once a seat of the Earls of Yarborough, and even now in its ruined state a wonderful Palladian shell. Then they came to Quarr (1907), acquiring the large Victorian house called Quarr Abbey, a mile away from the old abbey. This then became the nucleus of the new abbey – which indeed was raised to that rank in 1937, the community now being mostly English. The architect was Dom Paul Bellot, himself a member of the community. All his buildings are good, but his church is quite outstanding. The stone of the Binstead Quarry had by then become extinct and unobtainable; Dom Paul introduced bricks from Belgium of a rich peach hue, and designed a church of

59

tremendous originality and distinction, all built of this unusual warm-toned brick, inside and out. There is something Spanish about the form of Gothic – something almost Moorish. It is an extraordinarily powerful building, with its towers and pinnacles – one is tempted almost to say minarets. There is a short nave – then steps lead up into the long monastic chancel. Everywhere are these amazing and almost overpowering brick arches, which take our eyes and thoughts to Heaven. The thing to do, for us visitors (and perhaps Anglicans, or complete outsiders) is to sit in the nave for Vespers, or for Compline, indeed for any of the monastic Hours: the monks will be in their chancel, up all that flight of steps; here we can sit bewitched, as the voice of prayer, the voice of plainsong, is uplifted into the echoing vaults of those rose-pink arches. 'The voice of prayer is never silent' – but indeed it was, here in Quarr, for nearly four hundred years. But now, thank God, no longer.

Herefordshire

CLIFFORD PRIORY

Cluniac

This is remote Welsh borderland: here Radnorshire and Hereford-shire meet. Clifford is just in England, and the Wye is the boundary. The motte and bailey of the castle of the Cliffords and the Mortimers, with a few stone foundations, is still conspicuous; much less so is the site of the Cluniac priory, founded here in 1130. The house called Clifford Priory is a good-looking early eighteenth-century stone build-ing, with what are obviously older parts behind: it is altogether pleas-ing, but few would accuse it of mediaeval, let alone monastic, origins. Yet in the basement is a thirteenth-century doorway, and there is old masonry all round. Nearly everything else has vanished – church, cloister, claustral buildings – and it is hard to visualize the busy mon-astic life which flourished here, with prior and ten or twelve monks.

Francis Kilvert, in his *Diary*, describes visits to his friends the Allens at Clifford Priory in the early 1870s: 'At 5.30 started to walk to Clifford Priory to dinner,' he wrote on 7 July 1870, 'going to Hay across the fields. I arrived before any of the other guests and in the dark cool drawing room I found Mr Allen, his brother Major Allen, and Major Allen's two bewitching pretty little girls . . . It was a very nice pleasant dinner . . . Good champagne and the first salmon I have tasted this year . . . Clifford Priory is certainly one of the nicest most comfortable houses in this part of the country.' He was there again the following week, on 12 July: 'Walked to Clifford Priory across the fields . . . A crowd in the drawing room drinking claret cup iced and eating enor-mous strawberries . . .' Croquet followed, and then more iced claret cup, and more strawberries, after which they went out to watch the eclipse: 'we all strolled out into the garden and stood on the high terrace to see the eclipse . . . we were well placed . . . and the night was beautiful . . .'

CRASWALL PRIORY

Grandmontine

'This is the highest and wildest parish in Herefordshire. It reaches up onto the Black Mountains' – so wrote David Verey in his *Shell Guide to Herefordshire*. Beyond the remote tiny village with its little church, the road becomes a bleak mountain track, and rises higher and higher into the mountains, and a farm gate leads down into a valley – a very steep valley – at the bottom of which are the scanty relics of the priory, a house of the little-known Order of Grandmont, of which there were only three others in England, fragments surviving only here and at Alberbury. It is not at all easy to make anything of the low walls and lumps of stone that survive, but the church appears to have been small, aisleless and apsidal; to the south of the chancel is a fragment of what must have been the sacristy, and beyond that a fragment of the chapter house, so the cloister must have been on the south side. But much has to be imagined, as all is now half-smothered in trees and undergrowth. The track leads up again to the farm itself.

The priory was founded *c.* 1225, for a prior and ten monks, and though it survived the earlier suppression of alien houses it was dissolved in 1462, and the property was granted to Christ's College, Cambridge. It is a rare, solemn spot.

FLANESFORD PRIORY

Augustinian

The contrasting scenery of the Wye Valley: Goodrich Castle stands above, commanding a dramatic bend in the river, while half a mile upstream Flanesford Priory presides below over its quiet pastoral valley. Flanesford was an Augustinian house, founded in 1346. The only surviving building is the refectory, which stands erect and splendid, as though to provide for a community of some size; in fact it was quite a small house of perhaps half a dozen brethren. The Black Death, occurring soon after its foundation probably affected the community, and it never revived. Built of stone, with Decorated windows, and an unexpected pantile roof, the refectory, bereft of church and all its other buildings, makes a very attractive private house.

GARWAY PRECEPTORY

Templar : Hospitaller

Behind the interesting church of this Herefordshire village is a round tower – which at first sight could be taken for part of some fortification – part of a castle, or castellated manor house. In fact it is a dovecote, the remaining fragment of the preceptory of the Templars, founded here *c.* 1185. Garway was the most important house of the Templars on the Welsh border, and continued to be important under the Hospitallers, to whom it was transferred in 1312. The dovecote is a striking building, and most remarkably bears an inscription: '*istud columbarium factum fuit per Ricardum (1326)*' ('This dovecote was constructed by Richard in 1326'). Inside there are tiers of nesting boxes in groups of fours, divided by plain string courses, with a central tank in the floor for collecting guano. The Templars' church had a round nave, like so many Templar churches. Part of this has been excavated, and can be traced in the grass.

HEREFORD – BLACKFRIARS

Dominican

Behind the Coningsby Hospital in Widemarsh Street, and opposite the 'Hereford Snooker Centre' stands the fourteenth-century Blackfriars Preaching Cross. It is the only surviving friars' preaching cross in England, and so of exceptional interest. It stands on steep steps, a parapet of openwork panels providing, as it were, the sides of the pulpit, with the immensely tall hexagonal shaft of the cross in the centre and delicate shafts all round to support a shallow vaulted canopy to protect the preacher. Behind stands the ruin of a mediaeval building, probably a range of the friars' house, but greatly altered after the Dissolution, when it became the home of Sir Thomas Coningsby – many of the features, such as windows and fireplaces, are his. It was he who founded the Coningsby Hospital in 1614: this charming little quadrangular building, with its hall and chapel, was mostly built by

Sir Thomas, but he made use of some of the mediaeval hospital of St John of Jerusalem, which once occupied the site.

LIMEBROOK PRIORY

Augustinian Canonesses

Remote and wonderful Welsh border country: a lane off a lane off a lane reaches Limebrook, where there was once a priory for Augustinian Canonesses, founded here *c.* 1190. A couple of walls, the remains of a doorway, and one or two lumps of stone for ever entwined with roots of ancient trees – it is really very difficult to make anything of this. At the end of the lane stands the timbered Limebrook Cottage, perhaps fifteenth century in date, which may be connected with the priory. It was never a big priory, but somehow survived the suppression of the lesser monasteries; indeed there were still twelve holy women here at the Dissolution.

WIGMORE ABBEY

Augustinian

Wigmore stands in wonderful, romantic, well-wooded Herefordshire countryside, once dominated by the Mortimer family, that great feudal dynasty which held sway across the Welsh Marches, and built both the castle of Wigmore, and the abbey, where they were buried. Little remains of either castle or abbey, not a stone to mark their place of burial. Wigmore was bought in 1601 by the Harleys, Earls of Oxford, and as we stand in this green and pleasant land we may spare a thought for Wigmore Street, Harley Street and Oxford Street, in such close proximity in the distant metropolis; Harleys still live at Brampton Bryan, not far away.

From the village a road leads north, and a farm track takes us to the inner gatehouse, stone below, fourteenth-century half-timbered above. Beyond stand a tall fragment of the south transept, and part of the nave, some ten feet high, the south wall of an aisleless nave, with nothing left of chancel or chapels. Still, it is just possible here to imagine the grand tombs of the Mortimers; all is now grass.

Nor is there anything left of cloister or claustral buildings, which

Above: Hailes: fragments
of arcades and buildings
around the cloisters.
Left: the roof bosses
simply dropped into the
grass as the buildings
collapsed, so are well
preserved. Here Christ
is tearing apart the jaws
of Satan.

Kingswood: the mullion in the window of the 14th-century gatehouse
is carved as a lily in a long vase, for our Lady.

Opposite above: Godsfield: in quiet lanes between Alton and Winchester this tiny
fragment of the Hospitallers' Chapel survives.
Below: Mottisfont: walking along the south front of the Augustinian priory –
now a Georgian country house – there appear suddenly a 13th-century archway
and capital and a solid monastic pillar of the Canons' church.

Left: Netley: after the Dissolution the church was converted into a Tudor house, with the front door opening out of the cloister court.

Below: Titchfield: an incredible conversion – the monastic nave has become Tudor mansion and gatehouse, at the hands of Thomas Wriothesley, Earl of Southampton.

Wigmore: the monastic gatehouse has come into its own again as a gatehouse for sheep on a working farm in Herefordshire.

Canterbury: Greyfriars, the first Franciscan building in England (*c.* 1267), astride the infant River Stour.

Reculver: on the north Kent coast the fragments hang perilously over the sea shore.

Cockersands: marooned on the north Lancashire coast, the chapter house has survived by being used as the mausoleum of the Daltons of Thurnham Hall.

stood on the south side of the church. All that survives is the abbot's lodging, the long range which adjoins the gatehouse, and must once have been joined on to the refectory, which occupied the south side of the cloister. After the Dissolution this was converted into a house, with, at the east end, a domestic wing added at right angles in the sixteenth or early seventeenth century. All this is now a private house, and not open to the public – though learned societies may be admitted at certain times by appointment.

Wigmore Abbey was founded, originally at Shobdon, a few miles from Wigmore, in 1131 by Hugh Mortimer, for Canons of St Victor in Paris – later Augustinian – and after many moves finally arrived at Wigmore in 1171. The church was dedicated in 1179. The grandeur of the abbot's lodging is some indication of the importance of the abbey. There is a long low Great Hall on the ground floor, leading to other grand rooms above, lit by the traceried fourteenth- and fifteenth-century windows which are such a feature outside. There are more rooms above, some post-Dissolution insertions; there is a good deal of ancient woodwork, and the mediaeval roof is original. Heavily buttressed on the south side, and with some Georgian sash windows on the north, it is all a most attractive hotchpotch. The little summer-house on the terrace is made up of mediaeval fragments; from here there is a grand view of this adorable countryside.

Kent

BILSINGTON PRIORY

Augustinian

The high land overlooking Romney Marsh, with magnificent views across the Marsh, and out to sea: the Augustinian priory here was founded in 1253, an altogether charming little building, which at first sight might be taken for the church, with its heavily buttressed west end, and what looks like a long south transept; moreover there is a low tower in the angle, with tile-hung pyramid roof. It is not the church – the church has vanished, and even its site is unknown. In all likelihood this is the infirmary, set on its undercroft, with another domestic building adjoining to the south, and no doubt detached from church and cloister. The Augustinians often had these small houses in the countryside, with only a prior and a few canons: here at Bilsington there seem to have been six or seven.

BOXLEY ABBEY

Cistercian

Boxley is a wonderfully sequestered place, for all the proximity of Maidstone, and the heavy traffic on the M20 to the north. Through the village, a lane marked 'No Through Road' leads to the remains of the abbey gatehouse, and a long drive leads on to a tall brick Queen Anne house set in spacious gardens, adorned with cedars and other splendid trees. This does not at first sight appear in the least bit monastic. But wait.

Boxley was founded in 1143 for Cistercian monks, and colonized from Clairvaux. It possessed a very famous rood, and large numbers of pilgrims came to venerate it – so Boxley flourished. There was a fair-sized twelfth-century church of usual Cistercian plan, with a cloister on the south side: curiously, the refectory was parallel to the south walk (unusual for a Cistercian house); chapter house, sacristy, slype and warming house were in their usual positions on the east side, and the lay brothers occupied the west side.

After the Dissolution the west range was converted into a house, and most of the rest was pulled down. In the early nineteenth century the west range was pulled down, too, leaving the tall Queen Anne house, which indeed occupies the southwest corner of the cloisters. It is possible to stand at the front door here, get one's bearings, and envisage the church opposite. But in the early eighteenth century – novel idea – a terrace walk was made above the south aisle, from which to survey the garden and the house, and the nave and crossing became a water garden. This has disappeared, but it is delightful to walk along the terrace, and so into the chancel, where clipped yews mark the position of sanctuary and high altar.

The Best family first came to Boxley in the early eighteenth century; forty years ago the place was inherited by Sir John Shaw, 9th Baronet, whose ancestor, Sir John, 1st Baronet, 'rendered most essential services to Charles II by the advance of money during that Prince's exile'. The 9th Baronet assumed the additional surname of Best, and it is his family who live here today in the southwest corner of the Cloister. It is a charming house: the front door leads into a low hall, and a mediaeval arch into the dining room. A splendid early eighteenth-century staircase leads up to beautiful Georgian drawing rooms above. Nearby part of the refectory walls still stand, and a useful outbuilding turns out to be the monastic warming house. Everything is still enclosed within the impressive precinct wall, and to the southwest of the house is a magnificent late thirteenth-century monastic barn.

Boxley is a private house, not open to the public.

CANTERBURY – BLACKFRIARS

Dominican

What remains of the Priory of the Dominicans – the Black Friars – stands backing on to the Stour, at the end of Black Friars Street. We can ignore the notice *Black Friars Motor Co.*, enjoy the little early nineteenth-century stuccoed terraced houses, and then admire the imposing flint façade of the Dominican frater at the end of the street. It stands on an undercroft, and must date from the mid-thirteenth century. Henry III granted the Dominicans this site in 1237; the frater, it seems, occupied the west side of the cloisters, with the church on the south, and the dorter on the north – but neither of these survives.

CANTERBURY – GREYFRIARS

Franciscan

This is one of the most delightful of all monastic fragments. There are gardens off Stour Street in Canterbury, through which the little River Stour makes its way. Bridging this, and built on two pairs of pointed arches of which the pillars stand midstream, is a tall rectangular little building of stone and flint and brick – the first Franciscan building in England. The brethren first came to England in 1224, only fifteen years after St Francis had inaugurated his Order. This little building (of *c.* 1267) is probably the dorter – there is a fireplace in an upper room; the church lay to the north, but of this nothing remains. But this little building, astride the narrow river, is eloquent of the simplicity and beauty of Franciscan ideals.

CANTERBURY – ST AUGUSTINE'S ABBEY

Benedictine

Two imposing gateways, one dating from the early fourteenth century – the Great Gate – the other from the late fourteenth – the Cemetery Gate – led into the monastic precinct; both stand today, though only the Great Gate is in use. St Augustine's was in its day one of the very greatest of all Benedictine houses. But little survives, apart from the gatehouses and a labyrinth of foundations.

St Augustine founded the original abbey in 598, in which to bury archbishops and kings of Kent (the Romans forbade burial within city walls), and his church would have been a Saxon building of no great size, just outside the walls. But then, soon afterwards, another church, of St Mary, was added by King Edbald (*c.* 613), to be a royal mausoleum, some 50 feet to the east; then yet another, of St Pancras, was built soon after that, a further 250 feet to the east. Moreover, the original abbey church was later (*c.* 1000) extended to the west, and fifty years later this was all joined to St Mary's by an octagonal structure known as Abbot Wolfric's Rotunda. But all was swept away *c.* 1070 by Abbot Scotland, who built a grand new Norman abbey church on the site, leaving only St Pancras' on its own to the east.

At the Dissolution in 1538 part of the northwest end of the nave, together with the west side of the cloister and the abbot's house, were converted into a royal palace for Henry VIII, and remained a lesser royal residence until the late seventeenth century. It later became a brewery – until in 1844 the whole property was purchased by A. J. B. Beresford-Hope, who founded upon part of the site St Augustine's College, to be a missionary college for the Church of England. Here he employed Butterfield to design the college buildings, which were wherever possible sited on monastic foundations; the College Library partly incorporates the abbot's Great Hall. This was Butterfield's first great work: he and Beresford-Hope were to work together closely a few years later on the building of All Saints', Margaret Street.

But the foundations are the thing – at any rate for the archaeologically minded. Here can be seen what remains of the original monastic church, of the Rotunda, and of St Mary's – though on these was superimposed the crypt of the Norman church, and of this a little remains, and a little has been re-erected. To the east again are the foundations of the early sixteenth-century Lady Chapel, and farther east again the foundations of St Pancras' Church. Everything has been magnificently excavated, and everything is splendidly set out.

DOVER PRIORY

Benedictine

St Martin's Priory was founded for Benedictine monks in 1131: the church has disappeared, but it is extraordinary how much else survives, all well preserved and made use of by Dover College – the Victorian public school (founded in 1868). There is a fourteenth-century gatehouse, and the school chapel is the late twelfth-century monastic guest hall, which, with its six-bay arcade of pointed arches on tall round piers with scalloped capitals, is a building of some distinction. The monks' refectory, now the school hall, is slightly earlier, and a building of great Norman splendour. It is built of flint and Caen stone, with bays divided by pilasters and string course, and round-headed windows high up. Inside, these windows alternate with blank round-headed arches.

Jagged lumps of masonry outside tell the site of the monastic cloister – and much else can be imagined from the impressive buildings, still in use and full of life. But it is the life of squash racquets and piles of books and chattering schoolboys now – not of silent monks.

HORTON PRIORY

Cluniac

Inland from the Kentish coast, and not far from Hythe and Lympne, in countryside of fields and copses, stands Horton Priory, a mile or so from the village of Monks Horton. It is perhaps a surprise, at the end of the drive, to find a demure Tudor-style house of 1913 – accustomed as we are, in this search for monastic remains, to encounter surprises. Here a sophisticated, skilful hand has incorporated the remains of a Cluniac priory in the walls of his later house. Close to the front door is a part of the south half of the west front of the church, with the jamb of an archway now embedded in the front of the house, a fascinating fragment – the springer of a Norman arch, rising from triple carved capitals. There is more to see round the corner, where the west side of the house is indeed the west range of the cloister, with mediaeval and later windows, and mediaeval buttresses – all surveying a charming garden.

Horton Priory was founded in 1142 for Cluniac monks, dependent on Lewes. It was only a small house with a prior and perhaps eight or ten monks. The garden is sometimes open in aid of the National Gardens Scheme: it is a pleasure to see these monastic remains in such a beautiful setting.

LESNES ABBEY

Arrouasian

'Abbey Wood' the trams on the Embankment used to proclaim, emerging from that exciting passage of the Kingsway Tunnel. Some might only announce 'Elephant & Castle', some 'New Cross Gate', but the really adventurous trams were bent on reaching Woolwich, and, beyond Woolwich, 'Abbey Wood'. How many, watching the trams gliding along the Embankment, would pause to wonder where Abbey

Wood was? Or what it was doing on a London tram route? Abbey Wood really exists – unlike St John's Wood – and it is the wood that crowns the hill which overlooks Lesnes Abbey.

Lesnes was founded in 1178 for Arrouasian Canons – later becoming Augustinian. It was never a large foundation, and it was dissolved in 1525, and granted to Cardinal Wolsey to help endow his college at Oxford (later Christ Church).

What remains of Lesnes Abbey now stands in a public park approached from Abbey Road (B213) between Plumstead and Erith. The ground slopes up to the wooded hill to the south, the fragmentary walls spread out in front: the dorter nearest the road, of which one wall rises to some 12 feet, and the cloister court beyond, with chapter house, slype and sacristy opening out on the east side, the frater and kitchen out on the north. The church lay to the south, and it is possible to identify this from its low walls and foundations; nothing rises more than a few feet, and much of all this is the result of excavations during this century, and a little reassembling and reconstruction in the process.

It is a pleasure to walk around these very fragmentary remains, so curiously set down in one of outer London's public parks – with the intimidating blocks of high-rise flats not far away.

MOATENDEN PRIORY

Trinitarian

Headcorn has a long street with plenty of half-timbered houses, and a mediaeval church at one end to command its length: the place prospered in the Middle Ages on cloth and weaving. A mile or so to the north, just off the road to Sutton Valence, and down a farm lane, stands the fragment of the mediaeval Trinitarian Friary of Moatenden. Moatenden is a charming house of brick, with stone mullioned windows, perhaps fifteenth century in date. Inside, one room is divided from the next by a Tudor archway, with mullioned window adjoining – perhaps originally the outside wall of some monastic building. There are no clues, and all is conjecture. On the garden front what appear to be two mediaeval pillars lead towards the meadow, with copses beyond. Fragments of the church? Alas, they were bought in London by a former owner as garden ornaments.

The Trinitarian Friars followed the Augustinian rule, and were closer to the canons regular than to the mendicant friars. Their mother house was at Ingham in Norfolk, where their church survives. In Scotland they were known as the Red Friars: they only had three or four houses in Scotland, and eleven in England.

RECULVER ABBEY

Benedictine

The lane from Herne Bay, skirting the sea, is lined with an abundance of hedge parsley and other wild flowers in spring – and the sense of expectation is high as the twin towers of Reculver come in sight. But the lane descends to an anticlimax: an enormous and terrible caravan park, with all its attendant clutter and noise.

The site on the promontory, in the middle of what was a Roman fort – much of which is now under the sea – was given by King Egbert for the foundation of a Benedictine abbey in 669. Church and monastic buildings must have been built soon after. Though little survives of the church, enough of the foundations is preserved to give us some idea of the plan; and as the building was still standing, incredibly, until 1809, engravings exist to tell us more. In 1809, equally incredibly, the church was demolished by order of the incumbent in the belief that it was being used for a poppet show or some sacrilegious purpose – an amazing act of insanity and vandalism. We should otherwise be in possession of a very rare seventh-century church. As it is, we can see that it was symmetrical and cruciform, with an apsidal east end; a screen divided nave from chancel, and in front of the screen stood a remarkable stone cross, of which fragments are preserved in the crypt at Canterbury. The twin west towers, originally crowned with spires, were allowed to stand, as an aid to shipping.

Little is known of this Saxon monastery; the monks, it seems, were driven out by Danish raids, and escaped to Canterbury, merging with the Benedictine monks of St Augustine's. But here these precious fragments stand on the very edge of the sea, a reminder of the very earliest days of Christian England, as the waves break upon the shore below, and where in summer holiday-makers sun themselves in their deckchairs.

ST JOHN'S JERUSALEM

Hospitaller

Coming from London, here at last we leave suburbia behind, and reach the real Kent countryside – and this enchanting mediaeval moated house – once a commandery of the Hospitallers, now looked after by the National Trust. The chapel is at the east end, where thirteenth-century lancets light the sanctuary on its three sides. King Henry III ordered oaks from Tonbridge Forest for the roof of the chapel in 1234, so the building can be dated. At the west end the chapel dies into the later, seventeenth- and eighteenth-century house. But we know that there is some mediaeval masonry even behind the later brickwork and plaster.

In the eighteenth century Edward Hasted, the county historian, lived here, and much of the house we see must be due to him, but its beautiful name, for ever linking the place with the Order of St John of Jerusalem, lives on. Originally founded as a hospital in 1199, it was given to the Order in 1214. The wonderful garden, with its grand cedar tree and glorious copper beech, was created by the late Sir Stephen Tallents, public servant, traveller and author, and it was he who gave the place to the National Trust.

'I liked this place, and considered it worthy,' wrote James Lees-Milne in his diary for 27 January 1943 (*Ancestral Voices*, Chatto and Windus, 1975); he had gone down to St John's on behalf of the National Trust to discuss the gift with Sir Stephen and his wife.

ST RADEGUND'S ABBEY

Premonstratensian

The remains of the Abbey of St Radegund, founded direct from Pré-montré in 1192, stand lonely and forgotten high on the chalk downland between Dover and Folkestone, two miles from the sea. The back road across the Downs (B2060) passes through the village of Alkham: nearby a farm lane leads to St Radegund's. On a chilly early spring morning the sea mist makes the place seem even more remote, with the gaunt ivy-clad ruins looming ahead, farm buildings all around.

After the Dissolution the place passed through various hands, and in 1590 one Simon Edolph acquired it, and converted the refectory into a house. The church was unusual in one particular respect: it had a tower in the angle between the nave and the north transept – perhaps erected for purposes of defence. Much of the stone had already been cleared away for building Sandgate Castle (c. 1540): the tower Edolph converted into a gatehouse. This led into his courtyard – the former cloisters – and buttresses adorned with flint and stone flushwork made the perfect approach to the new porch which he added to the refectory, also adorned with flint flushwork. The other monastic buildings became his accessory buildings.

Over the centuries the fragments of the church and all the claustral buildings, built of local flint, crumbled – ivy and vegetation overwhelmed them, leaving the house to become a farmhouse as it is today.

SWINGFIELD

Hospitaller

An exposed lane on the North Downs between Acrise and Lydden, a large farm, and not far away, what is obviously a mediaeval chapel, all on its own in a field. This is St John's, all that remains of a house of the Knights Hospitallers. In the twelfth century this was a small house of the Sisters of the Order of St John of Jerusalem, but c. 1180 they were transferred to Buckland, Somerset, and the Knights took over. Its extraordinary survival can be explained by the fact that after the Dissolution the chapel was converted into a farmhouse, though still retaining many mediaeval features. It cannot have been a satisfactory farmhouse, and was later abandoned. So here it stands, with its lancet windows, north porch, aumbry and piscina within, beautifully textured flint walls without. Until recently inaccessible, protected by ivy and undergrowth, it has recently been rescued by the Monuments Commission, and is open to the public. A remarkable rescue.

Lancashire

COCKERSAND ABBEY

Premonstratensian

One of the smallest and oddest of all monastic fragments – but one of much beauty, lost, as it were, on the low shore of the Lancashire coast, itself romantic and beautiful. A lane leads off the road from Lancaster to Garstang, and a farm track leads off that; before very long a little rough-hewn hexagonal battlemented building comes in sight, built of warm red sandstone, surmounted by a cross. What is this? It is so unexpected that the question may well be asked.

This is the chapter house of Cockersand Abbey, which was founded first as the Hospital of St Mary in 1184, and then refounded as a Premonstratensian priory in 1190, becoming an abbey in 1192. Foundations largely covered in grass, the odd fragment of stone walling here or there, mark the site of the church to the north. Much imagination is needed to visualize the cloisters, which the chapter house adjoined. The survival of this precious relic we owe to the Dalton family, of Thurnham Hall, a mile or two inland, an ancient house with two hiding-places, for they were an old recusant family. They acquired the monastic property in 1556, and used the chapter house as their burial place. The exterior is plain – but the interior is beautiful, with its elegant rib vault, and central column with stiff-leaf capital. The date must be c. 1230 – not very long after the founding of the abbey: would that we could see the church itself, from which the remarkable canopied stalls now in Lancaster Priory are said to have come.

This is an extraordinary, romantic, solitary spot, with wide views across Lancaster Bay, a little lighthouse, and ships passing on their way to Heysham or Lancaster.

FURNESS ABBEY

Cistercian

A beautiful tree-hung, rocky, valley – called the Vale of Nightshade; it was a remote peninsula in 1126, when the first monks came here, and a remote peninsula it remained until the opening of the Furness Railway in 1846. What was a tiny hamlet called Barrow became the great ship-building town we see today. But in the Vale of Nightshade, a mile or two to the northeast, Barrow-in-Furness might be a thousand miles away.

The first monks who came here in 1126 were Savigniacs: this Savigniac house was originally founded at Tulketh near Preston two years before, and its founder was King Stephen (when Count of Boulogne). In 1147 the Savigniac Order merged with the Cistercian, so Furness became Cistercian, and certain changes in layout and design of church and buildings took place. Furness became second only to Fountains in wealth, and was second in precedence only to Waverley.

A very unattractive ticket office and 'visitor centre' has been erected here by the Monuments Commission but even this cannot quite destroy the beauty of the place, and the pleasure of seeing this great ruin, built of warm red sandstone, for the first time. Much survives: chancel, crossing, transepts, all stand upright – together with much of the claustral buildings, and the base of the impressive west tower, begun in 1500 and never finished.

Building of the church began in the twelfth century, and enough survives of the transepts and crossing to enable us to appreciate Transitional Norman at its finest – the first pointed arches, and clustered columns with waterleaf capitals; the soaring east arch of the crossing still stands, but only the bases of the nave columns, alternately round and clustered.

The chancel was rebuilt in the early fifteenth century: here there are long Perpendicular windows, and an enormous east window, which still retains a little of its tracery. Nearby, surviving almost miraculously, is the superb sedilia, with its piscina – a noble group of four canopied seats, with canopied piscina, and niches for the towels, all one exquisite composition.

The east side of the cloister court is remarkably well preserved, with an impressive row of late Norman round arches, splendidly ornate, leading into chapter house, parlour and slype – and above, the long line of lancets which lit the dorter. The chapter house itself is of great beauty, early thirteenth century in date, with paired lancet windows (or paired blank arches): one column stands to its full height, with stiff-leaf capitals crowning its eight shafts. There is little left of the south range: the refectory stood here (north–south, in Cistercian fashion), and there are only foundations of the west range, which was, as usual, the lay brothers' quarters. Farther south was the infirmary: here the chapel survives, vaulted still, and is now a museum, containing a number of carved effigies; there is another vaulted room next door. The abbot's house stood farther to the east, beyond the guesthouse. It was a large establishment.

The west tower was inserted within the west end of the nave after an abortive attempt to build a central tower (for which the crossing arches had never been designed). It was never completed: Furness Abbey was dissolved in 1537.

WHALLEY ABBEY

Cistercian

Whalley is a little old Lancashire town, not far from the Yorkshire border, watered by the River Calder. The Cistercian abbey was originally founded in 1172, at Stanlow in Cheshire, but moved here in 1296 on account of the flooding by the River Mersey of its original home. The rebuilding here was a slow business: the church begun in 1330 was not completed till 1380. Whalley is unusual for a Cistercian house in having been built so close to a town, and in having been built in the fourteenth century, a century and more after the great Cistercian foundations.

Little remains of church or claustral buildings, but there are two gatehouses to see – one, the outer, guards the western entrance, and is a long tunnel-like rib-vaulted gate; the other, the inner, is the entry from the town, and is late fifteenth century – perhaps completed after the Dissolution. If we enter here we shall come directly to the house known as Whalley Abbey, which is now the Retreat House for the Diocese of Blackburn. Originally the abbot's house – perhaps even pre-monastic, and adapted for conventual use when the brethren first came to Whalley – it was converted into a family house by Ralph

Assheton in the second half of the sixteenth century. A good deal was done to the house in the middle of the nineteenth century.

Little more than foundations survive of the church: it followed the usual Cistercian plan. More survives in the cloister – notably the archway, with its two accompanying windows, leading into the chapter house, or, rather the vestibule; a further arch led into the chapter house itself, which was octagonal – but only its outline in the grass is to be seen. On the south side, the refectory was unusually built east–west, and not north–south, which was the normal Cistercian way. The west range survives completely: it was the lay brothers' quarters, and is now used as a Roman Catholic church hall. So Whalley is once again much in use for religious purposes.

There are two other buildings of great interest: the first, close to the outer gatehouse, is the immense railway viaduct carrying the Blackburn–Clitheroe line across the valley, built between 1845 and 1850. There are fifty-three arches, and of these the ones close to the abbey are Gothicized in deference to the sacred site: what appear to be immense Gothic lancets, narrow and elegant, stand on clustered columns all of brick, and accompany the more sober round-headed arches which constitute the rest. It is an absolutely splendid conception, and much the most thrilling thing at Whalley.

The viaduct runs close to the outer gatehouse: close to the inner gate is the parish church, in itself a worthwhile mediaeval building, but doubly interesting on account of its furnishings. In the nave there are two delightful screened family pews, one in particular adorned with most accomplished carving, of 1697 – and in the gallery at the back is the organ in its immensely beautiful early eighteenth-century case. There is more to come: in the chancel is the magnificent set of early fifteenth-century canopied stalls, which came from the abbey church itself.

Leicestershire

GRACE DIEU PRIORY

Augustinian Nuns

The main road from Loughborough to Ashby de la Zouch (A512) makes a grand curve round the demesne of Grace Dieu, and from the road it is possible to see, not far across the meadow, venerable ivy-clad ruins against the backdrop of a well-wooded park. Here stands Grace Dieu Manor, built in 1833 for Ambrose Phillips de Lisle by William Railton and A. W. N. Pugin, and now a Roman Catholic prep school.

The Priory of Grace Dieu was founded in 1240 for Augustinian nuns, and dissolved in 1538. In 1539 it was acquired by John Beaumont of Cole Orton, later Master of the Rolls, who was deprived of office for corruption. He converted the priory into an Elizabethan mansion – which makes it hard for us to disentangle the monastic remains from the domestic house, let alone disentangle these mysterious ruins from the ivy that envelops them. They stand romantic and puzzling in the meadow at the northern extremity of Grace Dieu Park, to be approached on foot across a stream by a footbridge, and a footpath strewn with undergrowth and fallen trees. No whole part survives, except for a chapel (perhaps), with its wide four-centred arch at the entrance. For the rest, it is a wall here, a tall chimney stack there, an empty window or the fragment of a fireplace. Behind is the low viaduct of an extinct railway, romantic, too, like a Roman aqueduct in a Piranesi engraving. Sir Ambrose Phillips pulled down much of John Beaumont's house in 1696. The remains have crumbled quietly ever since.

ROTHLEY TEMPLE

Templar : Hospitaller

Rothley (pronounced Roathley) is a large village on the edge of Charnwood Forest, with many good houses of Leicestershire brick and pantile. To the west, gates lead into the pretty park of Rothley Temple, and the curving drive delivers us to the front door of what appears to be a charming Elizabethan stone gabled house, with later, Georgian, sash windows. It is surprising to find, attached to its north side, a grand mediaeval chapel. This chapel, lofty and spacious, was the chapel of the Templars, whose preceptory this was, and with long lancet windows must date from the end of the thirteenth century. There is a beautiful trefoil-headed piscina, and in the porch a much-defaced mediaeval figure under an ogee canopy. The east window is Perpendicular. The preceptory was founded in the reign of Henry III, and, on the suppression of the Templars, was transferred to the Hospitallers.

The adjoining house must incorporate part of the preceptory, but was converted into an attractive house by the Babingtons, who acquired Rothley after the Dissolution. There are sixteenth-century (and later) monuments to the family in the parish church, and later tablets in the chapel. Of special interest is the fact that Thomas Babington Macaulay, the historian, was born here in 1800, his mother being sister of the then squire. In 1857 he was created Lord Macaulay of Rothley. The house, surrounded by lovely gardens, is now a delightful country house hotel.

ULVERSCROFT PRIORY

Augustinian

The high wild country of Charnwood Forest: the rock-strewn hills rise in places to 800 feet and more, and there are beautiful, quiet, fertile valleys in between, the sides of the hills hung with oak woods. In such a valley stands Ulverscroft. From the B5330 a minor road descends past Green Hill to provide a perfect view of the valley below. There is a gate marked 'No Cars', and a drive leads across the meadows to the ruins – a wonderful collection of buildings, part monastic, part domestic, dominated by a noble fifteenth-century tower.

Ulverscroft Priory was founded by Robert Bossu, Earl of Leicester, for Augustinian Canons in 1134. A good deal of the south wall of the church survives, of Early English date, with larger Perpendicular windows inserted, and these are delightfully patterned, on the jambs and arches, with quatrefoils. There was no south aisle, as the cloister abutted on this side; of this, the west wall survives in part, and the refectory can still be recognized on the south. The parlour and prior's lodging on the east were converted into a house after the Dissolution, and this is now a private house. Across the moat the gates are all marked 'Private – No Admittance' – but it is possible to see most of these buildings without trespassing.

Lincolnshire

BARLINGS ABBEY

Premonstratensian

Samuel Buck's print of 1726, dedicated to Sir John Tyrwhitt, Baronet, 'owner of these remains', shows the fourteenth-century central tower still standing, handsome and pinnacled, on its four crossing arches, perilously poised in mid-air. How on earth did it stand up? How did it survive in this extraordinary position? In the background is the many-gabled Elizabethan Stainfield Hall, seat of the Tyrwhitts, with the little Classical church (1711) standing nearby. The tower fell in 1757, and all that remains now is a fragment of stone walling.

Barlings was founded for Premonstratensian Canons in 1114 by Ralph de Haya – here, in this solitary spot, not far from the River Witham, with distant views of the Cathedral of Lincoln on its hill. A splendid eighteenth-century farmhouse in the little hamlet of Barlings must have been built of monastic stone. Bumps in the ground, the monks' well – there is little else now to tell us of its great days, which ended with the execution of the abbot and four of his brethren in 1537.

BOSTON – BLACKFRIARS

Dominican

Boston in the Middle Ages was a place of great importance, and as a port second only to London in trade; but by the end of the sixteenth century things were very different. The new lands across the Atlantic brought greater emphasis to the western shores of England – and to Bristol in particular – and the increasing flow of silt from the Yorkshire coast into the Wash gravely affected the port of Boston. The place became a distressed area. The four Houses of the Friars suffered accordingly: the Dominicans (founded *c.* 1280), the Franciscans (*c.* 1260), the Carmelites (*c.* 1290), and the Austin Friars (*c.* 1317), all bursting with friars in the fourteenth century, were in low water at the time of the suppression. The only reminders of all these four Houses now are the tall timber-framed house in South Street called Shodfriars Hall, and, round the corner in Spain Lane, a building called Black-friars Hall. The actual purpose of Shodfriars, and in what way it was connected with the Friars, is uncertain. It is no doubt late fifteenth century in date, magnificently restored by Oldrid Scott in 1874. Black-friars Hall is probably thirteenth or early fourteenth century, and almost certainly the refectory of the Dominicans; so we can imagine it forming part of their cloister court, with their church on the side opposite. It is now part of Pilgrim College (Adult Education Department, Nottingham University).

LINCOLN – GREYFRIARS

Franciscan

Next door to St Swithin's Church (James Fowler's masterpiece) in Broadgate, Lincoln, is the Greyfriars, a long vaulted hall, or under-croft. It is an impressive building, and was probably the infirmary of the friars, dating from the thirteenth century; church and other build-ings would have been to the north. Upstairs there is another very fine room with a splendid roof; a piscina at the east end denotes that this would have been the chapel. The Franciscans came to Lincoln in 1230, and at one time there were over fifty friars in residence. It is now well used and cared for as a local museum.

LINCOLN – ST MARY MAGDALEN PRIORY

Benedictine

What is usually known as Monks Abbey is some way down the long and appropriately named Monks Road in Lincoln. It was, of course, not an abbey, but a priory cell, a cell of St Mary's Abbey, York. The remaining building stands on a wide green, and appears to be the chancel of the church, dating perhaps from the early thirteenth cen-tury, but with later traceried windows. There are fragments of the nave, but of little else. Founded *c.* 1120, it provided at most for a prior and two or three monks, who were especially responsible for supervising the estates of St Mary's Abbey.

NEWSTEAD PRIORY

Gilbertine

The empty countryside of Lindsey (northern Lincolnshire), between the Wolds and the Trent: here, in the parish of Cadney, there is what looks like an early nineteenth-century farmhouse called Newstead Abbey Farm. The name speaks for itself; and inside there is one splendid monastic room. It is vaulted, the vault upheld by a central octagonal pier. The site has not been excavated, so we know nothing about the plan; it must have been one of the cloister buildings – perhaps the parlour.

Newstead was founded *c.* 1164 for Gilbertine Canons; there were usually ten canons or so in residence, but only five and the prior in 1538, the time of the suppression.

This Newstead must not be confused with the better-known Newstead in Nottinghamshire (see *Collins Guide to Cathedrals, Abbeys and Priories*).

STAMFORD – GREYFRIARS

Franciscan

At the end of St Paul's Street, where the roads divide, one to Ryhall, one to Uffington, stands the handsome little gateway to what was Greyfriars. Built in Barnack stone, the archway itself is supported on either side by a bold buttress, of which the upper part forms a canopied niche for a statue, and which ends in a pinnacle. The canopied niche over the arch itself also ends in a pinnacle, and the parapet above terminates at either end in a little pinnacle. It is early fourteenth century in date.

The Franciscans came to Stamford *c.* 1230; after the Dissolution sufficient of the building survived for Sir William Cecil to entertain the Queen here in 1566. This site is now occupied by the Stamford and Rutland Infirmary, which was opened in 1828.

STAMFORD –
ST LEONARD'S PRIORY

Benedictine

This is the oldest building in Stamford, and one of the most beautiful in that most beautiful town – and the most forgotten, standing as it does, solitary on the very outskirts.

St Wilfrid founded the priory in 658, and bestowed it on his monastery at Lindisfarne; when the monks removed from there to Durham, St Leonard's was transferred to Durham with them. It was sacked by the Danes, but refounded in 1078 as a cell of Durham, to administer their southern estates. There would never have been more than two or three monks here, in addition to the prior.

This precious little church gives us some idea of what these small monastic cells were like. This is a grand Norman church in miniature. The monastic buildings must have stood on the south side, but have all disappeared. The church must date from the very end of the eleventh century; there is a north arcade of four bays, with simple, sturdy pillars, and the west front may be a little later, with its grand doorway, with blank arches on either side. There is an arcade of seven small arches above, which includes in alternate arches three small windows – every arch richly decorated – and a vesica window above. It is an exceptionally handsome frontispiece.

TEMPLE BRUER PRECEPTORY

Templar : Hospitaller

Even in the eighteenth century the Lincoln Heath – that high ground up and on top of the Cliff, south of Lincoln – was so desolate and such a haunt of highwaymen that Sir Francis Dashwood, of West Wycombe fame, but also of Nocton nearby, built the Dunston Pillar, surmounted by a lantern – 'the only land-lighthouse ever raised'. The Heath is still desolate and lonely, but beautiful with its beech trees and old tracks. It is always something of an excitement to find oneself on one of these unfrequented roads that pass near Temple Bruer, and see that splendid stone farmhouse, with its high gable and sash windows, walled garden and generous barns – and, rising mysteriously behind all this, a tall mediaeval tower, crowned with its wide flat pyramid roof. What is this? It is the former preceptory of the Knights Templar, founded here *c.* 1265. It was one of the richest of all the houses of the Templars, but suppressed like the rest of them *c.* 1308, when it was transferred to the Hospitallers.

The tower has the appearance of a castle rather than a church – but in fact it was the tower of the church (or in all probability one of two towers), and the nave was round, like the Temple Church in London, or the Round Church in Cambridge. The Buck print of 1726 shows the nave still standing, with its ambulatory: the chancel seems to have stood between the two towers. What is now the farmhouse must have been formed out of one of the domestic ranges. The buildings must date from the end of the twelfth century, and the tower is probably early thirteenth. In 1541 Henry VIII sojourned here with his brother-in-law Charles Brandon, Duke of Suffolk, on his way north to parley with the young King of Scotland, his nephew: the commandery had been granted to Charles Brandon at the time of the suppression in 1538.

THORNTON ABBEY

Augustinian

Thornton Abbey stands not far from the Humber: the cranes and hoists of Immingham, the tall chimneys of chemical works and refineries along the Humber bank appear menacing in the distance; but this is pastoral Lincolnshire, unknown, unappreciated Lincolnshire.

Suddenly the great gatehouse comes in sight, of overbearing, towering height, inexplicable, it seems, at the end of a quiet lane, and magnificent still, four and a half centuries after the Dissolution. Military? The entrance to a vanished castle? Despite the arrow slits, the figures of saints – the Virgin, St Augustine of Hippo, and (perhaps) St John Baptist – belie that, and proclaim its character religious.

Thornton was founded as a priory for Augustinian Canons in 1139, and raised to abbey status in 1148, becoming mitred in 1518: the first monks came from Kirkham. After the Dissolution Henry VIII refounded it as a secular college, with dean, canons and schoolmasters; but it was suppressed once more by Edward VI. In 1610 Sir Vincent Skinner purchased the place, and built himself a grand house, between gatehouse and church, but according to a contemporary account, when all was finished, 'it fell quite down to the bare ground without any visible cause'. Successive owners followed, and helped themselves to stone from the church, college and mansion – so that now there is very little left, apart from the gatehouse.

The grandeur of the gatehouse denotes the importance of the abbey: even at the Dissolution there were twenty-three canons in residence. In 1541 Henry VIII and his retinue were entertained here for three days in the college which he had founded: one longs to know a little more of this short-lived academic foundation, in some ways reminiscent of Christ Church. The gatehouse is of stone and mellow brick, and was begun *c.* 1380. It is approached by a barbican over 100 feet long across the moat – two stout parallel brick walls with arched recesses, probably built in the sixteenth century at the time of the establishment of the college. There are two grand rooms upstairs; the lower has an oriel window, and from the presence of a piscina in the wall, it was obviously used for an altar. It now contains a collection of bosses and carved stones from the church and elsewhere, and from the window there is a grand view of the whole monastic layout.

It is a walk of some 250 yards across the lawn to the church. Nothing remains of this, except the foundations – and a wall of the south transept. The 'new' church was begun in 1264, and, as can be seen, was of great size; adjoining the south transept are the remains of the parlour, and then the vestibule to the chapter house.

What remains of the chapter house is of great beauty: it is, alas, but the west and northwest walls of the octagon, but with its geometrical tracery in the blind windows above, and the blind arcading below, it is reminiscent of Southwell or York – two chapter houses which date from the end of the thirteenth century, the time when the Early English style was developing into the Decorated. There are remains of claustral buildings around the cloisters – warming house and so on – which are the earliest buildings of the abbey (late twelfth century). The dorter lay above this, and the frater on the south side of the cloister. Farther to the south, the farmhouse is built on a vaulted undercroft, perhaps a relic of the infirmary.

No book of this kind is complete without one gruesome story, true or no. An abbot of Thornton is said to have been walled up alive. Even the great Dr Stukeley (died 1765) records that *in his lifetime*, on the taking down of a wall here, a skeleton was found sitting, with a table and lamp at his side.

TUPHOLME ABBEY

Premonstratensian

A solitary spot: the lonely road from Bardney (B1190) leads towards Bucknall, when, suddenly, on the right, appear what could only be some almost forgotten monastic remains, standing forlorn in the meadows – a long, lofty wall pierced with tall lancet windows, a few scanty farm buildings behind. Tupholme Abbey was founded *c.* 1160 for Premonstratensian Canons, and what remains is the early thirteenth-century south wall of the refectory, standing above a fragment of the once-vaulted undercroft – five lancets, and, at the end, the pulpit, approached by its staircase contrived within the thickness of the wall. This is very well preserved – by pure accident, of course – with a pair of beautiful trefoil-headed arches above, and a small round-headed window beyond. A farmhouse which used to stand against the refectory has recently been pulled down; bumpy mounds in the grass on the north side must mark the site of the church and the cloister, and a track to the south leads to the River Witham, half a mile away.

London

THE LONDON CHARTERHOUSE

Carthusian

From the assertive Victorian Baroque of Smithfield Market, where porters in white aprons still push their barrows, great barrow-loads of flesh, and scavenging pigeons pick at left-over carcases, it is only a step into the college-like seclusion of the Charterhouse.

Most of what remains dates from after the Dissolution, adapted first by the Duke of Norfolk, who built the Elizabethan Great Hall, and then by Thomas Sutton, from Knaith in Lincolnshire, who acquired the place in 1611. He added the Master's Court, and founded the Charterhouse as we know it – part boys' school, part hospital. The school became one of the most distinguished in the country, and moved out to Godalming in the nineteenth century – while retaining its links with Charterhouse Square; but the Charterhouse retains its function as a hospital (in the mediaeval sense), providing accommodation for a brotherhood of 'aged men past work'.

The Carthusian priory was founded in 1371. Some of the west wall of the cloister walk remains, with three of the entrances into the monks' houses, and one whole court, part of the monastic outbuildings and known as Wash House Court, built in the early sixteenth century, half in stone, half brick. The priory gatehouse survives (with its oak door) from the fifteenth century: the upper storeys are eighteenth century.

The London Charterhouse had always been of great importance: in 1535 there were thirty monks and eighteen lay brethren, and Cromwell's fury descended upon them (and on other Carthusian houses, too). The prior of the London house was executed that year – as were the priors of Beauvale and Axholme, together with a monk of Sion, and, not long afterwards, three other monks whom imprisonment and torture failed to move. At this point even Cromwell, cruel man, fearing unpopularity, delayed; but after two years renewed the attack, imprisoning four monks and six lay brothers, chaining them hand and foot to posts to starve to death. One survived, and was executed.

It is a terrible story, hard to credit as we sit and absorb this unexpected and peaceful retreat from the London that bustles outside its walls. At its heart is a garden with an ancient mulberry tree, and old English roses.

Norfolk

BEESTON REGIS PRIORY

Augustinian

A wonderful position on the north Norfolk coast, between Sheringham
and Cromer: the remains of the Augustinian Priory lie in the valley
below the cliffs where the parish church stands. The priory was
founded *c.* 1216, and Abbey Farmhouse, a delightful eighteenth-
century flint farmhouse, must have been built of monastic materials;
all the same, a remarkable portion of the monastic church still stands.
There is the fourteenth-century aisleless nave, rather earlier (Early
English) chancel, north transept and north transept chapel, all of flint.
The cloisters stood on the south side of the nave, now represented by
the garden of the house. Beeston was only a small foundation, with
perhaps five or six canons and their prior; although the claustral buildings have disappeared it is possible to get some idea of the commodious
place which they occupied.

BROOMHOLM PRIORY

Cluniac

The road along the Norfolk coast is full of pleasures, not least the
village of Bacton. The great craggy broken lumps of the remains of
Broomholm Priory stand nearby – an extraordinary spectacle: Broomholm was in the Middle Ages a place of considerable importance,
because it possessed a relic of the Holy Cross, which brought pilgrims
from far and wide, including Henry III, who came on more than
one occasion. Now the impressive ruined gatehouse leads the modern
pilgrim to overgrown walls and forlorn fragments of a once-great monastic church. Only the north transept stands to any height. This is late
Norman, with round-headed upper windows, with narrow shafts and
stiff-leaf capitals as of earliest Early English – beautiful broken pieces
indeed. Less survives of the south transept, but there is a little Early
English arcading here, to adorn the rubble wall, and there is more

blank arcading in the chapter house. For the rest, it is not easy to identify much – just a fragment of the dorter undercroft perhaps, and a room nearby, which is probably the warming house.

Broomholm was founded for Cluniac monks in 1113: in its heyday there were more than twenty, but things declined, and at the time of the Dissolution there were only four remaining.

BURNHAM NORTON FRIARY

Carmelite

The north Norfolk coast has its own special charm, its own special atmosphere: the marshes, the dunes, the birds, the little harbours, the small flint villages, the churches, and, of course, the skies. Who can count the Burnhams? There is Burnham Market, and Burnham Ulph, Burnham Deepdale, Burnham Sutton, Burnham Overy; Nelson was born at Burnham Thorpe, and at Burnham Norton, by the roadside to the east of the village, stands the little gatehouse to the Carmelite friary, a building of particular delight. The friary was founded *c.* 1241; the gatehouse must be early fourteenth century, and is built of flint, with most decorative flushwork to adorn its front. It leads to the west wall – all that remains – of a small church also of flint, with fragments beyond of its east end. Nothing else survives, but this little gatehouse is very precious.

CARROW ABBEY

Benedictine Nuns

Our readers will by now be accustomed to finding their ruined abbeys in the oddest of surroundings – whether embedded in a stately home, or in use as part of a girls' school, or an old people's home, or a car breaker's yard. Carrow is also surprising: it is part of the celebrated works of Messrs Colman of Norwich, famed for mustard, for sauces, for lemon barley drinks, for Wincarnis Tonic Wine. All are made within a stone's throw of the abbey, and it is in the abbey dining room that the firm's employees are served their lunch day by day. No firm in England treats its employees better.

It should be said at once that of course Carrow is not, and never has been, an abbey. It was a priory of Benedictine nuns, founded in 1146 by King Stephen. There were usually about a dozen nuns in residence: numbers fluctuated little, and the reputation of the priory remained high. The commissioners, enforcing the Act of Dissolution (1536), looking eagerly for evil goings on, found wicked practices or irregularities in most houses 'save the nuns of Carrow in Norwich', who were said to be 'of very good name'. So we can find pleasure in the reputation of the ladies of Carrow.

During the fifteenth century the Lady Julian of Norwich was connected with Carrow. She lived in a tiny cell against St Julian's Church, as an anchoress, but she was associated with the nuns of Carrow, and took her vows in Carrow Priory church. This very holy solitary, author of *The Revelations of Divine Love*, must have been a tremendous influence on the nuns at Carrow, and this may perhaps explain some of the secrets of this holy place.

Another figure associated with Carrow at much the same time is the poet John Skelton, a native of Norfolk, author of most touching lines concerning the death of a nun's pet sparrow. The nun was called Jane Scrope, perhaps a member of the great Yorkshire family, and certainly a family friend of John Skelton; the convent cat had killed the poor bird:

> For the soule of Philip Sparow
> That was late slain at Carow,
> Among the nuns blake,
> For that sweete soule's sake
> And for all sparrowes' soules.

These lines give us a little insight into life at Carrow.

The only monastic building to survive is the prioress's house – a grand new building for Prioress Isobel Wygun (*c.* 1514). She has been criticized for indulging in this display of worldly ostentation – for it is a very fine building. But we must remember that Carrow, set as it is so close to Norwich, was a very important foundation, and its prioress an important figure in church and city. There are two splendid rooms downstairs – the guest hall, and the prioress's parlour, with a spiral staircase to the first floor.

After the Dissolution the property passed through various families until bought by the Martineaus (an important Huguenot family) in 1811; from them it was bought by Jeremiah Colman in 1878. He needed the priory, it was said, to house his books. At the turn of the century the large, but not unsympathetic, addition to the south was built, when the place became the home of Colman's daughter and son-in-law.

All this is now used by the firm as accommodation, and for guests, as is the enormous new Abbey Dining Room built on to the north – which partly straddles the nave of the church. Here careful excavation has been going on for some time – though there is nothing higher than 18 inches standing above ground.

But let John Skelton have the last word:

> That vengeance I aske and cry
> By way of exclamacion
> On all the whole nacion
> Of cattes wild and tame.
> God send them sorrow and shame.
> The Cat especially
> That slew so cruelly
> My litle prety sparow
> That I brought up at Carow.

CASTLE ACRE PRIORY

Cluniac

It is something of a surprise, on a first visit to Castle Acre, to find at the end of the village street a thirteenth-century gatehouse with two round towers. Was this a fortified village? In fact it is the gatehouse to the castle, one of the most impressive motte-and-bailey castles in the country: the village stands within the outer bailey of the castle.

The priory stands to the southwest, and, like the castle, was founded by William de Warenne, Earl of Surrey, for Cluniac monks, a daughter house of Lewes, the first Cluniac house in England (qv). Even in its ruined state it is a building of great magnificence, which is puzzling because there were never more than thirty monks there. The west front is well preserved, but the rest is a matter of great crags and lumps of flint and stone, standing like rocks on a rocky shore, battered into the weirdest shapes by an eternity of wild seas. It is, however, possible with an imaginative eye, to visualize the building as it was, cruciform, with central tower and two western towers.

The west front is a frontispiece of Norman splendour, with three doorways, the wall space adorned with all the Norman decorative features – blind arcading, interlacing arcading, round-headed windows

– and in the centre the relic of a grand Perpendicular traceried window. In the upper stage of the southwest tower there are pointed Early English windows. Inside, the only well-preserved part of the whole interior is the southwest bay of the nave, with a grand Norman pillar adorned with diagonal grooving as at Durham or Norwich.

The claustral buildings follow the normal plan: the cloister lay on the south side, and from this opened chapter house, dorter undercroft and dorter; the reredorter beyond was specially spacious. Little remains of the refectory, other than ragged ruined walls.

In the early sixteenth century the prior built for himself a residence of considerable size and splendour: this stands adjoining the southwest corner of the west front, and resembles any manor house of the period. The porch is of stone and brick and flint; the gable is timber-framed, with a wide four-centred entrance arch below a traceried Perpendicular window. Upstairs there are spacious rooms, and a chapel with elaborate canopied sedile, traces of wall paintings, the altar recess paved with mediaeval tiles – all this part of the earlier lodgings, now absorbed in the new house. The prior's house had now become a commodious, grand house – but then, by that time, the prior of Castle Acre had become a grandee.

COXFORD PRIORY

Augustinian

Opposite Tattersett church, in the fields of long grass and undergrowth in summer, stand fragments of the church of Coxford Priory, an Augustinian house founded originally at East Rudham, nearby, *c.* 1140, and moved to Tattersett *c.* 1216. There is one tall, elegant arch, later filled in with what must have been a Perpendicular window – perhaps a crossing arch into the north transept – with some walling and a lower arch nearby, which perhaps led into a chapel. There are lumps of masonry marking the position of the chancel, and bumps in the grass around. All else has vanished.

HICKLING PRIORY

Augustinian

The Norfolk Broads: Hickling is a charming spot, with boats tied up on the broad at Hickling Staithe, and the parish church presiding with its grand tower. At the end of a lane off the road to Sea Palling is Priory Farm. Here among the farm buildings there is the sudden sight of mediaeval masonry – the fragmentary remains of Hickling Priory, an Augustinian house founded in 1185. It is merely a forlorn stretch of flint walling with arched recesses, probably a part of the cloister, with remains of perhaps the parlour nearby; but all is overgrown, and long forgotten.

HORSHAM ST FAITH

Benedictine

Just north of the parish church at Horsham St Faith stands Abbey Farm. Almost needless to say, this was never an abbey, but a priory, the Priory of St Faith, and the farmhouse incorporates part of the monastic buildings, and indeed the refectory of the priory. Moreover, its walled garden is the cloister court, with remains of the imposing Norman doorway which led into the chapter house. The cloister lay to the north of the church, but that has disappeared.

The priory was founded *c.* 1105, and the story is romantic. The Lord of the Manor, Robert Fitzwalter, and his wife, Sybilla, went on a pilgrimage to Rome. On their way home through France they were captured by brigands, who threw them into prison. They were miraculously released, after praying to St Faith – and promptly made for the Shrine of St Faith at Conques in the South of France. Here they vowed that they would found a priory of St Faith at Horsham, and they brought two monks with them from Conques to form a nucleus of French Benedictines. The priory flourished: all through the Middle Ages a prior and six or eight monks were in residence.

After the Dissolution the refectory was divided horizontally, and became part of what is now the house. By chance, in 1924, the painting of the Crucifixion came to light on the wall of an upstairs room. More

Ulverscroft: cows now guard the monastic precinct of the Augustinian priory,
deep in a quiet valley of Charnwood Forest.

Thornton: sad but splendid survivals in Lincolnshire – the gatehouse, and chapter house.

Opposite above: Beeston Regis: wild flowers and long grass set off the 14th-century west front of this small Norfolk priory near the sea.
Below: Burnham: since 1916 contemplative nuns of the Anglican Augustinian Order of the Precious Blood have reoccupied the priory, founded for Augustinian nuns in 1266.

Overleaf: Castle Acre: most magnificent of Norman west fronts.

Above: Tattersett: a gaping window in the crossing of the ruined Coxford Priory, seen across the pond in winter.

Left: Horsham St Faith: wall paintings of the saint discovered on the walls of the refectory.

Right: Marham: two small round windows high up in what was the south wall of the nave of the nuns' church, now the tall garden wall of Abbey House.

Below: Hulne: the strong curtain wall built to defend the Carmelite priory in Northumberland, still standing against all comers above a deep ravine of the River Aln.

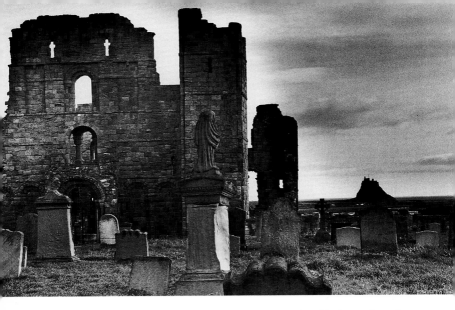

Lindisfarne: the Norman west front of the priory church, with the castle on its rock beyond, looking out to sea.

Tynemouth: the Early English east end of Tynemouth Priory in Northumberland, with a glimpse of the Tyne.
Right: the little Percy Chapel, attached to the east end of the priory – the low vaulted roof is adorned with heraldic bosses.

recently other wall paintings have been discovered, including one of St Faith herself, and a series of smaller paintings telling the story of the founding of the priory. Now the floor has been removed, revealing the whole end wall of the refectory. There are other paintings, too, which are in process of uncovering and restoration.

Abbey Farm is a private house, but it is possible to visit it by arrangement.

KING'S LYNN – AUSTIN FRIARS

Austin Friars

A single arch in a garden wall in Austin Street is all that survives of the house of Austin Friars, established here *c.* 1295. It is a four-centred Perpendicular archway, and now makes an ideal bus shelter: how many members of the public, waiting here for their bus, ever spare a thought for the Austin Friars?

KING'S LYNN – BENEDICTINE PRIORY

Benedictine

Under the very shadow of St Margaret's Church is all that remains of the Benedictine Priory, a cell of Norwich, established here *c.* 1100. It is a long line of buildings in Priory Lane, to the south of the church, and outside, apart from obviously mediaeval masonry, the only important feature is the tall archway which leads into a charming paved garden. Here are the doors to the cottages which have been formed here, recently restored by the King's Lynn Preservation Trust: a plaque under the arch records the restoration. There are many mediaeval features inside, but, of course, none of this is open to the public.

In the Middle Ages this little cell was used as a kind of rest-house for the priory at Norwich, and invalid monks were sent here for periods of recuperation. There do not appear to have been any other buildings, and probably only the prior and one monk would be in residence here.

KING'S LYNN –
CARMELITE FRIARY

Carmelite

Not far from the river, and standing solitary in wasteland, is the gate-way to the Carmelite Friary, a fourteenth-century archway of brick and stone with three niches over the arch, the centre one with an ogee top and pedestal, ready for a saint.

With incredible ill manners a concrete lamp standard as high as the gate has been erected within an inch or two of this historic little building. Who can beat that?

The Carmelites came to King's Lynn in 1261.

KING'S LYNN – GREYFRIARS

Franciscan

The remarkable octagonal tower of the Greyfriars Church stands in St James' Street. Built of brick and stone, it is, even in its truncated state, characteristic of the long narrow aisleless churches of the friars. The Franciscans came to Lynn *c.* 1230, and part of the church may have dated from that time; but the tower and the narrow vestibule beneath between nave and chancel are obviously late fourteenth century. As a landmark for shipping coming up the river it survived.

LANGLEY ABBEY

Premonstratensian

Langley Abbey near Lodden was founded in 1195 for Premonstraten-sian monks: it is one of the best camouflaged of all monastic sites anywhere. There is a farmhouse, and behind the farmhouse is what appears to be an enormous barn. This turns out to be the west range of the cloister, the cellarer's range, and a gap in the buildings to the right leads into the farmyard, which is really the cloister court. A gate in the far side leads into a field, which was the site of the church, now only marked by a few mounds in the grass. In its day the church was cruciform, and dated from the thirteenth century, with a tower added at the west end in the fourteenth century; here the crumbling remains of a spiral staircase can be discerned, at the point where church and claustral buildings joined. On the east side of the farmyard is a trefoil-headed doorway, with a window on either side – which is, of course, the entrance to the chapter house. Inside are traces of wall arcading, and a corbel or two to support the vault. But all these claustral buildings became ideal for the farm.

It is worth exploring the cellarer's range for further clues: here, among the farm stores and the agricultural implements, are the remains of vaulting on the ground floor, and unexpected mediaeval pillars – the undercroft – and nearby is the two-bay lavatorium, now part of a garage. A gatehouse adjoined the west end of the church, but little remains of this. There is still much unknown and unexplored about this fascinating place – which in its heyday housed an abbot, and sixteen or twenty canons. But now the music of the monks is silent, and the sounds and smells of the farm have taken over.

LUDHAM – ST BENET'S ABBEY

Benedictine

As extraordinary a monastic fragment as could be imagined – and as remote as could be desired – St Benet's was originally founded in the seventh century, and refounded in 1019 by King Canute, for Benedictine monks. It stands close to the confluence of the River Ant and the River Bure, down on the marshes some distance from the village of Ludham, and is the only English abbey never to have been suppressed. After the Dissolution, the last abbot became Bishop of Norwich, retaining the monastic revenues, and the Bishop of Norwich is still the titular abbot.

The church and all the monastic buildings soon fell into decay – but the gatehouse survived by having a windmill built inside it. There it stands, the fifteenth-century gatehouse, with its wide archway and niches for saints and other Gothic features, with the great round windmill rising from the inside. Sails and all have gone, but it is an extraordinary sight. Monastic church and other buildings have also gone; nothing survives, but a few lumps of stone among the undulations a hundred yards away.

MARHAM ABBEY

Cistercian Nuns

Marham Abbey was founded for Cistercian nuns in 1249. In the Norfolk village, opposite the church with its Perpendicular tower, there is an attractive farmhouse, called Abbey House. In the garden stands a considerable portion of the south wall of the nave of the monastic church, with two unusual round windows high up, one quatrefoiled, the other sexfoiled. The cloister must have stood on this south side; in the northwest corner is the fragment of some small room, perhaps the parlour. All else is lost.

NORTH CREAKE ABBEY

Augustinian

North Creake and South Creake are two of the great pleasures of this part of Norfolk, each with a distinguished church: in the *Shell Guide to Norfolk* Lady Harrod writes of South Creake Church as being in many ways the finest in Norfolk – 'This wonderful church . . . has the atmosphere of a very holy place, a sense of timelessness.' The little Burn river runs the length of both villages, and the road from North Creake leads to Burnham Thorpe, where Nelson was born at the rectory; a drive turns off to the right – to the farm, and to the abbey.

This is an enchanting spot – beautiful and solemn. The iron gate leads into the precinct: there is no vestige of the nave – only a high flint wall on the south side, where the aisle would have been, a lower wall on the left. Trim grass leads us to the crossing: here there are impressive remains.

Creake Abbey seems to have been dogged by bad luck: it was founded as an Augustinian priory in 1227, and raised to the rank of an abbey four years later. What was clearly an impressive Early English church was built, of which these eastern parts remain. But there was a fire in 1378, and another in 1490. The canons, disheartened, demolished the nave, walled off the crossing, and retreated into their choir and its attendant chapels. Ten years later all the canons, and finally the abbot, died of an epidemic, and Creake Abbey came to a sad end.

The high south wall of the nave was left, because the cloisters adjoined on that side. This cloister garth is now the garden of the Abbey Farm, which incorporates the south side of the cloister – no doubt the refectory. What remains of the church is Early English at its most delightful, with lancet windows – but Decorated windows in the north chapel, which was extended in the fourteenth century. A doorway in the south transept is now a gate into the beautiful garden of the farmhouse (all this is private): the chapter house, and other buildings of the east side of the cloister would have been here.

The last abbot died on 12 December 1506, and all the property and endowments reverted to the Crown -- to be bestowed in due course on Christ's College, Cambridge. The story of Creake Abbey is sad but the atmosphere of the place is holy, and timeless.

NORWICH – BLACKFRIARS

A remarkable and indeed tremendous building, now St Andrew's Hall, but in origin the Black Friars' church. The Dominican house was founded here in 1226, and this magnificent Perpendicular church was built between 1440 and 1470 – the kind of great preaching house the friars needed; in fact it is the only friars' church which we have inherited *in toto*. There is a great nave, and a great chancel; originally at the 'crossing' (in fact there were no transepts) there was an octagonal tower – the friars so often built an octagonal tower at a crossing – but this fell in 1712. As St Andrew's Hall it is used for concerts and so on. Adjoining the rump of the cloister on the north side is what is called Becket's Chapel, a very fine brick-vaulted undercroft, now used as a restaurant.

PENTNEY PRIORY

Augustinian

Rising from the Norfolk landscape stands the tall, wide, battlemented, flint gatehouse of Pentney Priory, an Augustinian house, founded *c.* 1230. Nothing else remains of what must have been a religious house of some importance; indeed, there were some twenty canons here, with the prior, in the fourteenth century, and some fifteen on the eve of the Dissolution.

Only small windows face the outside world, but within the arch there are larger windows, and rooms on three floors. The priory's survival may be explained by the existence of farm buildings adjoining – the gatehouse used no doubt for storage, a useful building. Standing here, it is as grand as it is unexpected.

THETFORD – BLACKFRIARS

Dominican

In 1959 Thetford had the misfortune to be designated a London 'overspill' town. Poor Thetford. Its great days, it knew, were over – Saxon days, mediaeval days, when it had been briefly the seat of a bishop, and a town full of parish churches and religious houses. After the Dissolution Thetford sank to the status of a quiet country town – but in the past thirty years the population has quadrupled, housing estates, industrial estates, have grown up, and the town is full of traffic, car parks, and dreary new shops. An 'overspill' town indeed: God save us from overspills.

The Dominicans came to Thetford in 1335. Thetford was, of course, an important town at that time; the friars would not otherwise have come here. It was a small house with a prior and five or six brethren. After the Dissolution Sir Richard Fulmodeston (or Fulmerston), refounding the old Grammar School, took over the friary, and incorporated it into his new school. So it is today – with an imposing east front built in the early nineteenth century. The tall narrow arch of what would have been the tower of the friars' church is easily discernible, together with what were the walls of the nave. Sir Richard Fulmodeston was a great Thetford benefactor (see Thetford St George's).

THETFORD – HOLY SEPULCHRE

Augustinian

The Canons, as it is still called, was founded in 1139 for Augustinian Canons. The remains – very fragmentary – stand close to the road to

Brandon, and comprise an aisleless nave, with virtually nothing of the chancel left at all. It was always a small house, numbering usually a prior and perhaps half a dozen canons.

THETFORD PRIORY

Cluniac

The site of the great Cluniac priory is still secluded, beautiful, peaceful. There is, in fact, remarkably little to see, except fantastic lumps of eroded flint, and strangely shaped piles of rubble. But all has been excavated, and is set amid well-tended lawns.

The priory was founded in 1103 for Cluniac monks, from Lewes (the first Cluniac house in England): such architectural clues as we have show that it was a Norman church, originally with an apsidal east end, and apsidal chapels to the transepts; with the change in fashions, these were all straightened out, and a long Lady Chapel built, parallel to the chancel. If the church itself dates from the mid-twelfth century, these alterations may be dated thirteenth century. But little stands upright, except in the sanctuary or transept – and even there, only a solitary arch or the fragment of a shaft.

It is, however, a pleasure to walk round and imagine the tall crossing or Norman nave, wander into the cloisters and consider all the familiar buildings in their accustomed places – the chapter house, slype, dorter, and just east of this the infirmary in its own little courtyard; the frater was on the south side, the stores occupied the west. The only later building, and the only one to survive, is the fourteenth-century gatehouse, three-storeyed and of flint. All else is a pitiable ruin.

Before the high altar the plain slab marks the burial place of the 2nd Duke of Norfolk. The 3rd Duke had intended to found here a mausoleum for his family, and his son-in-law, Henry Fitzroy, illegitimate son of Henry VIII, was originally buried here, but at the Dissolution his remains were removed to Framlingham, where indeed the 3rd Duke was himself buried. There are several gorgeous Howard tombs to be found at Framlingham, all of which might have been here at Thetford. Such has been the fall of this once great priory.

THETFORD – ST GEORGE'S PRIORY

Benedictine Nuns

On the far side of the river, three-quarters of a mile from the town, stand the remains of the Benedictine nunnery of St George. Hard to find, and approached by a private lane off the road to Brandon (B1107), the remains of the church can with some difficulty be recognized in the overgrown ruins of a barn; there is an early arch and walls nearby which seem aligned on the church. The house itself, in origin Elizabethan, was the home of Sir Richard Fulmodeston (see Thetford, Blackfriars above), a great Thetford benefactor, and founder of the Grammar School.

This house was originally founded for monks, a dependency of Bury St Edmunds, but the monks returned to their mother house. St George's was refounded for nuns soon after 1160. There were usually a dozen or so nuns here.

WALSINGHAM FRIARY

Franciscan

On the outskirts of the town, along the road to Houghton St Giles, stand the ruins of the friary founded by Elizabeth de Clare, a great Patron of the Franciscans, in 1347. A pretty nineteenth-century house of flint and brick was built among the ruins – but much can still be discerned of the friary buildings. The most important, and still the most conspicuous, was the guesthouse, or the Pilgrims' Hall, which stands with its high gables on the west; the kitchens stood to the south – though the Victorian house occupies part of the site – and to the east of the kitchen is the ruin of the Little Cloister, of which much survives. There is less of the Great Cloister, which adjoined this, and lay to the east of the guest-hall, and very little indeed of the church. This lay on the north side of the cloister, and comprised a large nave, and smaller, narrow choir for the brethren themselves, with the usual narrow space between to carry a steeple. The chapter house extended from the east side of the Great Cloister, and there are fragments of this, but none of any of the other claustral buildings. The house was founded for twelve friars and their Warden.

WALSINGHAM PRIORY

Augustinian

'Our Lady of Walsingham, pray for us' – such is the response of the faithful to the intercessions at the shrine of Our Lady, a response repeated with fervour still. The religious fervour which surrounded Walsingham – and which once again surrounds it now – the devotion to Our Lady, cannot be exaggerated.

In 1061 the Lady of the Manor, Richeldis de Fauvraches, saw a vision of Our Lady who directed her to build here at Walsingham a replica of the Holy House at Nazareth. In response to this – and the vision was repeated – the house was built, and two holy wells were discovered close by. So the shrine was established, with the celebrated statue of the seated Virgin. The Augustinians were appointed Guardians of the Shrine, and a priory was provided for them *c.* 1253.

Only the east gable of the priory church survives, with its enormous east window, empty now, set between two buttressed pinnacles, adorned with flushwork and canopies for statues of the saints. This can be dated late fourteenth century, and gives us some idea of the size of the church. It is set now on the smooth lawns of the eighteenth-century house of the Gurney family, known as Walsingham Abbey (which it never was). This incorporates at the back parts of the conventual buildings. There are considerable remains of the thirteenth-century refectory, with traceried windows, and the stairs to the pulpit. The 'abbey' is entered from the High Street by way of the Priory Gate, a fifteenth-century building of flint, aligned on the church, and adorned with shields and niches.

Walsingham became immensely popular for pilgrimages during the Middle Ages, and received many royal visits. It is still an enchanting little town, its streets, and especially the Common Place, full of delightful and ancient houses. Moreover, the twentieth century has seen a great revival of devotion to Our Lady of Walsingham: the new (Anglican) shrine was built between 1931 and 1938, by the Vicar of Walsingham, Father Hope-Patten. There is also a new Roman Catholic shrine (together with the mediaeval Slipper Chapel) at Houghton St Giles, a mile or two to the south. The Orthodox have recently opened a shrine, in the waiting room in the former railway station. All these twentieth-century shrines deserve a visit, and the cry goes up – as it has for many centuries – 'Our Lady of Walsingham, pray for us'.

WEST ACRE PRIORY

Augustinian

A delightful group at the end of the lane: the tall Perpendicular tower of the church, and the lower, solid, splendid gatehouse to the priory. This is of flint, patched with brick, and its wide arch leads down the drive to the comfortable farmhouse. It is difficult now to see any monastic buildings whatever – let alone imagine the great Augustinian house, founded in 1100, which in its day was even larger than the priory at Castle Acre. All now seems to be farm buildings, with a tall wall, perhaps, behind the pigsties – or a broken arch next to the hayloft. It is even difficult to get any idea of the layout in this setting of agricultural activity. There is, however, one enormous monastic barn, still serving the purpose for which it was built, and with a little ingenuity it is possible to identify the site of the church. It had a grand west front with two towers; the cloisters lay to the south, and here a fragment of the chapter house is still standing. The frater occupied the south range – it is all rather like a game of hunt the thimble on a grand scale. The little River Nar flows by: apparently the priory buildings extended on the farther side too – a long building, which was probably the school. And all around is the green and gentle Norfolk countryside.

YARMOUTH FRIARY

Franciscan

'The rows and the old houses on South Quay are best visited and studied as a separate town in themselves,' wrote Lady Harrod in the *Shell Guide to Norfolk*: '. . . the rows, narrow courts and alleys with their medley of mediaeval sixteenth-century, and more recent houses . . .' The rows are all numbered, and in No. 91 is the relic of the Franciscan friary. We have many Franciscan houses surviving, but very few cloisters. This represents part of the west walk of the cloisters of the friars, who first came to Yarmouth in 1271; this early fourteenth-century cloister, appropriately modest in size and beautiful in the simplicity of its shafts and vaulting, is a wonderful link with these early Franciscans.

Northamptonshire

DELAPRÉ ABBEY

Cluniac Nuns

That rare thing: a Cluniac nunnery. There were only two in England – the other was at Arthington in the West Riding, and is commemorated by a charming house called The Nunnery. But this was only built in 1585, on the site of the monastic house.

Here at Delapré the body of Queen Eleanor rested for a night on its long journey from Harby (Nottinghamshire), where she died, to London, in 1290; the Eleanor Cross at Hardingstone (standing close to the A508) commemorates the event.

Delapré in its park in the southern suburbs of Northampton now stands as a quadrangular house, undoubtedly incorporating much of the masonry of the cloisters of the abbey, if revealing now hardly a single monastic feature. Church on the north side, chapter house on the east, frater on the south, kitchen and guesthouse on the west – all may be there underneath, but all are now divided up into new rooms for secular purposes. After the Dissolution, first the Tate family, later the Bouveries, made Delapré their home. The last Bouverie died in 1943, and the place was bought by the Corporation of Northampton. It is now the Northamptonshire Record Office, and ideal for the purpose, with the rooms used for depositories, libraries, and reading rooms. Much of the exterior of the house is eighteenth or early nineteenth century, and delightful, the park extensive and beautiful. If we can't have Cluniac nuns, archives seem a good substitute.

Northumberland

ALNWICK ABBEY

Premonstratensian

The ducal park at Alnwick contains two monastic sites: the mediaeval gatehouse of Alnwick Abbey stands solitary above a beautiful stretch of the River Aln, half a mile from the castle, on the B6346 – and the Carmelite Priory of Hulne stands high up in the park, two miles northwest of the town above a deep wooded valley of the river.

The Premonstratensian Abbey of Alnwick was founded here in 1147. The gatehouse is a splendid survival, looking down on the river and the site of the abbey, which lay between them. It is fourteenth century in date, tall, square and forbidding, with four projecting towers at the angles, and, on the outside, a niche for the figure of a saint, to show that this was a religious house, not a castle, that it was guarding.

The site of the abbey was excavated in 1884 by W. H. St John Hope. The excavation revealed one or two oddities in the plan – a long nave, but a very short chancel (the canons' stalls occupying two bays of the nave, as well as the crossing), very shallow transepts, a strangely shaped chapter house (part rectangular, part circular), and no western range behind the cloister.

Cars are not permitted in the park – so a visit to the abbey makes a delightful short walk from the park gate; on the way will be seen, on the sloping ground to the north of the gatehouse, the only other monastic relic: the monks' well in its little wellhead.

CHIBBURN

Hospitaller

A lane from Widdrington leads east towards the sea, through open and desolate fields which merge with the sand dunes. On the left, standing starkly a field's length away, are the ruins of the preceptory of the Hospitallers. Within the moat there was a small courtyard, with ranges of buildings, and a chapel, of which, for the most part, little more than foundations remain. The most substantial fragment is the house built by Sir John Widdrington on the west side, probably after the Dissolution. The Widdringtons, of Widdrington Castle, were an important loyal Jacobite family, who lost all in the 1715 Rebellion; their castle was razed to the ground, and even their little house here is in ruins.

HULNE PRIORY

Carmelite

Hulne, founded in 1242, was the first Carmelite house to be established in England. The original Carmelites were hermits living on the slopes of Mount Carmel, but being obliged to leave Palestine they migrated westwards. Originally committed to a solitary life, they later became a more sophisticated, scholarly Order (like the Dominicans), but some continued to cultivate the solitary life, or at least the secluded life. So it was at Hulne.

Where better to live a life of seclusion than at Hulne? Two miles from Alnwick, in splendid isolation in the great park of Hulne, above a deep ravine of the River Aln, they were protected by a strong curtain wall against all comers – especially in this border country against the Scots. They could live here in wonderful seclusion.

The main gate is on the south side, and leads into the outer court. Close at hand is the infirmary, of which much is standing: beyond is the cloister court. Round this are grouped the church with its sacristy, then the chapter house on the east side; the dorter would have been above this, and the frater on the south – but these have gone.

All this is what we might expect: what we cannot have expected is the late fifteenth-century tower built to the west of the cloister garth by the 4th Earl of Northumberland. This was to be a strong tower of defence for the brethren in time of need.

Nor could we have expected the unusual erection in the northwest corner of the cloister garth – which turns out to be a summerhouse built by the 1st Duke in 1776; he must have added the elegant plasterwork in the upper rooms in the tower as well. The playful little Gothick gateway in the east (outer) wall is dated 1777, a charming little addition, especially with the exotic figures which stand on either side.

Hulne, perfect for the mediaeval Carmelites, intent on their

secluded life, must also have been fun for an eighteenth-century nobleman and his family, seeking a romantic place for a picnic on a summer
day.

LINDISFARNE PRIORY

Benedictine

Who can forget the thrill of a visit to Holy Island? The rocky coast of
Northumberland, the remote countryside, the empty roads, the small
stone-built villages, the castles, the hills? Who can forget eiders and
kittiwakes and cormorants on the Farne Islands, wild cattle at Chilling-
ham and kippers at Craster? All these contribute to the atmosphere –
and a quiet lane from Beal brings us to the causeway which leads
across the sands to Holy Island.

It was the Normans who gave the place this name: ever since AD 635
Lindisfarne had been famous as one of the earliest cradles of Christianity in England. It was in that year that St Aidan arrived at the
invitation of King Oswald, and established himself at Lindisfarne. The
light of Christ shone out from here – in St Aidan, St Cuthbert, and
the scholars who produced the Lindisfarne Gospels; until the Danish
raids two hundred years later extinguished the light. The monks
escaped to the mainland, bearing the hallowed bones of St Cuthbert
with them. This was 875. For two hundred years Lindisfarne lay
desolate: St Cuthbert's remains eventually found a resting place at
Durham, where they are today.

Yet St Cuthbert's successors never forgot Lindisfarne, and in 1073
Bishop William of St Calais refounded the monastery here, a Benedictine priory from Durham. So the light of Christ returned to Lindisfarne, or Holy Island, as it became known. And an enchanted place
it is, a delightful village, simple, unsophisticated still, uncommer-
cialized, with a spacious and beautiful thirteenth-century church, a
few shops and places to stay; and at the east end of the parish church
stand the romantic rose-red, weather-beaten ruins of the priory.

This austere Norman church must have been begun at the end of
the eleventh century, or in the very early twelfth. It has much in
common with the Cathedral of Durham, with many of the features –
such as the pillars in the nave with their strong and distinctive patterns,
which could well have been built by the same masons. The west
front is impressive, with its projecting doorway, one remaining narrow

southwest tower, and round-headed windows; an arrow slit or two are reminders that defence was still necessary – but now against the Scots. At the crossing, and most precariously balanced, one grand rib of the vaulting survives, but of the tower above nothing survives. The east end is square now, and the east window must once have been filled with fourteenth-century tracery; but originally the sanctuary was apsidal.

There is little left of the cloister, little of the monastic buildings. Beyond is a larger courtyard, with gatehouse and defensive precinct walls, for Lindisfarne was, and is, in a very exposed position, and the enemy could attack from the sea as well as from the land.

This is not all: from the churchyard there is the sudden and unexpected vision across the little bay of a fairy castle standing on a precipitous pinnacle of rock. The castle was built in the sixteenth century, and contained a small garrison until the nineteenth. A short walk will take us to the foot of this lofty craggy hill – then a steep climb up the cobbled path leads to the Lower Battery. In the early years of this century Sir Edwin Lutyens restored, indeed recreated, this romantic little castle for Mr Edward Hudson, founder of *Country Life*. It now belongs to the National Trust, and we can enter and enjoy its rooms, beautifully and appropriately formed in the Tudor bastion, and delightfully furnished. Lutyens was a genius – and his buildings are always fun. Making our way to the Upper Battery we can stand and absorb the incredible view – over the village, the parish church, the priory, the harbour, and across the sands to the mainland. Such is the view to the west and the north. To the south and the east along the coast is Bamburgh, and, out to sea, the Farne Islands. Here St Cuthbert spent many years as a solitary hermit, with only his eider-ducks for company, before being recalled to Lindisfarne to become its bishop. And then, below the castle, at a little distance, is the walled garden, created by Gertrude Jekyll for Edward Hudson, still carefully tended and full of flowers.

It is always a wrench to leave Lindisfarne; before crossing to the island it is important to check the tidetables, which are prominently displayed – or we may be marooned on the island until the next low tide. But even that would be a pleasure.

NEWCASTLE – FRIARIES

Dominican : Franciscan : Carmelite : Austin Friars

Seen from the Tyne Bridge, Newcastle rises up the steep north bank of the river in most dramatic fashion, to the skyline of mediaeval castle, and cathedral crowned with its corona. Narrow mediaeval streets from the waterfront lead uphill to the new city, with its grand streets planned by Grainger and Dobson in the early nineteenth century. Surprisingly, a good deal of the thirteenth-century wall survives – the best sections from Newgate Street, along the north side of St Andrew's churchyard, to West Walls.

Nearby was the house of the Black Friars, founded *c.* 1239; they obtained permission to make a postern through the wall in 1280, and a wooden drawbridge over an outer ditch in 1312. Of their house near Stowell Square, a yard surrounded on three sides by mediaeval buildings represents their cloister court: it is possible to identify the chapter house on the east side, and the refectory with its lancets on the south. This Dominican house was famous in its day; and to it came in 1334 Edward III – and Edward Baliol to do him homage. Later, the smiths had their hall here, and over a seventeenth-century door is their motto 'By hammer and hand, All Artes do stand'. Two arches of the priory church were re-erected in the churchyard of West Rainton, Co. Durham, in the nineteenth century.

The Franciscans were nearby in Pilgrim Street, but left nothing behind them; however in Forth Street, a mediaeval arch and some fourteenth-century masonry survive of the Carmelites, who first came to Newcastle in 1372. And in City Road, behind the charming Holy Jesus Hospital, with its long, brick, arcaded cloister (1683), is a quite unexpected survival: the thirteenth-century tower (with eighteenth-century top) of the Austin Friars, who came to Newcastle *c.* 1290. These minor relics are important – vividly recalling to us how active all the friars were in our mediaeval cities.

NEWMINSTER ABBEY

Cistercian

Barely a mile west of Morpeth stand the remains of Newminster – eldest daughter of Fountains, mother of Roche, Salley and Pipewell. Moreover Newminster produced its own saint, St Robert of Newminster. Robert, a monk of Whitby, hearing of the thirteen monks who had left St Mary's Abbey at York to set up a new house where they could re-establish a strict Benedictine rule, determined to join them at Fountains. Soon after, this small foundation joined the Cistercians. This was 1133, and five years later Ralph, Lord of Morpeth, so much impressed by the life of the monks at Fountains, built them another house, in Northumberland – their New Minster – and Robert became its abbot. Such was his saintliness and magnetism that Newminster grew, and became the mother of three daughter houses – Pipewell in Northamptonshire in 1143, and Roche and Salley in Yorkshire in 1147. Nothing survives at Pipewell, more at Salley, still more at Roche. Not much stands upright at Newminster: what does has been re-erected. This is fascinating.

After the Dissolution parts of the claustral buildings were converted into a house, but this was not long-lived, and both church and buildings were quarried away rapidly. During this century various excavations have taken place, and in 1924 whole sections of the cloister arcades were re-erected, a most remarkable achievement.

Newminster is private property, and permission to visit the remains must be obtained from the Abbey Farmhouse adjoining. Genuinely interested visitors are welcomed. It is difficult to make much of the church – except to see that it follows the usual Cistercian plan, with a grand nave (which would have included the monks' choir), transepts with straight-headed chapels, and short straight-headed sanctuary; there was a galilee at the west end. The lay brothers' range would have been in the normal position on the west side of the cloister; indeed it is possible to make out the bases of the pillars of its undercroft. The refectory, no doubt, would have been on the south side, and it is possible to imagine kitchen, warming house and dorter in their usual places; the position of the chapter house is easily seen, as we shall realize very shortly.

But it is the re-erected cloister arcades which are so remarkable and so memorable. Twin shafts, with narrow pointed arches on delicately carved waterleaf capitals – these are works of great beauty and elegance; moreover there is one doorway, on the east side, also re-erected, round-headed, its arch also resting on waterleaf capitals – the entrance to the chapter house. The sight of these wonderful and unexpected remains, rising from the long grass, the brambles, the wild flowers and the undergrowth, alone make a visit to Newminster abundantly worthwhile.

TYNEMOUTH PRIORY

Benedictine

There is an early eighteenth-century Buck print of 'Tynemouth Priory in the County of Northumberland' showing the ruins of the Benedictine church standing gaunt on their promontory, with tall sailing ships in the estuary, and out to sea, and the coast line of Co. Durham on the far side of the Tyne.

The original monastery here was founded in the seventh century (it is claimed), but was over the centuries mercilessly ravaged by the Danes. It was refounded as a Benedictine priory in 1090, depending first on Durham, later on St Albans. The remarkable thing about Tynemouth is the indissoluble connection between church and castle: they seem part of one another, and to get to the priory it is necessary to go through the castle. The priory is, in fact, a fortified church.

The castle, with its gatehouse and barbican and fortifications, stands forbidding, facing the seaward end of Front Street, near the Victorian clock tower. The gatehouse is a very fine introduction to the church, which stands across the lawn with its fragmentary Norman nave and magnificent Early English sanctuary. Nothing remains of the Saxon church – and of the Norman a blocked-up doorway here, an arch and a column there, and the crossing piers to support a central tower. But the Early English east end stands 72 feet high, a great composition of east wall and south wall, of lancets and wall shafts, and dogtooth and blank arcading. From here we can look out as Samuel and Thomas Buck did on the mouth of the river and shipping, on South Shields in Co. Durham opposite, and out to sea.

The cloister lay on the south side in the usual position, with only foundations visible of all the claustral buildings. The only wall to stand to any height is that of the prior's hall and chapel, with its four lancets intact. In the fourteenth or fifteenth century a high upper chamber was grafted onto and above the sanctuary – for what purpose is not clear: the bottom of its windows is visible above the lancets of the south side of the sanctuary. At the very east end itself the little low Percy Chapel was added in the fifteenth century. It has a low vaulted roof, heavy with heraldic bosses, and was over-restored by Dobson in the nineteenth century.

As an old-fashioned resort, with its nineteenth-century terraces with balconies and sash windows, Tynemouth undoubtedly has its charm. And Admiral Lord Collingwood, a distinguished native of Northumberland, stands on his tall column looking out to sea.

Nottinghamshire

BEAUVALE CHARTERHOUSE

Carthusian

A green valley, secluded, secret, despite the proximity of Eastwood, the colliery, and the M1 – the Carthusian house here was founded by Nicholas de Cantilupe in 1343 and was one of only nine Charterhouses in England. A farmhouse, built out of the stone of the priory, occupies part of the site, and against it are the remains of the church, its walls supported from collapse by wooden buttresses. Attached to this are the remains of a tower house, which was the prior's lodging. From here it is possible to make out the line of the cloister, round which were built the little individual houses of the monks, each with its own garden. The site has never been excavated, so we can only guess where the chapter house and frater might have been (see Mount Grace in Yorkshire, and Hinton Charterhouse in Somerset, for more details of the Carthusian plan). Protected by surrounding woodlands, it is still possible to imagine the seclusion and peace of the place; only the distant hum of the M1, which passes in a cutting nearby, infringes on its peace today.

MATTERSEY PRIORY

Gilbertine

As its name implies, Mattersey was once an island – an island formed by the embracing arms of the meandering little River Idle in northern Nottinghamshire: even now the Idle, the Chesterfield Canal, and (not very far away) the great River Trent make this a delightfully watery, misty, mysterious part of the world. A bumpy grass track leads east from the village, past the parish church, towards the river and the priory. This must be one of the least visited of all the monastic sites looked after by the Monuments Commission: a farmhouse, and fragments of the monastic buildings set in green lawns, close to the river. Not very much is left, but the ground plan is exposed, and it is possible to get some idea of this small Gilbertine house, founded for canons only, in 1185. The church lay to the north: it was small and aisleless, but had a tower added on its north side in the fourteenth century, of which a tall corner is still standing. The cloister was on the south side, and a good fragment of the east wall survives, with the responds of the vault of the dorter undercroft; fragments of the frater and kitchen are on the south. The situation is a special pleasure, with the River Idle flowing by, and views across the flat, lonely meadows and stumpy willows.

In the parish church, behind the organ, is a great surprise: two beautiful carved stone panels of the fourteenth century – dug up under the chancel floor in the eighteenth century. One depicts St Martin and the beggar, the other St Helen discovering the Cross. Could they have come from the priory church? The priory was dedicated to St Helen.

RUFFORD ABBEY

Cistercian

Driving along the road from Ollerton to Nottingham (A614), grand Baroque gates soon appear on the left; they are closed, but there is a glimpse of a half-ruined great house standing at the end of a long lime avenue. This is Rufford.

The Cistercian Abbey of Rufford was founded by Gilbert de Gant, Earl of Lincoln, in 1148, a daughter house of Rievaulx. After the Dissolution it was granted to the 6th Earl of Shrewsbury, Bess of Hardwick's fourth husband. Church, cloisters, and most of the monastic buildings were pulled down, leaving only the undercroft of the west cloister range – and above and around this a large Elizabethan house was built, much added to and altered in succeeding centuries; and the place descended through Bess's youngest daughter to Saviles and Lumley-Saviles, until 1938. Since then it has passed through many trials and tribulations. Eventually it was purchased by the Nottinghamshire County Council. Much was pulled down in 1956, and what remains was placed in the care of the Ministry of Works. Much restoration has been in hand in recent years, especially to the mediaeval undercroft, and all else has been tidied up.

The Elizabethan Great Hall stands above the undercroft, but it is roofless, as is the porch with its barley-sugar columns; but all this has been restored and is open to the public. We can enter here, and then descend to the undercroft. In a Cistercian house the west claustral range was always the lay brothers' – and here we have the exceptionally roomy undercroft, partly cellarium, partly lay brothers' frater, all vaulted and wonderfully preserved; to the south is what was probably the buttery and pantry. It is hoped to mark out the site of the church and cloister in due course. But already much reclamation has been going on in the grounds, and a beautiful garden recreated.

WELBECK ABBEY

Premonstratensian

Anybody visiting the great ducal demesne of Welbeck today might be forgiven if he does not at once detect a monastic presence here. The long drives, the avenues, the grand plantations, the ancient trees, the more than fifty lodges, the estate houses, 'The Winnings' – that delightful group of houses for retired retainers of the family, paid for out of the winnings from the turf – the riding schools, the stables, the kennels, the estate yards, the hot-houses, the walled gardens, the lake, three miles long with its bridge, the iron gates, the subterranean tunnels – all this without mentioning the mansion itself and its gardens, its state rooms, its Gothick hall, its libraries, its chapel, its underground ballroom: is there anything monastic here? Not much; but wait.

Welbeck Abbey was founded in 1153 for Premonstratensian Canons; it was an important foundation, and became recognized (1512) as the premier Premonstratensian abbey in England. After the Dissolution, and one or two rapid changes of ownership, it was acquired by Sir Charles Cavendish, who was Bess of Hardwick's third son – and so, through the families of Holles (Earl of Clare and Duke of Newcastle) and Harley (Earl of Oxford) to the Cavendish-Bentincks, Dukes of Portland. It is still the property of the family, though part of the house is used as a pre-Sandhurst army college.

The 5th Duke, who built all these fabulous underground rooms, also contrived a little tramway to run up and down the long passages underneath, to bring food hot from the kitchens to the dining room. The trams, alas, are gone, but the lines are still there, and will lead us, believe it or not, to the vaulted undercroft of the west range of the monastic cloister (*c.* 1250), with a round-headed doorway of *c.* 1200.

The other ranges of the cloister have gone, as have even the foundations of the church, which lay on the north side. But this undercroft survives: it is now divided into several rooms, which make excellent boys' studies – echoing now, not with plainsong, but with the cheerful music of their gramophones and wirelesses, the walls adorned with their pin-ups of pretty girls.

Oxfordshire

BRUERN ABBEY

Cistercian

Sequestered Wychwood countryside, and a handsome early eighteenth-century house of warm-coloured stone with sash windows and handsome Baroque details – a remarkably little-known house. And remarkably little is known of the Cistercian abbey which once occupied the site. It was founded *c.* 1147, and it is hard indeed to imagine Cistercian life here, a Cistercian church, Cistercian silence; the place has never been excavated. At the time of the Dissolution there were twelve priests here. It was acquired by the Cope family, Baronets of Hanwell (Oxon) and later of Bramshill, who built the present distinguished house. A hundred yards or so away, what appears to be an eighteenth-century cottage of little consequence contains a baffling groin-vaulted room. This must be monastic. But the place keeps its secrets.

GODSTOW ABBEY

Benedictine Nuns

Altogether baffling: an idyllic situation in the meadows on the west bank of the Thames, a mile or two north of Oxford, and opposite the celebrated Trout Inn – just a walled enclosure, with a small ruined building in one corner. The walls are high, and almost completely encircle the site: cows are in and out, grazing.

Godstow Abbey was founded in 1133 for Benedictine nuns: King Stephen and his Queen were present at its consecration, so was the Archbishop of Canterbury, so were four bishops; so it must once have been a place of importance. Apart from the little building already noted – perhaps the chapel of the abbess's house – nothing remains; apparently a little arcading of the cloister was standing until the eighteenth century, and the tower at the west end of the church was only pulled down in 1810 for building material. The church, it seems, stood on the north side, facing east towards the river, but the site has never been excavated, so little is known. For us today Godstow makes a delightful walk from Oxford, by the river bank, but it is withdrawn and silent.

THAME ABBEY

Cistercian

Driving along the quiet and delightfully uneventful road from Thame to Stokenchurch, we pass the demesne of Thame Park. Filled with mature and lovely trees, it looks every inch the nobleman's seat, and few would ever suspect that all this represents the policies of Thame Abbey, a Cistercian house founded in 1137. There are two charming little lodges along the road (*c.* 1830), with just a touch of the ecclesiastical about them.

Thame Park is private, and not open to the public, but if we are invited in we shall come face to face with a handsome house of *c.* 1745, built of stone, eleven bays wide, the three centre bays pedimented, the front door approached by a double flight of steps. This was built for the 6th Viscount Wenman by William Smith of Warwick, and is perhaps very much what we expected as we drove across the park. With its grand and beautiful eighteenth-century rooms with their Rococo plasterwork and marble chimneypieces, it is the perfect early Georgian country house. What comes as a surprise is to walk round to the back, and there discover the equally beautiful, but completely different late mediaeval wing behind. This is the abbot's lodging of Thame Abbey.

There can be no two opinions about this building: it is extremely beautiful, with its battlemented bay windows and staircase turrets and steep tiled roof. It was built in three stages after *c.* 1500, of which the third, at the east end, is in the form of a projecting battlemented tower built for Robert King, who became abbot in 1530. There is one particular room here, the abbot's parlour, which is richly decorated with panelling and plasterwork, and with the initials R.K. for Robert King. There is no more distinguished a room of this date anywhere.

'The monks of Thame Abbey', wrote John Piper, 'forsook learning for sheep shearing, and consequently amassed fortunes. It was the third richest of England's eighty-five Cistercian houses at the time of the Dissolution.' It was then granted to Lord Williams of Thame, and twenty years later was acquired by the Wenman family. To them credit is due not only for building so delightful an eighteenth-century house – but for preserving, in an age not yet accustomed to appreciate such things, this precious sixteenth-century jewel, the abbot's lodging.

WROXTON ABBEY

Augustinian

'Wroxton Abbey', wrote John Piper in the *Shell Guide to Oxfordshire* 'is not an abbey, but a large early seventeenth-century gabled house set in a bosky hollow': he is perfectly right – although some small remains of the Augustinian priory, founded here *c.* 1217 were incorporated in the seventeenth-century house. They do not amount to much: there is a mediaeval arch, and a mediaeval doorway in the cellar; and the masonry around, and probably above, is monastic. What is more, the site of the monastic church has been excavated (1964): it lay to the northeast of the house.

This was built by the Pope family, Earls of Downe. The founder of the dynasty was Sir Thomas, founder of Trinity College, Oxford; the eventual heiress married Francis North, 1st Lord Guilford, in 1671, and his great-grandson was Frederick, Lord North, Prime Minister 1770–81 (later 2nd Earl of Guilford). This grand, many-gabled house therefore became the country home of the Prime Minister. Much was done by Sanderson Miller, inside and out, and the gardens landscaped and adorned – not least with an obelisk to commemorate a visit from the Prince of Wales. So an abbey it became.

The mediaeval monastic house must seem small beer after all this. Little is known of it. On the eve of the Dissolution there were eight canons here, and their prior, plus three novices. Whatever happened to these young men?

Shropshire

ALBERBURY PRIORY

Grandmontine

Far away from the world, between the Severn and the Welsh border, and far from its village, there stands down a long lane a farmhouse called White Abbey, surrounded by its farm buildings. White Abbey? It looks an attractive, but perfectly ordinary farmhouse, solid, comfortable and Victorian. But come inside: the west front is merely a façade. Behind it, inside, facing east, is the choir of the monastic church, alongside it, on its north side, the Chapel of St Stephen. Kitchen or sitting room, bedrooms or bathrooms, are all inserted on different floors, on different levels – and Gothic shafts, carved corbels, elaborate bosses, mediaeval vaults appear beautifully preserved, delightfully inappropriate, in unexpected places.

Originally founded *c.* 1221 for Augustinian Canons, Alberbury joined the Order of Grandmont ten years later, and became one of only four Grandmontine houses in England. Dissolved as an alien priory, it was bought by Archbishop Chichele in 1441, and so became the property of All Souls' which it still is.

BUILDWAS ABBEY

Cistercian

Buildwas Abbey now shares the beautiful tree-hung valley of the Severn with a power station – a somewhat uncomfortable bedfellow. Whoever gave planning permission for this? Power stations, with their tall chimneys and gargantuan cooling towers, change the scale of everything around, and are like great pagan temples where the smoke of the sacrifices goes up day and night. Mercifully their lives are short, so the mediaeval abbey will long outlive its twentieth-century neighbour. All the same, it is incredible that the monster should have been built here.

Buildwas Abbey was founded as a Savigniac house in 1135, a daughter house of Furness. Like its mother it became Cistercian in 1147. Most of the buildings appear to be of the second half of the twelfth century: the church is remarkably well preserved; apart from the outer walls of the north and south aisles, the building is more or less intact. It is all built in the austerely splendid Transitional Norman style, and it is a pleasure to stand in the nave, and absorb its long arcades, with the arches just pointed, the crossing arches still in place, and bearing the remains of a squat tower, the short chancel beyond. Much of the transepts is intact, too, with their paired chapels still vaulted. There is everywhere the intriguing interplay between pointed arches and round-headed windows, the piers solid, the capitals scalloped. The absence of triforium and the simplicity of the architecture express the Cistercian ideals to perfection.

The cloister stood on the north side, and much less survives of this. But on the east side the sacristy, the chapter house, and the parlour still remain – the chapter house specially beautiful, its vault supported on four central columns. To the east again stands what was the abbot's house, and the infirmary beside it – converted into a private house after the Dissolution, and now the club house for the employees of the CEGB.

The north side of the cloister would have contained the frater; this has disappeared, and all is now absorbed into the garden of the club house. The west side would have been the lay brothers' range. Here the ground slopes away, and there must have been cellars here, with lay brothers' frater above them, and their dorter above that.

From here we can walk down to see the west front of the church: there is no west doorway, but the two long west windows are impressive and satisfying; and making our way round into the nave again, we can once more enjoy the grandeur of the building, and through the open arcades on either side absorb the beauty of the Shropshire countryside.

HAUGHMOND ABBEY

Augustinian

The visitor to Haughmond may well be surprised, on arriving at the gate, for this is clearly the garden gate to some seventeenth-century country house. And so it almost is. For through the gateway stands what must be a grand late mediaeval manor house, now in ruins. In fact this was the abbot's hall, with the abbot's lodging to the right.

This is a building of the greatest interest, and not only architecturally; it tells us how an abbot lived at the end of the mediaeval period – as a grandee, like a nobleman or more important squire. This is the finest surviving building at Haughmond, and, indeed, after the Dissolution, it became a gentleman's seat.

If we walk round its west end we can absorb some of its features, and its splendours – still so remarkably intact, and, walking north along the perimeter of the buildings, there is more to see – three magnificent chimney breasts, for instance. Behind was the kitchen, to provide for the refectory on one side, for the abbot's hall on the other; we can pass the west end of the refectory, pass the outside wall of the cloister, and reach the church. This is a great disappointment: there is nothing left. All was pulled down, and for us it is left merely to go round, absorb the foundations and the plan they unfold. It was the standard plan, with north aisle only, long nave and chancel, transepts with two chapels apiece. The ground slopes upwards to the east, so the worshipper would have ascended, up and up to the high altar.

But here we can enter the cloister court: here is the great reward for a visit to Haughmond – the entrance to the chapter house. There are three perfectly splendid Norman arches of the late twelfth century, the spaces between the shafts filled with fourteenth-century figures of saints standing in carved niches. The interior of the chapter house is of great interest, too – with its richly carved flat timber ceiling, more domestic than ecclesiastical. Its provenance is unknown, its presence intriguing; there is no other chapter house like this one: this ceiling is thought to be pre-Dissolution. But is this likely? There were only ten canons here in 1539.

The position of the whole place on the side of a rocky hill explains the odd irregularities of the plan, and its lack of symmetry. But it is a pleasure to walk back to the abbot's hall by way of the eastern terraces, and look across this mass of stonework to the distant spires of Shrewsbury.

Haughmond was founded _c._ 1130 by William Fitzalan, for Augustinian Canons. After the Dissolution, in 1539, the abbot's hall and lodging became the seat of the Baker family, and church, dorter and much else were pulled down. A farmhouse was formed in the kitchen court, and cottages elsewhere. The great house was abandoned in due course, but the farm continued to occupy, and to overflow, what else there was, and so continued until the Office of Works took over in 1933. That is how Haughmond survived.

LILLESHALL ABBEY

Augustinian

Lilleshall has great charm. It stands in one of the best parts of England – the Shropshire–Staffordshire borderlands, marked by such landmarks as the Shropshire Union Canal, 'that swollen bump, the Wrekin', and the Roman road, Watling Street, which draws off all the traffic; the countryside is undulating, well wooded, the villages unselfconscious, delightful. Such a one is Lilleshall – but Lilleshall is marked out in particular by its own great landmark, the obelisk on the hill, erected in 1833 to the 1st Duke of Sutherland. What on earth is an obelisk to a Scottish duke doing here, a reader may ask. All will yet be revealed.

Lilleshall Abbey is almost a mile from the village, down a dead-end lane, under the tree-hung hills. It was founded *c.* 1143, a few miles from Lilleshall, for Arrouasian Canons – but refounded here five years later, and later still became Augustinian. It stands a great aisleless church, its east end into the wooded hillside.

Who can forget arriving at the west front, with its enormous late Norman portal, and gazing up the whole length of the long aisleless church to the great Decorated east window, now framing the green foliage or bare branches of oak or ash or beech beyond? The church must have been begun *c.* 1150: the east window, of course, is a later insertion, but the windows of the chancel otherwise are round-headed, and the tremendous west doorway is very late Norman, too, though its stiff-leaf capitals foreshadow the Early English – and, alongside, in what was the massive buttress of the west tower, there is Early English arcading with delicate trefoil-headed arches.

There is an ancient yew tree occupying the cloister court, and in the northeast corner there is another remarkable late Norman doorway into the church, a triumph of late twelfth-century carving, almost Baroque in its detail. Nearby is the contemporary book cupboard; beyond this are slype and chapter house, with warming house and frater on the south side. Nothing survives of the west cloister range.

After the Dissolution Lilleshall was granted to the Cavendish family, who promptly sold it to James Leveson of Wolverhampton. It was he who gave twelve fifteenth-century Lilleshall choir stalls to Wolverhampton Church in 1546. Those who know the collegiate church there will remember the Leveson Chapel in the south transept, and especially perhaps the elegant figure of Admiral Sir Richard Leveson by le Soeur (1605).

The Levesons began by converting the claustral buildings into a house, and it was this (with the church) which another Sir Richard defended for Charles I in the Civil War. Later generations of the family built the Hall – rebuilt by Wyatville in 1829 (now occupied by the Central Council for Physical Education). The Levesons, later Leveson-Gower (pronounced Looson-Gore), graduated from being baronets to dukes in four generations; good going. Marriage brought the family immense territory in Scotland, including Dunrobin Castle. Hence the ducal obelisk above the village. But the family were (and still are) in reality an old Staffordshire family, despite the Scottish dukedom.

SHREWSBURY – GREYFRIARS

Franciscan

The few relics of the Grey Friars' house in Shrewsbury take a little finding, tucked away behind some brick cottages near the river. The street name gives the clue – St Julian Friars – a curious amalgamation, for St Julian, whose church is at one end, and the friars who were at the other. The Franciscans came to Shrewsbury in 1245, although the fragments of their buildings, when we find them, are probably of the refectory, which was rebuilt in 1520. They are worth seeking out, for the tracery in the windows facing the street, and for a private and ancient corner of Shrewsbury by the Severn.

WENLOCK PRIORY

Cluniac

This is adorable country – where Wenlock Edge joins Much Wenlock to the lands of Clun, 'the quietest places under the sun'. Much Wenlock is quiet, too, delightful with its mellow streets of Georgian brick and earlier timber, its Norman (and later) parish church, and Guildhall of 1577. The town grew up round the priory.

Wenlock Priory is the best preserved of the few Cluniac houses in

England. This remarkable Order, founded just before the year 1000 at Cluny, comprised a great number (at one time about 1,400) houses, which were all dependent on the mother house at Cluny. It was the Abbot of Cluny who ruled, and all the daughter houses were therefore only priories. Since the Dissolution, however, Wenlock has often been called Wenlock Abbey – which for its splendour it perhaps deserves.

The name Wenlock is derived from Gwyn-loc, the White Close. Here St Milburga, daughter of Merewald, King of Mercia, founded her nunnery in 680. Like so many early monastic houses, it was destroyed by the Danes two hundred years later, but refounded by Earl Leofric and his wife, Godiva, c. 1045, as a college of secular priests, dedicated to St Milburga. This in turn was refounded by Roger de Montgomery, Earl of Shrewsbury, one of the Conqueror's closest confidants, for Cluniac monks, c. 1070. The first monks came from La Charité-sur-Loire, next to Cluny the greatest house of the Order. Roger himself visited Cluny, entered the Order, and died in 1093. The foundations of St Milburga's little early church have been excavated, as have those of Earl Leofric's. There survive today a few magnificent fragments of the Early English church, the remains of the Norman chapter house, and the very distinguished late fifteenth-century prior's house, which has been continuously occupied since it was built. (It must be stressed at once that although the ruins of the church are open to the public, the prior's house is a private residence, and not open.)

The lane leads up from the town, past the tower of the mediaeval gatehouse, and delivers us to the north side of the church. The west wall of the north transept still stands, with the blank arches which formed part of a north chapel, of which only the foundations remain. The south transept is remarkably complete, with its Early English eastern arcade, the paired arches of the triforium, and its lancet windows.

Turning right, the three western bays of the south nave arcade are one of the unique features of Wenlock. Here the arches are blocked in their upper half, and low arches carry a low aisle vault – and above is a grand lofty vaulted chamber, with paired lancet windows overlooking both the nave and the cloister court. Its purpose is unknown; it may have been a chapel of St Michael, frequently honoured in upper storeys in French churches in this way – as indeed in other Cluniac churches.

A doorway here leads into the cloister court. The ruins of the church are now looked after by the Historic Buildings and Monuments Commission, but (as has been said) the Prior's House (with its garden) has always been, and remains, private. One of the great delights of Wenlock Priory is the beautiful garden, which has for so long been maintained round the cloisters and elsewhere.

In the cloister the three arches on the east side adjoining the south transept belong to the chapter house; they are Norman, and on either side the walls are adorned with elaborate Norman interlacing arches, reminiscent of similar work in the Norman chapter house at Bristol. In the court is another feature unique to Wenlock: the fragment of the Norman lavatorium. This would once have been an important little canopied building, with a fountain pouring into basins all round, its sides adorned with carved panels. Two of these survive and are of great beauty. One represents (perhaps) Christ walking on the water, with the Apostles in the boat with paddles, and Our Lord clutching one of them by the hand.

The blank wall on the south side of the cloister is really the north wall of the refectory; behind this is the (private) garden of the prior's house. This fascinating and indeed exceptional building was the work of Prior Singer in the last years of the fifteenth century, and adjoins at right angles the Norman infirmary, which in turn adjoins the chapter house. Prior Singer's new building comprises a long double-galleried front, with paired trefoiled windows divided by narrow buttresses. These run the full length of this east range, with a deep overhanging stone roof above. The northern end of this beautiful building supplied an addition to the infirmary (including a chapel which still survives): the southern was the prior's house. Here a long gallery on both floors facing the courtyard led into the prior's apartments; on the first floor is the spacious prior's hall, with an open timber roof. In all, the house, remarkably little altered over the centuries, must rank as one of the most important late mediaeval domestic buildings in England.

After the Dissolution the priory passed through various hands, the church becoming a valuable stone quarry; the prior's house, so new and so comfortable, a private residence. In time the surviving buildings became a farm, with the prior's house occupied by the farmer: this was, of course, the saving of the place – there is, after all, nothing like neglect for preserving a place. So this precious late mediaeval house survived. Then in 1857 it was bought by James Milnes-Gaskell, MP for Wenlock and a man of knowledge and taste, who not only came to live here himself, but instigated an admirable restoration of the whole building, and of the ruins. It is his descendants who live here today, and have done so much to preserve the place. We are much in their debt.

WHITE LADIES' PRIORY

Augustinian Nuns

'Upon further consideration by His Majesty and Council, and to the end the company might not know whither his Majesty directly intended, Mr Giffard was required to conduct His Majesty to some house neere Boscobel, the better to blind the design of going thither: Mr Giffard proposed White Ladies . . . lying about half a mile beyond Boscobel.'

Samuel Pepys' account of the flight of Charles II after the disaster of the Battle of Worcester (3 September 1651), dictated to him by Charles himself some thirty years later, tells a vivid story of those dramatic events, of how this obscure little nunnery, which had been dissolved over a century before, suddenly became famous in the annals of English history. White Ladies, Boscobel, the Royal Oak, have become legendary; the fragments of the priory church, Boscobel House itself, a great oak, descendant of the royal tree, still stand; moreover the Giffard family are still nearby at Chillington, as they were in 1651; they were present, as were descendants of the Penderels who befriended the King during those tragic days, at the tercentenary celebrations in 1951.

The famous picture of Boscobel, painted by Robert Streater at the command of the King *c.* 1670 and now hanging at Hampton Court Palace, shows the place as it was then, deeply surrounded by woods; on the left White Ladies appears, also deeply mysterious in its woods – a half-timbered house, with its little timbered gatehouse, attached to the nuns' church, the cloister on the north side of the church. In the picture White Ladies appears very close, and the King spoke of its being but half a mile away; in fact it must be a mile. A visit to Boscobel and the Royal Oak, if possible, should be contrived as well, either before or after White Ladies; but for us today it is White Ladies which must command our attention.

A bumpy, muddy track leads westwards from the road from Bosco-bel, as though leading nowhere: suddenly the little ruined church appears in the sloping meadow on the left. The Augustinian nunnery was founded here at the very end of the twelfth century: it was never a large house – at its height there were perhaps nine or ten canonesses, four in the fifteenth century, six just before the end. The spacious cloister in Robert Streater's picture has gone, so has the charming timbered house attached to the church; apparently the gatehouse survived longest, serving as a labourer's cottage into the eighteenth century. Now only the shell of the church is left: an aisleless nave, an aisleless chancel, an imposing Norman arch leading into a now-vanished north transept, small Norman windows everywhere. The little northwest doorway is of interest for the unusual lobed frieze to its Romanesque arch. A high wall on the south side of the church encloses what was the graveyard used by Roman Catholics until 1844.

But the most interesting and, indeed, most touching are the burial stones in the chancel. One is to William Penderel (1707), who sheltered Charles at Boscobel; the other is inscribed:

HERE LIETH THE BODIE OF A
FRIENDE THE KING DID CALL
DAME JOANE BUT NOW SHE
IS DECEASED AND GONE
INTERRED ANNO DO 1669

These recall so movingly the priory's hour of glory.

Somerset

BARLINCH PRIORY

Augustinian

Exmoor country: a long narrow valley, well wooded, quiet – and, below the road, a farm, a pleasant-looking Somerset farm; but it is more. In the farmyard wall there is what must be a mediaeval arch, and in the wall of a barn there is a traceried window. Another wall is inexplicably buttressed. This is a fragment of Barlinch Priory, founded for Augustinian Canons towards the end of the thirteenth century. It was a small house, with never more than nine canons, and now is a beautiful but puzzling relic.

CLEEVE ABBEY

Cistercian

A splendid Somerset setting: the Quantock Hills to the east, the Brendon Hills to the south, Exmoor to the west, the sea to the north – Cleeve, with its remarkably complete monastic buildings, stands in its own green valley, the Vallis Florida.

Cleeve was founded for Cistercian monks between 1186 and 1191, from Revesby in Lincolnshire (where nothing at all survives). Here at Cleeve stands the gatehouse, with the figure of the Virgin and Child to greet us, high above the window. Originally built in the thirteenth century, and partially rebuilt in the fourteenth, it was finally remodelled in the early sixteenth by the last abbot, William Dovell. Passing through the archway, and looking up, the figure of the Crucifix will at once be seen above the window on this side – two precious mediaeval sculptures safely out of reach of rapacious Protestant vandals. A short walk across the lawn will bring us to the cloister court.

On our right, as we approach, stands the charming seventeenth-century farmhouse, attached to the high gable of the frater. From the seventeenth century until the twentieth the monastic buildings were used as farm buildings; to this is due their preservation. Entering the cloister court it will be seen how much survives. The church, of course, has gone – but the east range stands remarkably complete, with a long line of lancets to light the dorter, the south range even more impressive, with its row of traceried windows to light the grand first-floor frater; the west range was in process of rebuilding by Abbot Dovell, and a section of this with its almost Tudor arches survives. The abbot's lodgings were above.

The church was of the standard Cistercian pattern: this we can see from excavations, as virtually nothing survives except for the outer wall of the south aisle and transept, which adjoined the claustral buildings. Walking along the east side of the cloister, the sacristy – approached from the church – comes first, then another small room, barrel-vaulted like the sacristy, and then the vestibule to the chapter house. This extended to the east, but only the vestibule survives. Next to this is the day stair to the dorter, then the parlour, and next to that the slype.

Above all this is the dorter, one of the finest surviving in the country, some 137 feet in length, and capable of accommodating thirty or more brethren. It is lit, as we have seen, by narrow lancet windows; the original roof has been replaced by a good eighteenth-century reproduction, when the building was used for storage. This splendid room extends to the south beyond the south range; beneath this, and entered by a doorway in the slype, is a vaulted undercroft, or common room. Here the vaulting has collapsed – two central piers alone surviving – but the vault has recently been rebuilt in concrete, and this gives us an excellent idea of what this impressive room was like.

The original refectory stood parallel to this, in the usual Cistercian way east–west. Nothing survives of this except the floor, a notable array of tiles, adorned with heraldic shields and other decorative designs, all still in their original position. The refectory was rebuilt, as we have seen, in the early sixteenth century as an upper floor of the south range, a magnificent but quite un-Cistercian position.

Stairs from the cloister court lead up to this grand room. Light and lofty, it is comparable with any late mediaeval Great Hall, or with a college hall at Oxford or Cambridge. The wonderful timber roof is original, adorned with carved angels and ornamental bosses. Beyond it to the west are two smaller rooms, one decorated with interesting contemporary wall paintings.

After the Dissolution Cleeve belonged for several centuries to the Luttrell family of Dunster Castle – and these useful buildings were for three hundred years or more a farm. The Luttrells not only maintained them in excellent order, but carried out the first excavations in the nineteenth century. In 1950 they passed the place over to the Office of Works. It is now the Historic Buildings and Monuments Commission who are continuing the work of preservation.

GLASTONBURY ABBEY

Benedictine

'The most sacred spot in England,' wrote F. H. Crossley in *The English Abbey* (Batsford, 1935); sacred, legendary, romantic, atmospheric – Glastonbury is all these; it is also very sad, and very beautiful. Who will not be moved by the first sight of Glastonbury Tor? To descend the hill at Pilton and suddenly to see the Tor, silhouetted perhaps against the setting sun, is unforgettable. Somerset is the land of towers; the churches are glorious, but the towers pre-eminent. 'Of all our towers,' wrote A. K. Wickham in *Churches of Somerset* (David & Charles, 1965), 'St Michael's on the Tor ... is better known and closer to the hearts of the people of Somerset than any other ... To those with an historical sense it is a perpetual reminder of the great abbey at its feet which lay there venerated, mysterious and powerful, for over a thousand years; and it recalls the fatal day when the last of its abbots fell a victim to Leviathan, the eternal enemy. To destroy so great an influence there was made so brutal an example. From that day no more fine towers were built in Somerset.'

'Venerated, mysterious and powerful' – in its day Glastonbury was the richest and most powerful abbey in England. It was also the most mysterious.

> And did those feet in ancient time
> Walk upon England's mountains green?
> And was the holy Lamb of God
> On England's pleasant pastures seen?

It is only a legend that Joseph of Arimathea – connected with the West Country tin trade – once brought the Christ Child to Glastonbury, a legend first added to the Glastonbury mythology in the thirteenth century. But it is a legend which helped to make the place more sacred, yet more venerated, and visited by the great ones of the earth.

The original monastic foundation probably dated from the early sixth century: there are those who maintain that it was even earlier.

We are on firmer ground with a date of *c.* 700 for a new foundation by King Ine of the West Saxons, and a refounding as a Benedictine house by St Dunstan, who became Abbot *c.* 945: he had been educated at the old monastery school here, and then became a monk – later Archbishop of Canterbury. It is certain, too, that a little wattle church – the *vetusta ecclesia* – existed, associated with St Paulinus (if not with St David, and even St Patrick): this stood on the same site as the later Lady Chapel. To this was added, to the east, a new church built by King Ine, which was enlarged by St Dunstan. But all was destroyed in a great fire of 1084.

Rebuilding began at once, and the new detached Lady Chapel at the west end, on the site of the little wattle church, was completed in 1189. The new chancel and transepts were completed *c.* 1220, and the nave, central tower and western towers early in the fourteenth century. To form a grand western entrance, and to join the Lady Chapel to the church, the galilee was added; and soon after that the chancel was lengthened. Building continued until the early sixteenth century, when the Loretto Chapel was added to the north transept, and the Edgar Chapel at the east end. There is a conjectural model of this tremendous church in the museum.

After rehearsing this remarkable history, it is miserable to have to say that there is very little left of the church itself, and, with one notable exception, nothing whatever of the claustral buildings. It is extraordinary, however, how much survives of the Lady Chapel.

This amazing building, magnificently ornate late Norman in style, could easily have been built half a century earlier. The elaborate interlaced arcading, both outside and inside, the unusual buttresses, the rectangular corner turrets (also decorated with interlaced arcading), the richly carved windows, and the gabled and many-arched doorways – the north doorway especially sumptuous in its carving – all this is most unusual and distinguished work, as though the builders put their whole hearts into this building. The galilee, built half a century later, marries happily with it. There is a crypt under the galilee, and – a skilful piece of engineering – a crypt was constructed under the Lady Chapel, too. On the south side is a holy well.

And so into the nave. It is, alas, but a magnificent grass sward, with only three bays of the south aisle wall still standing, with windows pointed outside, round-headed within. Beyond, still standing erect, are the eastern piers of the crossing, with St Thomas' Chapel in the north transept, and rather less surviving of the south. A beautiful early Gothic arch or two, the fragmentary triforium, the outer wall of the south chancel aisle, a relic of the east wall, the foundations of the Edgar Chapel, the hypothetical burial place of King Arthur in front of the high altar – there is only just enough of this to give us a very slight impression of what this great building was like. It is sad, indeed pathetic.

There is nothing whatever to see of the claustral buildings – merely foundations in the grass. The one exception is the abbot's kitchen, which stands complete and wonderful to the southwest. It was built *c.* 1350, and there is only one other mediaeval kitchen surviving in England – that of the Harcourts' house at Stanton Harcourt near Oxford – and one in France. The kitchen, with its four fireplaces in its four corners, tells us everything about the power and importance of the abbots of Glastonbury, of their wealth, and the important guests whom they had to entertain.

There is little else to see, save the small Chapel of St Patrick (*c.* 1500), close to the gatehouse, and, nearby, the thorn tree, a descendant of the legendary thorn brought here by Joseph of Arimathea. It flowers on Christmas Day.

In the town, the George Inn must be inspected – one of the few mediaeval hostelries to survive in England – and the two ancient parish churches: St John's with its noble Somerset tower, and St Benignus' with another handsome tower. St Benignus, it may be noted, was friend and companion to St Patrick. With St Patrick he may have come to Glastonbury. It is a very rare dedication.

The last abbot, the saintly Richard Whiting, was beheaded with two of his brethren on Glastonbury Tor on 14 November 1539; the abbey was sold to Edward Seymour, Duke of Somerset, who cared so little for the sanctity of this holy place, this incredible church, that nearly all was destroyed and carried away.

HINTON CHARTERHOUSE

Carthusian

Travelling towards Bath from Warminster there suddenly appears, on the left-hand side of the road and across a meadow, what is obviously a small but important mediaeval building – tall and gabled and of unusual plan. What can this be? It is the chapter house of the Carthusian Monastery of Hinton Charterhouse.

We are lucky to be able to see this precious and beautiful fragment from the road – because access is forbidden. The gate nearby leads to a gabled Tudor house, what was the monastic gatehouse, converted after the Dissolution into a secular house; a private house it remains. From careful excavations carried out half a century ago we know a good deal about the plan of this Carthusian house, which was one of only nine in England. The great cloister was 225 feet square, and around it were fourteen cells, or little houses, in their gardens, for the brethren. The foundations of one or two have been excavated. The small church (Carthusian churches were always small), sacristy, frater and chapter house were in their usual positions; the undercroft of the frater survives – the frater itself became a barn.

Hinton Charterhouse was founded in 1232, and church and chapter house must have been built soon after. This chapter house is the special glory of the place; above the room itself was the library, and above that the dovecote, altogether an unusual and delightful arrangement.

MONTACUTE PRIORY

Cluniac

Most people go to Montacute for the house, and few will realize the existence of the splendid Perpendicular gatehouse of the Cluniac priory, founded here *c.* 1102. It was one of the earliest Cluniac foundations in England. But nothing remains of this date, and nothing remains of church or monastic buildings of any date, only this grand gatehouse. This must be fifteenth century: the gateway itself is very tall, and above, both on the outside, and on the in, there is a handsome oriel window, adorned with quatrefoils and battlements. On either side is a domestic range, perhaps originally the guesthouse; in any case the building has survived intact, converted early and easily into a private house.

MUCHELNEY ABBEY

Benedictine

As its name implies, an island in the marshes – the marshes of Sedgemoor; there is much to see here: a parish church with a Somerset

tower, and an unusual seventeenth-century painted ceiling, a mediaeval vicarage (a great rarity), and, of course, the rump of the abbey.
And what a rump!

The plan of the church may be made out in the grass: the first
apsidal east end, the transepts with their first apsidal chapels, the later
rectangular Lady Chapel, and transept chapels. Muchelney must have
been a wonderful church – dwarfing the parish church, dwarfing the
claustral buildings. It is only the southwest corner of the claustral
buildings that survives – but they make Muchelney famous, and different. The rest of the buildings round the cloister were in their usual
places – chapter house, sacristy, parlour – and all today are mere
foundations.

The first monastery here was founded *c.* 700, by an early king
of Wessex. It was sacked by the Danes – but refounded as a
Benedictine priory by King Athelstan in 939, and became an abbey
c. 950. For a time it was overshadowed by its powerful neighbour
at Glastonbury, but became prosperous in its own right, and early
in the sixteenth century, rebuilding of the south range of the
cloisters began, together with the refectory and abbot's house. The
refectory has disappeared, but the stone panelling of what was its
north wall, backing on to the cloister, survives, together with most
of its south walk. After the Dissolution the abbot's house became
a farmhouse: after all, it was all too new and all too good to
destroy. They were practical men in those days. And the existence
of three rooms over the cloister saved the cloister. It was used for
cider-making. It has lost its fan vault, but the springers remain,
and it makes a wonderful fragment with its Perpendicular traceried
panelling and windows.

The abbot's house adjoins: a low anteroom connects with the cloister, and a stone staircase leads up to the abbot's parlour, a room of
some splendour, with a very fine fireplace with elaborate carved frieze,
and a pair of lions *couchant* to crown the overmantel. The three rooms
over the cloister open out of this room, all with remarkable and different ceilings, and two with fragments of wall paintings. And from the
windows on the north side there is a view across the foundations of
the other cloister ranges, and the church.

The survival of these splendid rooms is entirely due to the fact that
the house was used as a farmhouse for very nearly four centuries, and
so were forgotten and neglected. (Neglect, after all, is one of the most
important ingredients of preservation.) No hand has been laid on its
handsome exterior, either, with its battlemented parapet, and grand,

almost domestic, windows on the south front – now merely overlooking a farmyard.

Muchelney has always been a place apart, a holy, withdrawn, mysterious place. This elusive quality clings to it still.

STAVORDALE PRIORY

Augustinian

Up a long lane in deep Somerset countryside, not far from the Wiltshire border, stands Stavordale Priory. It is clearly visible from the lane. A church? A house? It could be either at first sight. Founded in 1263 for Augustinian Canons, the church was rebuilt by Sir John Stourton in 1443. The commission from the Bishop of Bath and Wells is dated 4 June 1443, and Sir John Stourton was later the 1st Lord Stourton, of Stourton, only a few miles away across the border in Wiltshire. He performed this rebuilding as a descendant of Sir William Zouch, founder of the priory, and one of the canons of Stavordale was to pray daily in the chapel under the campanile for the souls of Lord Stourton's grandparents and parents, and other members of the family.

After the Dissolution the church was converted into a house: the bellcote at the east end of the nave, and fifteenth-century traceried windows betray the ecclesiastical origins of the buildings; in the long chancel what were traceried windows upstairs were converted into cross windows in the seventeenth century – with smaller mullioned windows below. A piscina, even an Easter Sepulchre survive within: it was a sympathetic conversion. Outside, the campanile has disappeared, but the beautiful texture, the slim buttresses, and the setting in a lovely garden, in delectable countryside, make Stavordale, whether house or church, unforgettable.

TEMPLECOMBE PRECEPTORY

Templar

The name Templecombe brings back memories of Waterloo Station, with a magnificent Southern Railway engine, steaming and hissing, ready to depart, a long train behind it, all in S.R. green, and on the guard's van a single notice in red lettering to announce its destination: 'Templecombe'. One longed to throw away one's ticket to Wimbledon or Windsor, and join the train to Templecombe. What visions of a little valley, a stream bubbling down, a temple of the muses close at hand.

Templecombe is not quite like that; in fact it is a rather bleak stretch of railway landscape, the track poised above a village of no special charm, a church tower, a bridge across a main road, the station itself, with trains passing by – to Yeovil Junction, Crewkerne, and Exeter Central, or to Tisbury and Salisbury.

Not far from the railway bridge is Manor Farm, a small seventeenth-century house, it seems, built on the site of a Templars' preceptory. This was founded in 1136, a small community of four brethren. On the suppression of the Order in 1308 three were thrown into the Tower – what had they done? – and the buildings were transferred to the Hospitallers. So they continued until the Dissolution.

Behind the farmhouse a long range of buildings survives, of much earlier date it seems, the quarters of the knights: refectory, kitchen and so on; and at the very end the ruins of the chapel, probably dating from the thirteenth century – the Templars' chapel all right. So hence the name.

WOODSPRING PRIORY

Augustinian

The long, long track, itself hard to find, in the flat countryside north of Weston-super-Mare, leads on and on across marshy fields to reach Woodspring. At first the church looks intact, with its tall tower and the body of the building itself still roofed. Then a chimney stack appears rising up from the roof of the nave, a dormer window, too – then mullioned windows, on two floors below, where once large traceried windows would have been. Woodspring is a house!

Woodspring Priory was founded in 1210 by William de Courtenay for Augustinian Canons of St Victor: in the fifteenth century the church was rebuilt. Somerset is famous for its grand church towers: here is a beauty, with its parapet of pierced quatrefoils to match the parapet of the church. The rebuilding was completed a short while before the Dissolution (1536); the building so recently completed, was rapidly converted into a house, with an additional domestic wing added on to the west end. The walled garden to the south of the church represents the cloisters; to the southeast is the infirmary, a handsome fifteenth-century building in itself, now used as a cowshed, and the magnificent monastic barn to the northwest is still used for its original purpose.

In 1969 Woodspring was acquired by the Landmark Trust, and a most careful restoration has been carried out. Writing in *The Landmark Handbook* (1986), Sir John Smith, himself the founder of the Trust and the inspiration behind it, speaks of the 'large tranquil rooms' built into the church, which are available for letting, and the orchard where visitors may picnic, and contemplate 'the serene atmosphere of an isolated religious community, surrounded by a working farm lying next to the sea.'

Staffordshire

CROXDEN ABBEY

Cistercian

Croxden lies in its own lush valley a mile or two from Denstone, in remote, unfrequented Staffordshire. It was founded *c.* 1176 for Cistercian monks by Bertram de Verdun. Farm buildings, a handful of cottages, and a small Victorian church comprise the tiny village. After the Dissolution the useless church, of course, became a stone quarry, and that heartless age put a road right through the ruins, from northwest to southeast.

However, the west front still stands upright, austerely splendid with its doorway of clustered columns below, and long sparsely set single lancets above. Fragments of the nave connect with the south transept, of which the tall south wall is still standing, again pierced by long lancet windows, and this leads to the cloister court. Here the wall of the east range survives, with three arches on clustered columns – the middle one the entrance to the chapter house. In the centre of the nave stands a great sycamore, and here the lane now cuts through the middle of the church, with the sparse fragments and foundations of the north transept and quire on the other side. The east end, visible in the grass, was apsidal, with a cluster of five apsidal chapels and an ambulatory – a chevet, rare in England, but to be found in another Cistercian church, at Hailes. There are remains of the dorter, the abbot's house, and the infirmary farther to the south, and to the southwest a good-looking Georgian farmhouse sits inconsiderately across the southwest corner of the cloister garth.

How beautiful the interior of the church must have looked with its chevet, and how very French!

DIEULACRES ABBEY

Cistercian

Leek stands in magnificent country, in rural northern Staffordshire. It is a town of immense character, with its steep streets and cobbles, its houses of blackened stone, its silk mills, its chimneys. But it is not a large town, and all around is moorland. A mile northwest of the town is Dieulacres Abbey: 'May God give it increase!' the Countess of Chester remarked to her husband, the founder, in 1214. Originally founded at Poulton in Cheshire *c.* 1135, for Cistercian monks, it moved here in 1214. All that survives is a pair of bases of the crossing piers, with the farm lane running through the length of the church. The farmhouse is an early seventeenth-century timber-framed building, one of those half-timbered houses which are such a speciality of the Cheshire–Staffordshire borders; it was built by the Rudyards, who acquired the monastic property after the Dissolution. Everything, it seems, was 'tidied away' in the early nineteenth century, and the stone used for farm buildings – with 'innumerable carved and moulded pieces built in nightmarish patterns' as Anthony New has remarked. As for the Countess's prayer, there were only seven monks here in 1377 – but *fifteen* at the suppression.

RANTON ABBEY

Augustinian

Ranton lies in a little-known stretch of quiet country between Stafford and Newport. The Augustinian priory here was founded in 1149 by Robert and Celestia Noel of nearby Ellenhall, and there were usually half a dozen canons in residence – seven at the time of the suppression (1539). The monastic tower survives, an imposing fifteenth-century addition to a much earlier church; but of this nothing but a Norman doorway and a little walling of the nave survives. In the early nineteenth century the first Earl of Lichfield built a shooting lodge attached to this, an attractive late Georgian house; but, greatly enlarged later in the century, it is now ruinous. The present Lord Lichfield has plans to reduce the house in size and restore it – once again incorporating the tower. All this stands in a wooded private park; it is not open to the public, but the tower is visible in the trees from the road to Knightley.

Suffolk

ALNESBOURNE PRIORY

Augustinian

Alnesbourne was a very small Augustinian priory, founded *c.* 1200, close to the east bank of the River Orwell. 'Private Road to the Priory,' states a signpost off the road from Orwell village to Ipswich: a long drive leads down the valley, with mown grass and twee lampposts, to an ancient barn of stone and brick, all that remains of this little Augustinian outpost overlooking the river. 'Priory Club circa 1100,' reads the notice here: 'Three Bars Food Dancing'. This is all that survives, surrounded now by all the amenities of a caravan park.

BUTLEY PRIORY

Augustinian

The Suffolk coast, legendary and lonely: Aldeburgh, Orford, Shingle Street; and the sea was much closer when the priory at Butley was founded in 1171. Then the tidewater came up to within 200 yards of the priory, and the wharf and canal have been excavated where the barges tied up, bringing the stone for the priory from the valley of the Yonne, far away in France. But transport by water was much easier then than transport by road.

Very little survives of the church or monastic buildings, but excavations have revealed the plan of the church, which dated from the twelfth century. The monastic buildings stood on the south side, and parts of these can be identified in the farm buildings which occupy the site.

But the great thing at Butley, of course, is the superb fourteenth-century gatehouse. From the heraldry this can be dated *c.* 1320–5, and is therefore one of the earliest examples of flint flushwork in the country. The gatehouse is a building of considerable size, with the centrepiece ascending to a high gable, with slightly lower wings on either side, and in front of these, again lower, buttressed projections on each side of the entrance – a capacious archway, with a smaller pedestrian archway at its side. All this frontispiece displays a magnificent show of flushwork. Immediately above the arch there are five rows of no less than thirty-five shields of arms – the arms of, for instance, England and France, the great baronial families of England, and the great families of East Anglia. Above there is a grand traceried Decorated window, with on either side the pattern of a similar traceried window all in flushwork, and in the gable itself a gorgeous triple-gabled and canopied niche for figures of saints. The same theme of windows, and patterns of traceried windows in flushwork, and niches and chequerwork is to be found in the lower projections. The inner façade of the gatehouse has an only slightly less magnificent display of decorative flushwork.

After the Dissolution the gatehouse became what it has ever since been, a most desirable, and delightful, if slightly inconvenient, country house.

CLARE PRIORY

Austin Friars

Clare itself – the little town – is a great pleasure, set in Suffolk countryside, a land full of pleasures. There is a grand church, and a wealth of houses, big and small, of every period, in many a delightful street.

Of special interest is the priory – so called; it was not in fact a priory, but a friary, the house of Austin Friars, and indeed the first house of Austin Friars to be founded in England – founded by Richard de Clare in 1248. It was only after the Dissolution, as home for generations of the Barker family, that it became known as Clare Priory; and names stick. Thirty-five years ago the friary was reacquired by the Austin Friars, so is once again in religious hands, used as their English novitiate. Yet, in spite of this, so much of the mediaeval house is in ruins – so must qualify for this book: the return of the friars is just a joyous postscript.

Approaching from the west, the guesthouse stands to greet us: originally the cellarium, the western range of the cloisters, it was built up in early Tudor days to serve as the guesthouse wing, and further embellished after the Dissolution, when it became a small mansion; indeed its appearance is that of a Tudor country house, and one of great charm, with Tudor mullioned windows and a decorative Tudor chimney, pretty gabled dormers and some seventeenth-century chimneys at either end; only mediaeval buttresses and a fourteenth-century front door betray its earlier origins. The back of the house is also delightful, but, with later accretions, completely conceals all traces of its claustral origins.

The church, of course, occupied the north side of the cloister, and enough of this stands to sufficient height to enable us to enjoy it, embraced as it is by a wonderful old wistaria. The church had a long nave and a long chancel, with an aisle only on the north side, and, as was the way with friars' churches, a narrow central tower. There is still a sedilia on the south side of the sanctuary, with the monument to Joan of Acre, daughter of Edward I, curiously impinging on it. Through the empty windows of the church we look out into the cloister garth, now a lovely garden. The chapter house and checker were on the east side, with the dorter above, and the frater was upstairs on the south side – all very much as we might expect.

What we might not expect is the infirmary, now standing detached, but once attached to the south end of the dorter wing. This is a charming building of flint, heavily buttressed, with fourteenth-century windows upstairs and down, and with a tiled roof. We enter to find the friars in their stalls, reciting their office. The monastic infirmary has survived through four centuries and more to serve the friars on their return as their chapel. It is a romantic story.

DUNWICH – GREYFRIARS

Franciscan

Sandy paths along the edge of the cliff – roads that reach the coast and peter out: such is Dunwich. One such road leads to the friary, which was founded in 1277, but, already in the thirteenth century, had to move almost at once further inland, and was re-established here in 1290. There was a church, there were refectory, dormitory, and everything else all round the cloister – but all is, save for a substantial wall, and the fragment of the gatehouse with its archway, and smaller doorway. But so, too, have nine parish churches, a Dominican priory, a preceptory of the Templars, and so on. All went into the sea: that was the end of a great mediaeval town and port.

EYE PRIORY

Benedictine

Eye has one of the greatest of all flint flushwork towers: beyond the church and the little town, to the east, is what is called Abbey Farm, or Priory Farm (there was always a tendency to promote priories to abbeys after the Dissolution). There is a tall, lovable early eighteenth-century brick farmhouse, built on the site of a Benedictine priory, and in the garden there is indeed a fragment of the south transept – a very small fragment – some low walling, which may be of the church, and some fragments of a small detached building, which could have been the guesthouse. Excavations have established that the church had an apsidal east end, and that the transept chapels were also apsidal.

Eye Priory was founded as an alien priory *c.* 1080, but later became an independent Benedictine house (*c.* 1385), with a complement of nine or ten monks. The house is now famous for its nurseries – and especially for its auriculas.

HERRINGFLEET PRIORY

Augustinian

Herringfleet is in that narrow northern pocket of Suffolk beyond Lowestoft; St Olave's Priory is a mile or more northwest of the village, above the River Waveney, and was founded for Augustinian Canons *c.* 1216. There were never more than ten canons, and often less, so it seems a spacious church with its transepts, and nave of five bays; the south aisle was added in the early fourteenth century to an aisleless nave. The lane now runs through the middle of the church, cutting off the crossing and all beyond. The small cloister court is on the north side, and of this the one interesting feature is the undercroft of the refectory, which despite its early date (*c.* 1300) is vaulted in brick.

IXWORTH PRIORY

Augustinian

Ixworth is a busy village, where two main roads meet. 'Ixworth Abbey', as it is called – it never was an abbey – is down a quiet lane off the main street. But first it might be of interest to visit the parish church. Here stands the Elizabethan tomb of Sir Richard Codington (died 1567) and his wife. The inscription records that he exchanged his manor of Codington in Surrey with Henry VIII for the dissolved Priory of Ixworth. Cuddington in Surrey (now spelt phonetically) is now overwhelmed by the labyrinthine roads of suburban housing which have sprung up in this century, but originally it was ruthlessly destroyed by Henry VIII, who pulled down the church and Sir John Codington's manor house to build Nonsuch Palace in its place. When the site of Nonsuch was excavated a few years ago, the foundations of the church were discovered, and many graves unearthed.

Ixworth Priory stands a good-looking house, outwardly eighteenth century: the front door leads into a staircase hall of good Georgian proportions. Only just round the corner is the entirely unexpected undercroft of the monastic dorter. This would have formed part of the east range of the cloister. The chapter house has gone, and the slype was made into a chapel in the seventeenth century, and the parlour and warming room have become other rooms for the house. Little remains of the south range, and nothing at all of the west, but these beautiful vaulted thirteenth-century rooms, now inextricably interwoven with the sixteenth- to eighteenth-century house above and around take us back to its monastic past. Part of the dorter above has been formed into an Elizabethan panelled room, and elsewhere unsuspected mediaeval fragments suddenly turn up in later rooms. Foundations of the cruciform church are to be seen on the lawn to the north of the house.

Ixworth Priory was founded *c.* 1170 for Augustinian Canons; what, one wonders, did Sir John think of his new home?

KERSEY PRIORY

Augustinian

Only at the last minute does Kersey reveal its charm, for the village street is built down one side of a steep valley of a little tributary of the River Brett, and, past the water splash, continues up the other. It is a street lined with little houses, some of brick, some timbered, some plastered – with the church at the top on the south side, conspicuous and erect with its lofty tower. The priory is at the top of the north side, completely inconspicuous, indeed invisible from the road.

Kersey Priory was founded for Augustinian Canons *c.* 1218. It numbered about nine canons, but seems to have been under-endowed, and to have fallen on hard times in the fourteenth century. Monastic life ended here in 1441, and the property and its endowments were bestowed on King's College at Cambridge, founded that very year by Henry VI. The remains are attached to Priory Farm, and indeed what appears to be a nineteenth-century farmhouse incorporates a mediaeval aisled hall, perhaps part of the prior's lodging. The church was of flint, and cruciform: there are fragments of the transepts and central tower, and a good deal more of the south chancel chapel, with its arches still standing.

The priory is private property, and not open to the public.

LITTLE WELNETHAM

Crutched Friars

There is so little in all England to remind us of the Crutched Friars – a street in London, a memory here or there – that it seems worth mentioning this most fragmentary fragment. Chapel Hill Farm, a mile southwest of the village, is an unusually ornamental small Tudor brick house, with step gables and highly decorative chimneys. In fact it incorporates what remained after the Dissolution of the house of the Crutched Friars. An angle buttress of flint and stone on the east side, together with more flint and stone on the east side, together with more flint walling nearby, dates back to the friars, established here in 1274. The Crutched Friars were the Fratres Cruciferi, or Friars of the Cross.

SIBTON ABBEY

Cistercian

A remote Suffolk valley, the only Cistercian abbey in the county, and the most overgrown and forlorn fragment of a ruin one could imagine. Virtually nothing survives of the church – merely a south wall, presumably of the nave: parallel with this, the other side of what must be the cloister, is a considerable portion of what is probably the refectory, unusually for a Cistercian house standing east–west. Presumably the refectory survived by being used as a barn.

Sibton Abbey was founded in 1150: such architectural features as can be discerned appear to be late Norman. The abbot and seven monks sold the place to the Duke of Norfolk in 1536, although (being a larger monastery) it was not then due for suppression; but they read the writing on the wall to their own benefit. In 1610 John Scrivener purchased from Thomas, Earl of Arundel, and his brother Lord William Howard, the Abbey of Sibton, and the original surrender signed by William Fladbury, the last abbot. The family are still in possession, and live nearby.

SUDBURY – BLACKFRIARS

Dominican

In searches like this, there are always clues. Here in Sudbury there is a street called Friars' Street, which can boast several charming timbered houses – one in particular with a timbered archway. Moreover it is called The Friary, and a friary it was of Dominican Friars, founded *c.* 1248. This was their gateway, but all else has gone. In its heyday it was an important house, with no less than thirty friars.

SUDBURY PRIORY

Benedictine

A lane leads up to the tiny chapel, all that survives of a small Benedictine house. It is not easy to find, and the lane leads off the road into the town from the north, the road from Long Melford. It is a very little, perhaps fourteenth-century, flint chapel of what was no more than a Benedictine cell – with only three monks – founded from Westminster *c.* 1115.

Surrey

NEWARK PRIORY

Augustinian

Across the quiet waters of the River Wey, Newark Priory looks perfect – like an eighteenth-century folly. In fact it is the real thing. The priory was founded for Augustinian Canons in the late twelfth century, and what remains is the Early English chancel, much of the south transept – with long lancet windows – and rather less of the north. The flint is beautiful, but it has crumbled so badly that architectural features are poorly preserved. The curious thing is that the transepts are oddly placed, not in a way to form a crossing, but extending almost accidentally from the chancel. Moreover, the canons' choir is walled in, which is unusual. It is all solitary and romantic.

There is a tradition that the remarkable east window of Ockham Church (only a few miles away) was the east window of the priory. It is thirteenth century, and comprises seven lancets, each lancet divided internally by a marble shaft; what is more, the capitals of the outer shafts appear to have been altered to fit, and, outside, the east wall has obviously been altered to take the window. If this is indeed the east window from Newark transferred, it is a most interesting early example of the English conservationist instinct.

WAVERLEY ABBEY

Cistercian

The first Cistercian house in England, and as such celebrated: Waverley stands in the meadows of the River Wey, not far from Farnham; a short walk through a field gate close to Waverley Mill, and along the eighteenth-century lake of the late Georgian house called Waverley Abbey (in eighteenth-century manner), and the ruins come in sight. The footpath turns left, and we come to the foundations, very difficult to decipher, of the church. Farther on, to the right, stands a considerable ruin comprising an undercroft, with a hall above – and, to the left, a crumbling gabled fragment, with three long lancet windows. There is not much else, but the setting is perfect: fine trees, eighteenth-century parkland, water, all delightfully sequestered and silent.

Waverley was founded in 1128 by William Giffard, Bishop of Winchester, a daughter house of l'Aumône in Normandy. The first church was long, narrow and aisleless, cruciform, with straight-ended sanctuary and flanking chapels forming shallow transepts – expressing in its simplicity and severity the ideals of the Cistercian movement. It was consecrated c. 1160, but early in the thirteenth century a new and much grander church was begun, and completed in 1278. There was a long aisled nave, a long aisled quire, a retroquire with five altars, and north and south transepts with three apiece. Moreover, the north wall of the first church became the south wall of the second. It is the rough foundations of this that we stumbled on as we approached the site. At the east end, where the five chapels once stood, the southeast corner is now clutched by the roots and gnarled trunk of an ancient yew tree, which is growing there happily in Bayham fashion. A good deal more masonry is standing of the south transept, but there are few architectural features to observe. Next to it can be imagined the chapter house, and next to that is a room, still with its barrel vault, which was the parlour.

We are standing in fact in the cloister court – but everything has to be imagined. On a line with where we are is the monks' dormitory, far ahead, close to the river bank, with its crumbling gable with the three long lancets which we noted before; the long dorter wing extended far beyond the cloister; the refectory and kitchen occupied the south cloister range, following usual Cistercian plan – but all this has to be imagined, too, as has the west range, which would have been the lay brothers' quarters. And here we are on a line with that vaulted undercroft and hall above, the first building which we noted on our arrival.

This is indeed the finest fragment of Waverley to survive, the undercroft of the lay brothers' refectory. It is of great beauty, with four bays of most delicate thirteenth-century vaulting resting on slender circular piers with the simplest of circular capitals. A certain amount of the upper floor survives – the lay brothers' refectory – notably the south gabled end, with its coupled lancets below, and the remains of traceried windows above, and a roundel in the gable.

Waverley 1128, Tintern 1131, Rievaulx and Fountains 1132 – such was the force of the Cistercian movement. It is sad to reflect that there were only thirteen monks here at the time of the Dissolution (1536).

Even if Waverley never became so powerful as Rievaulx, so grand as Tintern or so wealthy as Fountains, Waverley was the first Cistercian house in England. Walter Scott fell for the place – its setting and its ruins – so his twenty-four novels were named after it, as have been an important railway station, countless houses and suburban roads, and even a fountain pen.

Sussex

BATTLE ABBEY

Benedictine

Battle is a delightful small town: the long High Street is lined with charming houses of warm red brick, some of them tile-hung like so many in this part of Sussex. At the southern end it broadens into a triangular Market Place, presided over by the grand gatehouse to the abbey.

As everybody knows, Battle marks the site of the Battle of Hastings, and the Benedictine abbey was founded in 1067 by the Conqueror to celebrate his great victory, and to pray for the souls of the fallen, especially of King Harold. The high altar was placed exactly on the spot where Harold fell. Monks were brought over from Marmoutier in Touraine.

The gatehouse, forbidding with its turrets and battlements and arrowslits, is of *c.* 1350. Building and rebuilding seem to have gone on continuously: most of what we shall see – and so much has disappeared – is thirteenth century.

After the Dissolution the abbey was granted to Sir Anthony Browne, one of Henry VIII's executors. His descendants lived here till 1779, when it was sold to the Webster family. It is now the well-known girls' school. Every generation, it seems, has laid heavy hands on the buildings. Sir Anthony Browne soon demolished the church, and used the materials for his own building: he rebuilt the east wing of the gatehouse as a court house, and the abbot's house he adapted and expanded for his own use. He also built a house for Princess Elizabeth (later Queen Elizabeth) – whose guardian for a while he was – and this he erected on top of the guesthouse undercroft: she never spent any time there. Little survives of the monastic buildings, all destroyed by Browne or his descendants, who became Viscounts Montague (see Easebourne Priory). In the nineteenth century the Websters employed Henry Clutton to alter the abbot's house still further.

The abbot's house occupied the west range of the cloister, the church (in normal fashion) the north. Of this practically nothing survives. It was large and cruciform, with apsidal chapels to the transepts, and a chevet at the east end, in French fashion. A stone on the site of the high altar marks the place of Harold's death. The crypts of the three chapels of the chevet have been excavated, and can be entered. Only foundations remain of the chapter house and parlour, on the east side; but next to this comes the best-preserved part of the monastic ruins.

The dorter is a magnificent roofless shell, with long rows of lancet windows, and a dramatic gable at the south end. And underneath is the equally magnificent undercroft, consisting of three main rooms, vaulted, their simple rib vaults resting on round pillars. The ground slopes steeply to the south, so the farthest room is an impressive, lofty spacious room, with a fireplace; it may have been the novices' room. Why was this splendid dorter allowed to survive? One longs to know.

Only foundations remain of the south cloister range – the refectory, and – farther south again, the kitchen; but walking along the terrace here the undercroft of the guest-house is reached. Nothing remains of Princess Elizabeth's house, which was built above this, except for the tall polygonal turrets, which must have punctuated the west end of the building, and still stand rather oddly all on their own. But from the terrace here the wonderful view of the Sussex Weald can be enjoyed – across which William's army advanced to meet Harold here.

(See also Easebourne – Sussex.)

BAYHAM ABBEY

Premonstratensian

Bayham must have been a very striking church in its heyday: long, lofty, narrow, aisleless, nearly all of purest Early English style. Standing at the west end now, with part of the south wall still standing upright, it is possible to get some impression of this very unusual interior, which terminates at the east end in a polygonal apse, rare in England at this time. It is highly unusual today, with a magnificent beech tree taking the place of the east window, growing out of the stone wall, clutching the sides with its roots, as though with old gnarled fingers. The crossing is of great beauty with its tall, clustered crossing piers, and two Early English arches giving entry to the two north transept chapels, which are still vaulted. Not quite so much survives of the south transept. In fact these two transepts, and the extension to the chancel, date from the late thirteenth century: at this time the earlier thirteenth-century transepts were shortened, and walled off like passages behind the nave. Everywhere in the chancel are very finely carved corbels – stiff leaf or foliage – and remarkable decorative blank sexfoils, almost Gothick in feeling, a very unusual feature of this late Early English rebuilding. About a century later the nave was remodelled, with large Perpendicular windows, and slender shafts to carry the vault; to support this, at some stage, great buttresses were built across the cloister walk.

Little remains of the cloister, except for the claustral buildings on the east side: sacristy, chapter house, and slype. In the chapter house a three-bay arcade divides the building; above all this was the dorter. Very little remains of the south or west range: the former would have held the frater; the latter the abbot's lodging, or the guesthouse.

Bayham was one of two Premonstratensian houses in England to have been founded direct from Prémontré: it was founded by Robert de Thornham in 1208, absorbing two other little foundations, which had fallen on hard times. It also had the distinction of being suppressed by armed force – in 1525, when it was given to Wolsey to endow his new colleges. But local feeling ran high, and for a time resisted the suppression, and reinstated the abbot. But in the end he surrendered.

In 1714 the property was purchased by Sir John Pratt, the Lord Chief Justice: his son became Lord Chancellor and 1st Earl Camden (1768), his grandson Lord Lieutenant of Ireland, and 1st Marquis Camden (1812). To them and their descendants is due the preservation of the ruins we see today. They built the charming Gothick house, known as the Dower House, to the west of the church (a very sympathetic addition), and towards the end of the century employed Repton to landscape the place. The ruins, of course, became the principal feature of the scheme, and the north gatehouse was enlarged and romanticized, with the addition of a (genuine) mediaeval arcade – probably removed from the chapter house. This made a lovely loggia, with a view of the lake, which was formed by damming the little River Teise. Further to the northwest they built the Victorian house called Bayham Abbey (by David Brandon, 1870), looking down from its hillside on all this romantic creation.

Lord Camden gave the ruins and the Dower House to the Ministry of Works in 1961: much excavation has been carried out since.

CHICHESTER – GREYFRIARS

Franciscan

The friars' church will be found in Priory Park, not far from the Ship Hotel, not far from the Festival Theatre. Originally founded in 1225, nearby, the friars moved here in 1269, and their church, of which this is the chancel, was completed perhaps by 1280. It is austerely beautiful, with its grouped lancets, and simple, strong proportions, a spacious church for preaching. Two doors on the north side led into the cloister. The house was dissolved in 1538.

EASEBOURNE PRIORY

Augustinian Nuns

Easebourne (pronounced Esbourne) more or less adjoins Midhurst, with the ruins of Cowdray House set back, and the great park surrounding it; it is, in fact, very much an estate village, the church at the top, the priory buildings attached. The priory was founded for Augustinian Canonesses *c.* 1238; oddly enough, it had no church, merely using part of the parish church; indeed, as time went on, usurping it. The nuns' part – the east end of the south aisle – became ruinous after the Dissolution, and was only rebuilt to serve as the burial place of the owners of Cowdray: here is the tomb of Sir Anthony Browne, 1st Viscount Montague – originally in Midhurst Church, and much altered when transferred here; it closely resembles the tomb of Sir Thomas Wriothsley at Titchfield (qv), but lost its obelisks in the removal. Very extensive rebuilding of the church took place in 1876 onwards at the hands of Sir Arthur Blomfield, for the 7th Earl of Egmont, whose family acquired Cowdray on the extinction of the Montagues.

It was the Egmonts who began the restoration of the priory buildings. They form a long range to the south of the church, and are, in fact, the east range of the cloisters: in the centre is the familiar tripartite entrance to the chapter house, attractive work of the second half of the thirteenth century; sacristy, parlour and warming house adjoined, and above all this was the dorter. On the south side, above an undercroft, was the frater. This in course of time degenerated into a barn

– but the whole range was restored for parish use in this century, becoming vicarage, parish hall and so on. Nothing remains of the west range, but a beautiful garden fills the space of the canonesses' cloister court. Here is a 250-year-old espalier apple tree, Sussex Nanny, and much else to give pleasure in this secluded spot.

Sir Anthony Browne, 1st Viscount Montague, of Cowdray, was the son of Sir Anthony Browne to whom Battle Abbey was granted at the Dissolution. As he drove the last monks out at Battle in 1538, one turned on him and pronounced a curse – that his line would expire by fire and water. The last (7th) Viscount was drowned in the Rhine in 1793; a week later Cowdray House was destroyed in a great fire. His sister, who married Stephen Poyntz, succeeded – and their two sons were drowned, bathing at Bognor.

HARDHAM PRIORY

Augustinian

Water meadows by the Arun, between Arundel and Pulborough – a lovely spot: the Augustinian priory was founded here *c.* 1250, and what appears at first sight as a long, low Sussex farmhouse is, in fact, in part, the refectory, rebuilt and adapted; the forecourt, where we stand, is the cloister court. Within is a vaulted undercroft. More exciting, and indeed of great beauty, is the chapter house, standing in its familiar position on the east side of the cloister. The entrance screen, with its three elegant arches, the side arches paired under a quatrefoil, and all standing on delicate short shafts with carved foliage capitals, is a masterpiece. At the east end there are three long lancets, and on the side walls there are still fragments of the vaulting. The church and all else has disappeared: if this was the chapter house, what must the church have been like?

LANGNEY PRIORY

Cluniac

Langney is now caught up in the most dismal Eastbourne subtopia: council estates, supermarkets, jazzy public houses and unceasing traffic. But off the main road from Pevensey, amid all this horror, a

Above: Beauvale: the
[...]s of the 14th-century
[...]thusian church,
[...]ported by wooden
[...]resses, provide a
[...]g shelter for a farm
[...]tor.

[...]t: Buildwas: through
[...] open arcades of the
[...]e it is possible to
[...]rb the beauty of the
[...]opshire countryside.

Haughmond: the late Norman triple entry into the chapter house.

Lilleshall: the tree-hung hills provide an incomparable setting for Lilleshall Abbey, Shropshire.

Stavordale: a subtle 17th-century conversion of a monastic church into a two-storied country house in Somerset.

Croxden: the long single lancets of the west front, a fragment of the chevet, and a great sycamore to occupy the nave.

Opposite above: the gatehouse at Butley in Suffolk is one of the earliest examples of flint flushwork in England, *c.* 1325.
Below: Newark Priory: the chancel and transepts across the River Wey in Surrey.

Battle: as Sir Anthony Browne drove the last monks out in 1538, one turned on him to pronounce a curse, which was duly fulfilled.

Bayham: a magnificent beech tree grows out of the east wall, clutching the sides with its roots, as with old gnarled fingers.

Michelham: gatehouse and bridge lead across the moat to the remains of the priory beyond.

Above: Winchelsea: the early 14th-century church of the Grey-friars, still standing in a garden on the edge of the ancient Cinque Port.

Right: Lacock: the 14th-century cloisters – still the heart of the house.

side road is marked 'Priory Road' – a clue! And Priory Road leads to the priory.

It must be stressed at once that Langney is not a priory as such, but a priory grange, a grange of Lewes Priory. But so little survives of that, and so much of this, that it seems right to include it. Moreover, it is an important little building, undoubtedly monastic, the perfect example of a monastic grange – of which there were once hundreds throughout the land. The house is of great antiquity, as is the chapel, and the preservation of both is remarkable.

The west front of the house is gabled and pretty, with early nineteenth-century timbering and barge boards. The house, however, is genuine mediaeval, and in fact a timber house, extended on the north side in the eighteenth century, and partially encased. In the east wall of the drawing room is a door: 'Now we step down eight hundred years in history,' says the owner, leading us down into the chapel. This is indeed twelfth century, lengthened in the fourteenth. After the Dissolution it was used as a barn – and thus it has survived. Now it is used for worship once again: it retains all its architectural features, and is beautifully furnished.

Above the chapel is the Great Hall, another mediaeval room, and outside, with its buttressed east end, and walls of stone and flint, it is a little building of great charm, and looks very much as it did in 1785 when S. H. Grimm drew it – a delightful drawing, now in the Manuscript Room at the British Museum.

LEWES PRIORY

Cluniac

Lewes is a town of many pleasures – the castle, the ancient churches, the Georgian houses, the setting, the river, the small streets and alleys, the brewery. In addition to the High Street with its distinguished houses, there is Southover below, with its own charming High Street; there are delightful houses here, and there is less traffic. First, a visit should be paid to Southover Church. This was originally the *hospitium* of the priory, and only became the parish church in the fourteenth century when the original church within the priory gates became too small. The tower of mellow brick is of 1714, with an elegant cupola. This is not all: in it are set three stones from the priory, carved with the rose and crown, the arms of de Warenne (for the founders), and a mitre with the letters I.A.P.L. (for John Ashdown, Prior of Lewes). In the Victorian pseudo-Norman chapel are the two little leaden caskets which contained the bones of William de Warenne and his wife, Gundrada; their bones now lie under the beautiful black Tournai marble tomb slab to Gundrada.

There is so little to see of this celebrated priory that it is some compensation to be able to venerate these relics, and revere the memory of the founders. William de Warenne was one of the Conqueror's chief barons – to whom the rape of Lewes was granted. He built the castle and, after matters military, turned his mind, with his wife, to matters spiritual. So they set out on a pilgrimage to Rome, but got no farther than Cluny, where they were so impressed by the abbey, and the Cluniac Order that they vowed to found a Cluniac house at Lewes. The Abbot of Cluny sent one Lanzo to be Prior, and three other monks to establish the first Cluniac priory in England; it grew, and de Warenne bestowed on it many endowments – and the manor of Castle Acre in Norfolk, destined to be the second English Cluniac house. There were, of course, ups and downs of fortune, but its importance in the history of English monasticism cannot be exaggerated. There were still twenty-three monks here at the time of the Dissolution.

There is little to see except cliffs of eroded stone and flint – and these are all railed and wired off impenetrably to prevent entry: one wall, supposedly, is a wall of the refectory, another the reredorter, another the infirmary. All remained forgotten and overgrown till the railway, in 1845, tore right through it to build the line to Brighton. The founders' leaden caskets – now in Southover Church – were discovered: Gundrada's tomb slab was discovered in Isfield Church (a few miles to the northeast) – and returned to Southover. So some attempt at reparation has been made.

MICHELHAM PRIORY

Augustinian

Michelham stands in an ideal sequestered setting, away from main roads in beautiful weald countryside. The priory was founded in 1229 for Augustinian Canons, but was never very large, nor very prosperous; however it has bequeathed to us today something of very great charm, redolent of the spiritual ideals of a religious house. Its special charm is its gatehouse, which stands astride its moat, fed by the River Cuckmere. It is tall and commanding, and must date from the early fifteenth century. Across the moat the considerable monastic fragment turns out to be the south side of the cloister court – the refectory, converted into a house after the Dissolution, together with the taller building, which filled the angle of the south and west ranges and the prior's house, over the cellars. All else has gone: church, chapter house, dorter, but the site of the church has been excavated, and is marked out. For over 300 years Michelham was used as a farm, forgotten and protected from the world; thus it has survived, to recall the secluded but active and scholarly lives of its canons.

Michelham was rescued and beautifully restored earlier this century, and now belongs to the Sussex Archaeological Trust; it is open to the public regularly.

ROBERTSBRIDGE ABBEY

Cistercian

It must be said at once that there is really very little to see at Robertsbridge Abbey, that it is a working farm, and private; moreover, visitors are, not surprisingly, discouraged. But, for completeness, Robertsbridge must be included in this book.

The Cistercian abbey here was founded in 1176; it is one of the comparatively few Cistercian houses in the south of England, and the only one in Sussex. It was famous in its day, and twice visited by Henry III – with a fairly consistent complement of a dozen monks in residence, and always, it seems, a high reputation. Now almost the only surviving building is the Abbey Farmhouse, which was probably the abbot's house. The thirteenth-century undercroft survives, together with other mediaeval features, and a king-post roof. Otherwise, there are but crumbling walls of what was once the frater, of what was once the warming house (and later converted into an oast), and the parched lines in the grass that appear in a hot summer to indicate the foundations of the church. All very sad, no doubt, but very beautiful. Let us leave some monastic sites unexcavated, some ruins in a state of 'pleasing decay', let Robertsbridge join Jervaulx, in its setting of meadows and wild flowers.

RYE – FRIARY OF THE SACK

Franciscan

There stands in Church Square, in this ancient town and Cinque Port, a house called the Friary of the Sack. An offshoot of the Franciscans, they were called the Friars of the Sack because they wore sackcloth – they were officially the Friars of the Penance of Jesus Christ. After 1317 they were absorbed into other Franciscan bodies, and of their seventeen houses in England only this house at Rye survives. It was founded *c.* 1263. It is unquestionably a mediaeval house, and in recent years was the home of Dr Alec Vidler, the distinguished Cambridge scholar and Dean of King's. It was also his birthplace.

SHULBREDE PRIORY

Augustinian

The romantic and beautiful fragment of an Augustinian priory in an idyllic setting, isolated and embowered in woods, where the hills south of Haslemere fall away gently into the Weald: Shulbrede is in Sussex, but very close to the point where Sussex, Surrey and Hampshire meet. There are two fishponds, and a moat surrounding the place, still partially filled with water, and what appears to be a farmhouse or small manor house of ancient stone with old brick chimneys and warm red tiles. Then a mediaeval doorway will be seen, and early mullioned windows, denoting the mediaeval, monastic origins of the house. What we see is in fact the southwest corner of the cloisters of an Augustinian priory, founded here *c.* 1200. The church, apparently cruciform with a central tower, stood on the north side, but that and the other claustral ranges have all disappeared. But round the corner from what is now the front door is the lavatorium, three trefoiled arches in the outside wall of what was the refectory: here the monks washed their hands before meals. So what is now the house was the prior's lodging with its impressive vaulted undercroft, with the refectory adjoining, now divided into two floors.

For centuries after the Dissolution Shulbrede was used as a farm-house, and, thus forgotten, survived until discovered early in this century by Sir Arthur Ponsonby, later Lord Ponsonby of Shulbrede. It was he who by careful restoration made it the beautiful house that it now is, and laid out the enchanting garden with its impressive yew hedges. It is his family who live here today, and treat the place with such understanding.

It makes a most lovely house. The undercroft must date from the early thirteenth century: it is a beautiful groin-vaulted room, the vault resting on a Purbeck marble column. But the great thing at Shulbrede is the parlour upstairs, where are to be seen the fascinating wall paintings illustrating the legend that animals could speak on Christmas Day.

The scene is set in rolling Sussex downland, all painted in soft green. The cock proclaims: 'CHRISTUS NATUS EST.' 'QUANDO? QUANDO?' calls the duck – to which the raven replies: 'IN HAC NOCTE.' 'UBI, UBI?' asks the bull; 'IN BETHLEM,' replies the lamb. A text from Isaiah is painted above: 'ECCE VIRGO CON-CIPIET, ET VOCABITUR NOMEN EJUS EMANUEL' – and, below, the words, 'GLORIA TIBI, DOMINE, QUIA NATUS ES DE VIRGINE, CUM PATRE ET SANCTO SPIRITU IN SEMPITERNA SAECULA. AMEN.'

What date can be assigned to these paintings? About 1550 is usually suggested, but who would have painted them here, after the suppression of the monastery? There are women, too, in Elizabethan dress, and the arms of James I (perhaps a later addition). Whatever the date, they are charming, and deeply moving; they provided the inspiration for a recent stained-glass window by John Piper.

TORTINGTON PRIORY

Augustinian

Close to the Arun, and only a few miles southwest of Arundel on the west side of the road is Priory Farm, and on the north side of the house is a barn. Against that is what remains of the nave arcade: three beautiful Early English bays, with clustered columns, curiously marooned here in the middle of the farmyard. What is much odder, however, is that all around is what appears to be a depot of reproduction Italian classical statuary, splendid maybe, but unexpected and perhaps a trifle bizarre here.

The priory was founded here *c.* 1180, for Augustinian Canons.

WILMINGTON PRIORY

Benedictine

Wilmington was an alien priory, established before 1110, when the manor was given to the Abbey of Grestain in Normandy by Robert of Mortain, half-brother of the Conqueror, and Lord of the Rape of Pevensey. It was only a very small foundation, and was obviously used as a kind of headquarters for the collection of their local rents and duties by the Norman abbey; probably only the prior and one or two monks would be in residence; they had what was more of a manor house than a conventional house. There was no church, no cloister, no chapter house or refectory. The mediaeval house contains a vaulted room, whose purpose is unknown; there is another room, which is usually called the prior's chapel, and a ruined wing to the north, which may have connected with the parish church, which they used rather than building one of their own. On the west side is the rather grander façade of a fourteenth-century gatehouse, now only leading to a pretty garden. It is altogether a most charming building, of stone and flint and brick. The Anglo-French wars cut off Wilmington from its mother house in Normandy, and in 1414 it was suppressed by Henry V.

Wilmington is an idyllic spot, with the slopes of the South Downs to the south, and the Long Man looking down on church and priory and village. The priory now belongs to the Sussex Archaeological Trust, who look after it beautifully, and open it to the public on certain days.

WINCHELSEA – GREYFRIARS

Franciscan

A day in Winchelsea is always a pleasure – New Winchelsea it should be called, for the old Cinque Port stood down on the marshes, close to the sea, victim always of French raids, or storm damage from the sea. This is Edward I's new town, a town which somehow never grew up and remained the grandest and most beautiful of villages, a great parish church never completed, a town hall never built. The three gatehouses – the Strand Gate, the Land Gate and the New Gate, this last far out of the village, down a country lane – speak of its embryonic greatness. So does the Greyfriars: the Friars only settled in places of importance.

The house called Greyfriars is an attractive nineteenth-century rebuilding; in the garden, at the back, is the chancel of their church, a fragment of great beauty. It is early fourteenth century, and apsidal: the chancel arch survives, the bell turret on its south side, and Decorated windows, which have lost their tracery. This beautiful sanctuary is deeply moving, and with its surrounding garden, its trees, its daffodils in spring, its simplicity, recalls St Francis himself, and his ideals.

Warwickshire

COMBE ABBEY

Cistercian

Combe in its day became one of the wealthiest of monastic houses –
on sheep; the Cistercians were, of course, great farmers, and their
sheep at Combe brought great wealth to themselves, and to the ancient
town of Coventry, not far away.

There is very little monastic left at Combe Abbey now. The
approach from the south through the park (now the property of the
City of Coventry) leads us to the moat, and so into the open quadrangle, which was the cloister court. The moat may seem mediaeval,
but in fact this and the 'mediaeval' bridge are the creation of Eden
Nesfield, the talented Victorian architect, who between 1861 and 1864
rebuilt part of the house for the 3rd Earl of Craven.

Combe was founded for Cistercian monks in 1152, and after the
Dissolution, and two rapid changes of ownership, was acquired by
the 1st Earl of Craven. The church, occupying the south side of the
cloister, stood where Nesfield's moat now is; on the east side the
Norman doorway to the chapter house remains with its accompanying
windows, with slype and warming house adjacent. That is all there is
left of the monastic house. The church soon disappeared, and what
remained was converted into domestic accommodation.

Of course, this was not good enough for the Cravens, in the seventeenth century one of the great building dynasties of England: the
array of theatrical gatepiers at Hamstead Marshall, round the site of
a vanished house, and their tall romantic hunting lodge at Ashdown
on the top of the Berkshire Downs will come to mind. In the 1670s
and 1680s William Winde built handsome new ranges on the west
and north sides of the cloisters; the fascinating thing is that much of
the correspondence between Sir William Craven (later 2nd Lord
Craven) and William Winde survives in the Bodleian. In these ranges
beautiful rooms with sumptuous panelling and plaster ceilings were
contrived.

Nesfield's building was concentrated on the east side round the chapter house, and was appropriately Victorian mediaeval in character. In 1923 the 4th Earl died, and the place was sold: Nesfield's work was pulled down, and much of the wonderful seventeenth-century panelling removed. The house later became a hostel for the General Electric Company.

COVENTRY – GREYFRIARS

Franciscan

The spire of Greyfriars – one of the famous three spires of Coventry – still stands, bereft of its original church, bereft of its later church, bereft of all its claustral buildings, bereft of its friars. The Franciscans came to Coventry in 1234, and this spire must date from *c.* 1350. It is octagonal, 230 feet high, and stood above that narrow cross-passage which was always the great feature of Franciscan churches, the wide-aisled nave (for preaching) on one side, the narrow quire (for the friars) on the other. Only this spire survived the Dissolution, and in 1830 Rickman and Hutchinson built a new nave, and converted the base of the spire into the chancel, for a new church called Christ Church. The nave was destroyed by bombing in the war. Once again the spire survives.

COVENTRY – ST MARY'S PRIORY

Benedictine

This great building once dwarfed all the parish churches around. It was the first Cathedral of Coventry, and stood roughly parallel with Holy Trinity and St Michael's, and just to the north. But today we have to look carefully to find even the slightest remains. There are the foundations of two of the radiating chapels, once part of the east end, set in cobbles close to the steps down to the present cathedral refectory. To the right of the tree-lined path by Holy Trinity stands the wall of the west end, with piers set against it, the responds of the nave arcade: the base of one or two piers have been discovered. In a small courtyard near the junction of Trinity Street and New Buildings is the base of the northwest tower, now part of the wall of a later building. This is all that is left of what was once the richest monastic house around here, founded in 1043, its privileges confirmed by William the Conqueror.

COVENTRY – WHITEFRIARS

Carmelite

In Gosford Street there stands what at first sight appears to be a red sandstone house, Elizabethan or thereabouts, with the usual mullioned and transomed windows, and an oriel at the centre. It is, in fact, the east range of the Carmelite friary; the Carmelites settled in Coventry in 1342. They built a cruciform church with central tower – but this has vanished, as have the north and south ranges of the cloister; but here in the east range the early sixteenth-century vault of the cloister survives, together with the vaulted chapter house and dormitory above. After the Dissolution all this was converted into a house by John Hales, citizen of Coventry, who entertained Queen Elizabeth here. After having served as part of the workhouse, it is today the local history museum.

KENILWORTH ABBEY

Augustinian

Kenilworth, of course, is dominated by ruins – but it is the tremendous ruins of the castle that dominate: the ruins of the abbey are forgotten.

Standing outside the south porch of the parish church, and walking down the churchyard path to the southwest, the foundations of the abbey church will soon be seen. The priory of Kenilworth was founded c. 1125 for Augustinian Canons, and raised to the rank of an abbey c. 1440.

There is, unfortunately, little to see of church or monastic buildings, and the churchyard path carries on regardless across both north and south transept, then through the cloister, and on through the frater. We can pick out a few features – a little walling of the north transept, a little more of the south, and a long low stretch of the south wall of the nave. As sometimes with Augustinian churches, both nave and chancel were originally aisleless; the chancel appears to have been given aisles in the thirteenth century, and to have been extended east-ward in the fourteenth. What was unusual was the fourteenth-century octagonal northwest tower.

Walking on down the churchyard path, we can see clearly the foundations of the apsidal chapter house, with slype between it and the transept, before proceeding to inspect the only two buildings which still stand upright: the guesthouse to the southwest, and the gatehouse due west of the church. Both are fourteenth century, the guesthouse of stone, brick and timber, and the gatehouse of stone. This is still an impressive building, with its four-centred archway, and vaulted carriageway, to lead us back into the town from a vanished world.

MAXSTOKE PRIORY

Augustinian

An imposing fourteenth-century gatehouse by the road, a peep through the vaulted archway – and across the courtyard stands what appears to be an Elizabethan manor house with gabled porch. In fact it is the inner gatehouse to Maxstoke Priory, converted into a house after the Dissolution. There are farm buildings all round, and, beyond, standing in the meadow, is the crossing tower of the church – or as Douglas Hickman describes it in the *Shell Guide to Warwickshire*, 'a tall slice' of the tower. Square at its base to accommodate the crossing arches, it becomes octagonal above, and half of it has collapsed. Nothing else survives of the church, but not far away stands the west wall of the infirmary, with its empty window above, arched doorway below.

The priory was founded by William de Clinton – who also built the moated castle to the north of the village – for Augustinian Canons in 1336. There are wide views over pleasant open country, with the cooling towers of Hams Hall Power Station looming on the horizon.

STONELEIGH ABBEY

Cistercian

Most people thinking of Stoneleigh think of the great eighteenth-century house, the home of Lord Leigh. Its grand Baroque front was built for the 2nd Lord Leigh by Francis Smith of Warwick, and finished in 1726. It is not often realized that much of the monastic house survives behind this west front; few would guess that it is a rebuilding of the west range of the cloisters, or that a fragment of the Norman nave arcade actually remains, embedded in the north front of the house.

Stoneleigh was founded for Cistercian monks *c.* 1135. What must have been basically a Norman cruciform church conformed to a normal Cistercian plan; cloisters were on the south side, with the east range occupied by sacristy, chapter house, slype and so on, with dorter above; the south no doubt by frater and kitchen. Now the south aisle of the church is absorbed into the north side of the house, with Norman arcade included in the outer wall, and Norman doorways, still in position, opening into what was the cloister court, now the inner court of the house. The east range, in similar way, has been absorbed into the domestic life of the house. The south front is partly by Francis Smith, and partly later eighteenth or early nineteenth century. The four-teenth-century gatehouse, with guesthouse attached, is particularly delightful, and is still the gatehouse to the place.

After the Dissolution Stoneleigh was granted to Charles Brandon, Duke of Suffolk, but after his death was acquired by Sir Rowland Hill and Sir Thomas Leigh, who married Sir Rowland Hill's niece, and thus acquired it all. His son was created a baronet, and his grandson was created the 1st Lord Leigh (1643). In the Civil War he was a great supporter of the King in this bleak Parliamentary county, and entertained Charles I at Stoneleigh 'when the gates of Coventry were shut against His Majesty'.

A later member of the family was Cassandra Leigh, wife of the Reverend George Austen and mother of Jane; it is to Cassandra that we owe a delightful account of Stoneleigh in the early nineteenth century. Life here must have influenced Jane, too, and it is a pleasure to associate her with Stoneleigh, which is still the home of the Leigh family.

Westmorland

SHAP ABBEY

Premonstratensian

A mile and a quarter from the village of Shap, in a quiet secluded valley of the River Lowther, stand the remains of Shap Abbey, founded originally at Preston Patrick (near Kendal) in 1192 as a Premonstratensian house, and moved to Shap in 1201. What remains of the church, begun in the thirteenth century – a nave of six bays with north aisle, transepts and chancel – faces east towards the river. The cloister lay to the south, with sacristy, chapter house and claustral buildings reaching to the river bank. These were completed in the early fifteenth century. The east end of the church was rebuilt later in the century, and *c.* 1500 the dominating west tower was built. This is remarkably intact, a tall, heavily buttressed Perpendicular tower, with a big west window, and three-light bell openings above. After the Dissolution, the place became a useful stone quarry, and the buildings were used as barns – only the great tower, more difficult to demolish, being left to stand upright. After being held by the Lowthers, Earls of Lonsdale for two or three centuries, the ruins were taken over by the Office of Works in 1948. The farmhouse and cottages and accompanying barns nestle in the valley close to the abbey, an extraordinarily beautiful ensemble.

Wiltshire

BRADENSTOKE PRIORY

Augustinian

The village of Bradenstoke is on a ridge, rising from the north Wilt-shire plain – a surprisingly attractive place, with many old half-timbered cottages. But what remains of Bradenstoke Priory, after being pillaged by William Randolph Hearst in the 1930s?

Bradenstoke Priory is not easy to find, not at first even easy to locate: it is possible to get lost in a long-disused airfield, where there are ruins and remains in plenty, but of the wrong kind. Strips of tarmac, once perhaps the floors of hangars, now almost invisible beneath tufts of grass, are not the mediaeval foundations for which we are searching. But at last a dark tunnel of long-neglected lime trees leads us to the priory, and here is the entrance to a surprisingly well-preserved mediaeval undercroft, with octagonal pillars supporting a plain ribbed vault.

Despite the notice warning us what Terrible Danger we are in, we can clamber down, over heaps of rubble, and long-abandoned beer tins, and admire what is part of the west cloister range, clearly built in the fourteenth century, with, at the north end, part of a tower of much the same date, which seems to have stood at this corner of the cloister; somewhat unusually, the church stood on the south side of the cloister.

Bradenstoke Priory was founded in 1142 for Augustinian Canons; there were a dozen at the time of the foundation, and more at the time of the dissolution. The church soon disappeared, as did much else. Then Mr Hearst came along, bought the guesthouse, the prior's lodging, and the tithe barn, and removed them to St Donat's Castle. So what we have left are merely the remains of the remains.

KINGSTON ST MICHAEL

Benedictine Nuns

The beautiful Wiltshire–Gloucestershire border country of golden stone villages, golden stone houses: Priory Farm at Kingston St Michael at first sight appears such a one, of early seventeenth-century date, no doubt. Only the discerning eye will notice earlier features, fifteenth-century windows, perhaps – even one tiny trefoil-headed lancet – or the odd mediaeval buttress or doorway, and mediaeval masonry everywhere. The house, in fact, is all that remains of a priory of Benedictine nuns, founded *c.* 1155. The church lay to the north, and the present house seems to have formed one part of the claustral buildings – indeed, the west range of the cloister. As such it would have been, probably, the guest hall, and the prioress's lodging – ideal for conversion after the Dissolution.

John Aubrey, the seventeenth-century antiquary, writer, and historian of Wiltshire, was born in the parish, and through his mother's family, the Lytes, had a long connection with Kingston St Michael.

Priory Farm is a private house, and not open to the public.

LACOCK ABBEY

Augustinian Nuns

Lacock is a perfect village, with streets of mediaeval, Elizabethan and Georgian houses and cottages in happy unison. The abbey stands just beyond the village, surrounded by wide lawns and meadows. Founded in 1232 by Ela, Countess of Salisbury, for Augustinian nuns, it became an abbey in 1241; the foundress became the first abbess, and died in 1261. The abbey was dissolved in 1539, and bought by Sir William Sharington: his niece married a Talbot, and Lacock remained with his descendants until given to the National Trust by Miss Matilda Talbot in 1944. Henry Fox Talbot (1800–77) was 'the father of photography', and here made the first photographic negative in 1835.

Much remains of the claustral buildings, but nothing of the church, which was entirely pulled down by Sharington. The stone he used to construct the stables – a most charming courtyard, which stands to the north of the monastic buildings, and around the cloisters he formed his house. Passing first through the delicious Gothick arch (by Sanderson Miller (1756) for John Ivory Talbot) we reach the west front of the house. This is enchanting, and is dominated by Sanderson Miller's Great Hall, with its pair of ogee-headed windows, and a double stairway leading up to the front door in between. To the right are the more sober sash windows of the Georgian dining room; to the left the lower mediaeval monastic kitchen with its simpler Gothic windows.

But to appreciate what lies behind all this, it may be best to pass on, and reach the south front of the house. This south front is really the north wall of the church, which was aisleless and occupied the site of what is now the spacious lawn. Here there are three Gothic oriel windows, inserted in 1830, and at the far end Sharington's octagonal tower. All this makes a most happy composition: one would like to know who designed – but did not over-design – those three oriel windows. Inside Sharington's tower are two rooms, one above the other, containing extraordinary stone tables, one supported by fantastic squatting fauns: what do these tell us about Sharington the man? He was a strange successor to the other-worldly nuns.

But a low door in this south front leads into the fifteenth-century monastic cloister court – the heart of the nunnery, and still the heart of the post-monastic house. Three sides survive, with their Perpendicular traceried windows, and superb lierne vault. Here we are back with a jolt in the mediaeval abbey. Around the cloister, doors lead off to a series of vaulted rooms – the chaplain's room, the sacristy, the chapter house, the warming room, this last containing the amazing metal cauldron made at Malines in 1500. Above the north walk was the refectory, now divided into smaller, domestic rooms. Indeed, above this cloister quadrangle are to be found the many smaller rooms of the Talbots, rooms of great charm.

But their grand rooms are those on the west front, built above the monastic range. At the southwest corner the dining room is a splendid, somewhat earlier, Burlingtonian room of perfect proportions, altogether quieter, more restful than the room it adjoins. This is a glorious Gothick fantasy, for which the long ogee-headed windows (which we saw outside) will have prepared us: the shallow-vaulted ceiling is adorned with the coats of arms of Ivory Talbot's friends, set in plaster quatrefoils, and all around the walls are elaborate canopied niches, filled with terracotta figures by the German sculptor Alexander

Sederbach. They cannot all be identified, but one is certainly the Abbess Ela, the foundress herself.

MONKTON FARLEIGH

Cluniac

The east front of the manor house is early Georgian and very handsome, standing on its terrace, looking down on the avenue which crosses the park below. Few would suspect that underneath this – apparently – calm eighteenth-century house the remains of a mediaeval Cluniac priory would be embedded. There are few clues: a little mediaeval masonry on the west side of the house, a heap of carved stones in a back yard, two free-standing lancets in the garden nearby, perhaps part of the refectory, and three mediaeval effigies. It is difficult to make much of all this: the remains are so very fragmentary. It is difficult, too, to imagine that this was quite a large priory, with a prior and twenty monks in the middle of the fifteenth century, and a dozen at the time of the Dissolution. But so it was. Monks' Conduit, to the north, is the little conduit house, rebuilt in 1784, which houses the spring from which the monks drew their water.

Worcestershire

DUDLEY PRIORY

Cluniac

This was a very small priory, on the slopes of the Castle Hill, owing allegiance to the Lords of Dudley, by whom it was founded *c.* 1160. It was a daughter house of the great Cluniac priory of Much Wenlock.

Dudley has always been in Worcestershire, and in the diocese of Worcester – although an island in the middle of Staffordshire. Yet, mystery of mysteries, Dudley Castle has always been in Staffordshire. The ruins of the castle are worth looking at, perched as they delightfully are on their wooded hill overlooking the busy town. Besides, the priory is not the only attraction on the way up; there is also, most unexpectedly, a zoo, founded in the 1930s, with fanciful concrete buildings in a playful, amusing, 1930s style. Here seals splash about in the moat, and there are endearing penguins and polar bears.

The priory is a more serious pleasure. There are fragments of the church – an aisleless nave, a straight-ended chancel, a south transept with twin chapels. From what survives, this must be thirteenth century in date. There is very little of the claustral buildings to see – just the plan of the cloisters marked out, with a few low walls to show the position of the domestic buildings. There is nothing unusual in any of this; it must have been comfortable and commodious for so small a community, which normally seems to have numbered but a prior, and one or two monks.

EVESHAM ABBEY

Benedictine

The orchards of Worcestershire: the River Avon flowing through the town – Evesham is attractive with many good houses in its streets, and at its heart the precinct of the great Benedictine abbey, founded by Bishop Egwin, third Bishop of Worcester, in 714. Here Eove, the Bishop's swineherd, saw a vision of the Virgin; a similar vision was granted to the Bishop shortly afterwards. '*Ecce locus quem elegi*' – 'Here is the place which I have chosen,' were her words to him; the earliest church and its accompanying buildings were established on this spot, but nothing remains of all this – nor of the churches which succeeded it. Indeed it is tragic how little of this great foundation survives. But there is compensation in the survival of the magnificent bell tower, built by Abbot Clement Lichfield and completed in 1539, the very eve of the suppression of the monastery. It is 110 feet high, and was built as a free-standing campanile with an open archway at its base, its sides panelled all over, its windows and bell openings all crowned with ogee gables, its top adorned with open-work parapets and pinnacles. To the south of the tower is the entrance arch to the chapter house, now in a garden wall. This is distinguished work of the end of the thirteenth century, the arch itself adorned with little canopied niches containing (now) decapitated figures of saints.

To accompany the tower, and on its either side, are the two churches of All Saints, and St Lawrence – two churches in one churchyard. Both are mediaeval, All Saints the parish church, St Lawrence built as the cemetery chapel; St Lawrence is now in the care of the Redundant Churches Fund. To both of them Abbot Lichfield built a sumptuous addition: to St Lawrence the Chapel of St Clement (the Abbot's Christian name was Clement), to All Saints a chapel for his own burial.

Of the two gateways, Abbot Reginald's led from the churchyard into the town: the upper part is fifteenth-century timber work, but below, with its blind Norman arcading, it is twelfth century. The Great Gate leads to Merstow Green: here the almonry, partly stone, partly timber-framed, is fourteenth and fifteenth century, and is now an interesting museum.

A unique account of the dissolution of Evesham Abbey exists in the annotations of the Evesham Abbey Bible, which reads: 'The yere of our Lord 1539 the monastery of Evesham was suppressyd by King Henry VIII the XXXI yere of his rayene the XXX day of Januari at Evensong tyme the convent beyng in there quere at thys verse Deposuit potentes and wold not suffer them to make an end phillip Lawford beyng abbot at that tyme and XXX were at that day a lyre in the said monastery . . .'

'The abrupt and unceremonious end to the conventual life of Evesham is without exact parallel, so far as I know, in the records of the Dissolution,' writes Professor Knowles. The Evesham Abbey Bible was the first edition of the Matthew Bible (1537: printed in Antwerp), and enjoined by Bishop Latimer of Worcester for reading in monasteries in his diocese. This copy of the Bible came into the possession of John Alcester, former Sacristan, and eventually into the hands of Mr Philip Robinson. It was sold at Sotheby's in 1972 to Evesham.

A letter at the time from Mr Robinson (to Dr Arnold Taylor) concludes: 'This is unique in monastic history in that the annotations in it give the precise moment when the monastery of Evesham's long history ceased . . . the precise moment when the troops took over – the year, the day, the hour, the minute, and precisely the words the monks were singing at that moment . . .'

HALESOWEN ABBEY

Premonstratensian

The traffic on the dual carriageway of the Kidderminister–Birmingham road (A456) rushes past unceasingly; nobody cares whether the remains of a Premonstratensian abbey are hard by the road, just over the hedge, or not. Nobody has ever cared much about Halesowen Abbey, anyway, at any rate since the Dissolution. What remains has until recently been embedded in a workaday farm, with silos in the nave of the church, lancet windows peering up unexpectedly above cowsheds. It has been merely Manor Farm, on Lord Cobham's Hagley Estate – but now it is being taken over by the Historic Buildings and Monuments Commission and no doubt will all be tidied up, before being opened to the public (summer 1992).

Halesowen was a daughter house of Welbeck, founded for Premonstratensian Canons in 1215. The buildings followed the normal Premonstratensian plan, with the church on the north side, cloister court and claustral buildings on the south. Of the church, the outer wall of the south aisle is still standing, as is much of the west wall of the south transept, with its two lancet windows. Nearby is the doorway to the night stairs, which led up to the dorter, which was in its usual position. Red-brick farm buildings on the south side of the church in the form (more or less) of a quadrangle represent the cloisters. The most impressive remains, however, are those of the refectory, on the south side of what was the cloister. Here the south wall still stands, with small lancets below, taller lancets above. Part of the north wall of the quire of the church is still recognizable, too, with a single lancet window.

The farmhouse to the south of the cloister is post-Dissolution, but to the east is another mediaeval building, which may have been the abbot's house, or the guesthouse. In more recent years it has given good service as a piggery.

WORCESTER – GREYFRIARS

Franciscan

Somewhere beyond the roundabout in the middle of the terrible new road at the east end of the cathedral, and behind the multi-storey car park, is a narrow street called Friar Street, which has somehow been allowed to survive the general destruction of this part of the city. On its east side stands a long half-timbered black-and-white house, The Greyfriars, the guesthouse (it is supposed) of the Franciscan friary, founded *c.* 1227. It is a building of distinction, and must date from *c.* 1480, with its long front gabled at either end, over-hanging first floor and archway into a court behind. It now belongs to the National Trust, and may be visited at certain times; there are pleasant rooms within, sympathetically furnished, and a charming garden in the court-yard behind.

WORCESTER – THE WHITE LADIES

Cistercian Nuns

Within the main courtyard of the Royal Grammar School in Upper Tything are two fragments of The White Ladies, a Cistercian nunnery founded *c.* 1250 by Bishop Cantelupe. Facing the school hall and library – imposing neo-Jacobean buildings of 1915 – is a long early eighteenth-century brick house; round the corner it will be found that its west wall is supported by the mediaeval red sandstone east wall of the monastic church, its two lancet windows blocked; at the other end it will be seen that the west wall also survives, again with blocked-up lancets, propping up another later building. A charming garden now occupies the site of the church itself.

Yorkshire – East Riding

BEVERLEY – BLACKFRIARS

Dominican

In an unpromising position close to the railway line stands a range of buildings which once formed part of the Dominican friary. Long unrecognized for what it was, and concealed by later encroaching buildings and houses, it has only recently been rescued, and is in process of restoration. Partly of stone, partly of brick and timber, its mediaeval quality is asserted by its stone buttresses; these probably represent one side of the cloister court. This house of Black Friars was founded *c.* 1240, and in the early fourteenth century there were as many as forty friars here. Interesting wall paintings have been discovered, and are in process of restoration. The house has now been opened as a youth hostel.

WATTON PRIORY

Gilbertine

In the flat country, south of the wolds – a quiet sequestered setting for a great monastic foundation – Watton was the largest of all the Gilbertine houses, with seventy men and a hundred and fifty women inhabiting its two cloisters. Moreover St Gilbert himself, founder of the Order, would often visit Watton in its early days, as did St Aelred, Abbot of Rievaulx. Except for the prior's house, nothing exists of this great place above ground; but the site was fully excavated by Sir William St John Hope at the end of the last century, so at least the plan is known.

The prior's house stands at the southwest corner of what was the canons' cloister: it is a building of considerable magnificence. What appears as the smaller wing on the left of the entrance front is the original prior's lodging, a beautiful and indeed quite impressive building, standing on an undercroft. But to its right was attached a most imposing brick tower-house in the fifteenth century, with large octagonal corner turrets, and a very grand oriel window of stone, five-sided, to light ground-floor and first-floor rooms, its parapet ornately carved, and with fanciful gargoyles at the angles. Monastic prosperity? Monastic decadence? In any case, it made a desirable gentleman's residence after the Dissolution, and thus has survived. For the rest, it is all grass with an occasional hump or pile of stones to remind us of a great church, two cloister courts, two sets of claustral buildings.

Yorkshire – North Riding

BYLAND ABBEY

Cistercian

Byland stands in its own wide and beautiful valley: tree-hung hills descend to the road which leads from Ampleforth to Coxwold, and the ruins stand impressive above the road as it turns the corner past the little inn. Here a narrow lane to the west lands us at the abbey gatehouse – now but a solitary arch across the road, and stranded, it seems, a little way from the rest of the ruins. We can leave the car here, and walk back to the west front of the church.

Even in its ruined state this west front is magnificent, with half of a grand rose window surviving, and, below this, three lofty lancets, and below them a superb trefoil-headed west doorway. Too little survives of the church itself – no arcades in nave or quire, no crossing arches, only that impressive north aisle wall standing almost to full height, more or less the whole length of the building, which stood above the road as we approached; a fragment of the east end; a fragment of the south transept; that is all. But in spite of this it is an imposing interior – imposing for the impression it gives of great spaciousness, imposing for its double-aisled transepts, imposing for its unity of design. This church was all built within fifty years, in that austere and lovely Transitional–Early English style which seems to reflect so perfectly the ideals of the Cistercian movement. Here there is none of the grandeur of Fountains, none of that exquisite elaboration of Rievaulx: Byland is quiet, composed, calm; herein lies its charm. These may be our thoughts as we make our way to the site of the crossing, and on to the ambulatory at the east end.

Byland had an odd and disturbed beginning. It was founded first at Calder, a daughter house of Furness, and, like its parent as a Savigniac house: this was 1135. There the monks were harassed by the marauding Scots, and moved south, first to Old Byland, near to Rievaulx – too near, it seems for peace and happiness – and then to Stocking, near to Coxwold, finally arriving here in 1177. Meantime the Savigniac order had merged with the Cistercian, and it was as Cistercians that they built and established themselves here. So they built fast, and with evident determination: so much, if not all, was complete by the middle of the thirteenth century, a fact worth remembering.

We were standing in the church: we can make our way into the cloister court. As with the church, the claustral buildings proved too tempting a stone quarry, and as with the church nearly everything has gone – merely a cliff of masonry here or there, and foundations everywhere. Suffice to say that the monastic buildings follow the usual pattern, with the usual offices in the usual places. The lay brothers' 'lane' is of interest, the walk which adjoined their quarters in the west range, and led to a small yard to the south of the kitchen – independent of, and behind, the cloister itself. To the south of all this a museum has been built in recent years, containing so many things which we have not seen among the ruins. There are beautiful waterleaf capitals and carved corbels, the remarkable fragment of a stone lectern, and many immensely attractive tiles. Byland specialized, it seems, in these; there are many still in situ, in the crossing, and in the south transept – browns and greens and yellows – and there are more of them here.

COVERHAM ABBEY

Augustinian

East Witton is a delightful estate village, built in the early nineteenth century by the Brudenells, Earls and Marquises of Ailesbury, with cottages lining the long village green; at one end the road leads to Jervaulx, at the other the lane leads to Coverham. It is a magical, narrow winding lane, through the valley of the little River Cover. On one side it passes a perfect, gabled, seventeenth-century house, Braithwaite Hall – and on the far side there soon appears a handsome late Georgian house called Coverham Abbey. A mediaeval bridge crosses the river, and a sharp right turn leads to Coverham – house and ruins. The lane leads under the gatehouse arch, past a nursery garden on one side, past the gatepiers and garden entrance to the house on the other, past stone walls everywhere – when a long back wing to the house appears, clearly monastic in date and character. There is a remarkable nine-light mullioned window, and a number of carved decorative panels bearing the IHS symbol, or other inscriptions: Coverham seems to have specialized in these. This long wing was in fact the guesthouse, and formed the west side of the cloister. Round the corner, and a greater surprise is in store for us: two fourteenth-century arches of the south nave arcade come striding towards us across the garden; nearby is what must be the west wall of the north transept. It is just possible to imagine it all; the cruciform church, with its cloister court and guesthouse, which now forms the back wing of the Georgian house. Round the corner, propping up the garden wall and facing the front door, are two magnificent fourteenth-century knightly figures, originally, no doubt, recumbent in the church.

The Augustinian house was originally founded at Swainby (a few miles away) in 1189, and moved to this incomparable little valley in 1212. Lying here in this sequestered spot, with its two nave arches still standing, its guesthouse wing preserved, its nursery garden, old trees and stone walls, Coverham must be one of the most poignant monastic fragments anywhere.

EASBY ABBEY

Premonstratensian

The quiet road from Richmond descends slowly, then turns, to reveal the sudden view of Easby – parish church, abbey, gatehouse, the River Swale, all against the backdrop of the hills. Easby was founded in 1101 for Premonstratensian Canons: it is built in an awkward situation in the valley of the Swale, so that buildings are on different levels, and (very unusually) advantage is taken of this to provide accommodation in the claustral buildings on different levels, too. Again, it is unusual to find the parish church within the abbey precinct, but the church was here first, and one of the canons was normally incumbent.

After the Dissolution the gatehouse was used as a granary, and so has survived: it is the road that has been moved to the side. The gatehouse can be dated *c.* 1300: it brings us to the parish church, a long, low bellcoted building, outwardly in no way unusual, but inside full of things of interest: wall paintings, a copy of the Easby Cross, and so on. So we come to the abbey.

The refectory makes a wonderful frontispiece. From where we stand we can see at once that the sloping ground is going to provide all kinds of problems in a lay-out which is normally somewhat conventional. Here we can appreciate the lofty undercroft with its good-sized windows; the refectory itself has lofty (originally) traceried windows, and must date from *c.* 1300. The whole building towers above us, and is exceptionally delightful.

We can enter at the west end through what was the guest hall (with the prior's room, as it was, above). Here steps go up into the cloister garth (again note the levels), but others go into the refectory undercroft; the vaulting has gone, and we can gaze up into the refectory itself, admire the size of the great room, and the large window at the east end, which still retains much of its tracery.

From here, ascending into the cloister, we can see what an extraordinary shape it is. Most cloisters are square, or rectangular, courts. Here it is of no known shape: the position of the various claustral buildings dictate this. On the east side chapter house and sacristy are in their usual positions; behind us, on the west side, is (unusually) a three-storeyed block — again making use of the lie of the land — which contained not only the stores (as usual), but also the guest hall on the ground floor, the prior's hall on the first, and the dorter on the top.

Nothing survives of the church, which occupied the north side, but we can from its foundations appreciate its plan — long and austerely simple. This, and much of the claustral building, dates from the early thirteenth century, though we can see in some places later adaptations and additions, as in the east cloister range, where obviously important upper rooms were added in the fifteenth century, complete with private staircase and garderobe.

Beyond the church, on its north side, is a large and important block, containing the infirmary (with its kitchen, misericord and chapel), and, above that and curiously placed, the abbot's lodging, with his gallery, hall, and chapel; and here, as elsewhere, the provision of fireplaces (usually fifteenth-century additions) is some indication of the relaxing of the rules of austerity.

From here we can make our way back to the west range, and see how remarkably complicated the domestic planning was: the prior's apartments, the guest hall, guests' solar and dorter, together with the canons' dorter were all situated here. The explanation of these unusual arrangements is simple: on the west side runs in its valley the Swale, and this is where the main lavatories had to be; the great drain is clearly visible.

Walking round this extensive west range and enjoying the view of the river and the hills beyond, we shall come to the most beautiful feature of the whole abbey. Above the doorway of the south front is a most elegant thirteenth-century façade — composed of three wide interlacing arches, with clustered columns and stiff-leaf capitals, which form four pointed arches, two open to provide windows, two blind, with quatrefoils above. It is an Early English equivalent of a familiar Norman design. Above, to the left, is a group of three lancets. The rest of the upper floor has fallen: it must have been a most elegant façade.

This must have been the entry for the abbey guests. All monastic houses – even the Carthusian – laid great emphasis on hospitality, inspired by St Paul. Here is hospitable Easby opening its doors in welcome to its guests.

EGGLESTONE ABBEY

Premonstratensian

The valley of the Tees is magical; the river is the natural frontier between Yorkshire and County Durham, and on either side are well-known prizes: Greta Bridge and Wycliffe, Rokeby and Mortham, Barnard Castle and Egglestone. Egglestone is in an idyllic position, where the Thorsgill Beck runs into the Tees. The road from Rokeby crosses the river by the Monks' Bridge, and a lane leads up to the abbey. There are glimpses of the ruins through the trees, and suddenly the abbey is above us – the east end first, then a substantial part of the chancel, then a less substantial relic of the south transept. And the setting is incomparable.

Egglestone Abbey was founded for Premonstratensian Canons at the very end of the twelfth century. The church is cruciform and aisleless, and much of nave and chancel survive – the chancel with elegant Early English double-lancet windows. The east window with its straight mullions is a great curiosity. It *can't* be mediaeval: it must be seventeenth century. But who would have done this in the seventeenth century? Walls of nave and chancel still stand remarkably high, and standing at the west end it is possible to get some impression of what a beautiful church this must have been. Not much survives of the cloisters: this part of the building is oddly misshapen, with what remains of the west range extending beyond the west end of the church; and owing to the widening of the nave in the early fourteenth century this west front is no longer symmetrical. But the east range of the cloister was converted into a house after the Dissolution; this still stands in its ruined state, and with its mullioned windows looks every inch an Elizabethan manor house. It is possible that someone at this time, being archaeologically minded, repaired the east window of the church.

Egglestone, with its farmhouse and simple cottages nearby, its stone walls and wide views, with the river rushing below, seems indeed an enchanted spot: the stone mediaeval grave slabs, some beautifully carved, are reminders of its holiness.

ELLERTON PRIORY

Cistercian Nuns

The lonely road west from Richmond follows the valley of the River Swale: it is a lonely road, and a holy road, with the Benedictine nunnery at Marrick, and, two miles short of that, the Cistercian nunnery at Ellerton. They were both founded at much the same time, Marrick a few years earlier. Would that we could hear their bells, echoing down the valley.

Ellerton was founded *c.* 1170, but little survives of that date, except perhaps the late Norman arch leading from the tower into the nave. The tower itself is Perpendicular, robust and buttressed. Very little survives of the aisleless church, nothing of the monastic buildings. But two great cedars of Lebanon fill the body of nave and chancel: whoever was the genius who planted these?

GUISBOROUGH PRIORY

Augustinian

The tremendous eastern gable of the church still stands erect and splendid to tell us what a great church this was. A terrible fire in 1289 destroyed the earlier church. It's an ill wind that blows nobody any good, and as a result of this disaster one of the grandest of all monastic churches rose to take its place. Only a still greater disaster robbed us of the chance to see this church today. But this east end stands to delight us, and inform us.

Guisborough Priory was founded for Augustinian Canons in 1119 by Robert de Brus. If we go into the parish church nearby we shall see the wonderful Brus cenotaph, which once stood in the priory church, a monument to the founder, erected four hundred years later, an act of *pietas* indeed. On each side of the tomb chest are the little figures of five knights bearing the arms of the Brus family, with smaller figures of bishops set between, with other symbolic emblems – a chalice for a priest, a shell for a pilgrim, a cock for Prior Cockerell (prior 1519–34) who must have erected it; round the corner is a portrait of the seated prior, another of the seated Virgin. It is a work of art; moreover it was another act of *pietas* to salvage it from the ruined church, and re-erect it here.

Guisborough was a rich and powerful foundation. In 1535 it had an income of £638, far exceeding that of most foundations; Henry III granted it a weekly market in the town; at the end of the fourteenth century there were twenty-six canons in residence; just before the end, twenty-five.

We can stand at the west end of the church, where two towers once stood, and see their foundations: perhaps this west front resembled Beverley or York; we know that this enormous church took a century to complete; and moving up the empty nave, the empty quire, can stand before this grand east end, and gaze at the east window – empty now, but once filled with late thirteenth-century geometrical tracery. We can think of Lincoln, think of Ripon, or slightly later traceried windows like Carlisle, or Selby or Heckington. Even in its empty state, this east window is a masterpiece.

After the suppression Sir Thomas Chaloner, a powerful, influential, wealthy civil servant, leased the monastic property in 1547, and purchased it outright in 1550. His descendants have continued to live here. Was it they who preserved this noble east end? as a folly? or a landmark? Certainly an eighteenth-century print of their house next door shows the east end of the monastic church as a prominent feature of their garden. If so, this was an act of *pietas*, too.

There is little else to see: cloisters and their surrounding buildings must have stood on the south side. To the west is the early thirteenth-century gatehouse with its round arch; nearby is the octagonal monastic dovecote, of the same date perhaps, but crowned now with its eighteenth- or nineteenth-century slate roof and cupola – with its fox *courant* weather vane. What more charming finale could there be?

JERVAULX ABBEY

Cistercian

Jervaulx is captivating: there is no village, no parish church, no public house, no post office nor shop, no commercialism of any kind, only the Old Hall, which is a privately run hotel. It is rather like the 1930s, when we could visit these divine places without those crowds, without all the 'tourist' tarnish, without the conservationists, or all the talk of 'heritage'. Thank God for Jervaulx, which is privately owned, and privately loved, not over-organized, and indeed allowed to be itself. There is just the ruined abbey, and the park with its ancient trees.

There is a car park on the far side of the road. Opposite, a gate leads into the park, past the remains of the gatehouse, now converted into a cottage. A walk across the park towards the abbey, a gate into the precinct, a stall (unattended) with guidebooks and postcards, and a box for 'conscience' money – and the venerable ruins are upon us.

The great thrill about Jervaulx is that, as private property, it has never been tidied up too much, and there is none of the standardized treatment associated with the usual preservationist bodies. So Jervaulx is different, and full of atmosphere. Walking across the park, the ruins appear as an incredible conglomeration of jagged stonework hard to interpret. There is just one long line of lancet windows in an upper room – the only part of the building to retain any height – otherwise it is a case of a fragmentary arch here, a broken pillar there, silent walls everywhere.

The best thing to do is to walk straight up the path along the west wall of the lay brothers' refectory, crossing the drain (Jervaulx is especially strong in these) to the church. Very little remains of this: the base of a pillar here or there, the external walls largely made up of fragments, often of carved stonework. At the Dissolution the abbot and one monk were executed, and the church blown up, the stone quarried away. We are lucky to have anything. From here we can move easily into the cloister, and so into the chapter house, where the columns have been re-erected – four of them complete with capitals. Sacristy, parlour, slype – all these can be identified in their usual positions; then comes the site of the refectory, in normal Cistercian habit running north–south, then the kitchen – and so we are back at the lay brothers' range. Parallel with the lay brothers, parallel with the refectory, is the dorter undercroft, with the dorter above, still standing aloft with the high lancet windows which we saw from afar. Beyond all this is the spacious infirmary, and nearby is the abbot's house.

Jervaulx was originally founded a few miles away, and as a daughter of Byland was originally Savignac: all the houses of this Order joined the Cistercians in 1147; Jervaulx moved to its present site in 1156. The name Jervaulx means 'the valley of the Ure', and a wonderful valley it is. Jervaulx is celebrated for its wild flowers in the spring: they grow in the crevices, they dangle down the walls, they overflow everywhere, white, and gold, and red and blue. There is a booklet on sale describing them. So, come in the spring – or come in the autumn when the ancient trees are gold and yellow. Or come in the winter to see Jervaulx under snow. It is always open, the box there to receive our 'conscience' money. And what we owe to Jervaulx – for its beauty, its detachment, and, so often for its silence.

KIRKHAM PRIORY

Augustinian

A minor road to Kirkham leads off the A64 (York to Scarborough): this is glorious countryside. The Castle Howard Mausoleum, where Horace Walpole almost advocated being buried alive, is visible to the north – even the dome of the house, with luck – and the road leads down the hill to the River Derwent, and the railway. There is a charming Victorian signal box, and an ancient bridge, rebuilt by John Carr in 1802, to cross the river. All the time the ruins of the priory are clearly visible on the rising ground beyond the river. Entering by the grand late thirteenth-century gatehouse, the whole outer court is a wide expanse of grass, leading up to the west door of the church, the river murmuring and bubbling below.

Little survives of the church. The nave was narrow and aisleless – dating from the twelfth century, soon after the founding of the place by Walter l'Espec, Lord of Helmsley in 1110, and the transepts were of the same date. At the west end were twin towers: nothing remains of the north tower, but the grand entrance to the cloister, still partially vaulted, is the base of the south tower.

The chancel was built in the thirteenth century, and was altogether grander: eight bays in length, with aisles, eastern chapels and ambulatory, it was all built at a time when the priory prospered under the

Byland: across a meadow bedecked with cowslips, the west front of the abbey still stands prominent and distinguished.
Below: the 14th-century tiles – browns and greens and yellows – form intricate patterns to adorn the floors.

Opposite above: Easby: the grand 14th-century refectory makes a wonderful frontispiece for Easby Abbey in Swaledale, Yorkshire.

Below: Jervaulx: wild flowers and blossom adorn the day stairs at Jervaulx, Yorkshire.

Right: Kirkham: the view through the arch of the SW tower to the river and John Carr's bridge.

Below: Richmond: the tower of the Franciscan church with its slim buttresses, and narrow archway between the nave and the friars' choir.

Above: Rievaulx: the
ruins of Rievaulx Abbey
in the North Riding
stand white and ethereal
across a field of Queen
Anne's lace.
Below: fragmentary
flying buttresses still
support the clerestory:
the Rievaulx terrace
looks down from the
tree-hung hillside on the
left.

Whitby: the abbey stands supreme on its cliff-top, exposed to all the winds of heaven – and to every snow storm.

Fountains: in the snow, on a short December day, recalling the day in December 1132 when the monks first came to this desolate valley.
Below: the Lay Brothers' undercroft, the largest such interior in Europe.

Left: Kirkstall: the austere Norman west front – only the Perpendicular pinnacles are a later addition.

Below: Monk Bretton: a fragment of a Norman arch, and the triple piers and carved capitals of the priory church, now embedded in the frontispiece of a much later house.

Roche Abbey: a fragment of Cistercian perfection stands in a secluded valley landscaped by Capability Brown.

Sawley: rugged lumps of stone, all that remains of the Cistercian church standing against the dramatic backdrop of hills on the borders of Yorkshire and Lancashire.

patronage of the de Roos Lords of Helmsley, whose burial place the chancel became. The fragment of one elegant lancet window survives at the east end.

The cloister court is on the south side of the nave, and although only the external walls are standing, it is altogether charming with a spreading cherry tree occupying its northeast corner. On the east side is the chapter house, with, beyond and below, the walls of the infirmary to the east, and the prior's house closer at hand. Alongside the chapter house is the undercroft of the dorter, with the reredorter beyond. In the southwest corner a Norman doorway commands the view over the undercroft of the frater, with the foundations of the kitchen and guesthouse beyond. A spiral staircase here leads down to the undercroft, necessitated by the fall of the ground. On the west wall is the most beautiful feature of the place: the late thirteenth-century lavatorium, where the canons washed their hands before entering the frater. There are twin arches with a blind geometrical traceried recess behind; only the lead basins and pipes have disappeared. At the far end steps lead down under the vaulted arch of the southwest tower; we can walk down from here to the river bank.

So we depart by the gatehouse – a building we can put in our minds alongside Colchester, and St Osyth, Battle and Thornton, Cleeve and others. This has a splendid frontispiece to the outside world – the archway itself, with little crocketed gables above to enclose the windows, still complete with their tracery, with niches for statues (some of them surviving) and heraldic shields. The arms of Espec are there, as are those of de Roos, and Scrope, and England. Opposite is a good-looking eighteenth-century stone farmhouse, its front adorned with carved figures which must have come from the priory – as must the stone for the house itself.

MOUNT GRACE PRIORY

Carthusian

The traffic along the A19, to or from Middlesbrough, is relentless: a signpost points to Mount Grace Priory – a signpost to a different world, a signpost not merely to monastic calm, but a signpost to Carthusian silence. Mount Grace lies just below the Cleveland Hills, just below the Moors: as we approach, a steep backdrop of hills hung with oak woods stands behind the ruins. It is a wonderful setting.

193

Mount Grace is the best-preserved Carthusian priory in England – and only nine were ever founded here. It is here that we can best understand the ideals of the Carthusian life, and appreciate its workings. The Carthusian Order was quite different from all the other monastic Orders: founded at La Chartreuse by St Bruno in 1084, the rule was based on the hermit ideal of each monk living almost entirely by himself in his own tiny house. Grouped around the cloister, these little houses, or cells, afforded almost complete isolation for the brethren, who only met in church, or for occasional gatherings in chapter house or refectory. Such was the life at Mount Grace, a life of silence.

The priory here was founded in 1398 by Thomas Holland, Duke of Surrey, half-brother of Richard II. A wooded path leads to a gatehouse, which stands between two long ranges, the guesthouse on the left, porter's lodge, additional guesthouse and grain store on the right; a further range of barns completed the precinct on the south. Entering the gatehouse, the ruins of the church face us – modest in scale, like all the buildings here. There is a short aisleless nave, with a chapel on either side, and a narrow crossing with lofty arches supporting a tower, battlemented and pinnacled, but again modest in size; little remains of the longer chancel and sanctuary beyond. On the north side of the church is the Great Cloister, with five cells on three sides, each with its own walled garden. On the fourth side, adjoining the church, stood the small chapter house (adjoining the chancel), with sacrist's cell to the east, prior's cell, frater and kitchen to the west. A small extra court was formed, southeast of the church, in the early fifteenth century, with six more cells – of which the foundations can be seen. But everything was small, to cater in all for a mere twenty or twenty-one monks.

In 1654 the guesthouse was converted into a mansion by Thomas Lascelles: it was added to, and delightfully embellished by Philip Webb for Sir Lowthian Bell, the great industrialist, in 1900. Much credit is due to him for preserving the ruins in the early years of this century. He actually reconstructed one of the cells in the Great Cloister most effectively: we can see how a Carthusian monk lived – with his four little rooms on two floors, small garden, and private lavatory at the end of the garden. Close to the door of each cell is the dog-legged hatch, through which food was passed, brought from the kitchen: it was dog-legged so that the monk could not see the face of the bearer. Such was the austerity of the Order, such was the silence.

But it was this austerity, from which the Carthusians never wavered, which kept the Order pristine to the end; alone among the religious

Orders the Carthusians remained high in the nation's esteem until the Dissolution.

RICHMOND – GREYFRIARS

Franciscan

Richmond is a great pleasure, with its long market place, its delightful eighteenth-century houses, its castle, its river, and its setting. The parish church is in rather an odd position down the hill, and is not conspicuous: the two great landscape features are the castle keep, and the tower of Greyfriars, which stands in an attractive position not far from the Market Place.

The Franciscan Friary here was founded in 1257, and the church was of the usual Franciscan type, with nave and narrow chancel, and lofty tower in between. Nothing remains of nave or chancel, except for two windows of the south aisle chapel, fourteenth century in date. The wonderful tower is late fourteenth or early fifteenth century, standing on its tall narrow arches – looking every inch a Franciscan tower. It has strong yet tapering buttresses, twelve elegant pinnacles, and an open-work parapet. Nothing remains of its claustral buildings, which housed a warden and fourteen friars at the time of the Dissolution.

RICHMOND – ST MARTIN'S PRIORY

Benedictine

Standing on the south bank of the River Swale, its existence little known, is St Martin's Priory, a small Benedictine house, founded in the early twelfth century. It never seems to have held more than a prior and a very few monks. It is surprising what remains: the west front of the church is clearly recognizable, with its Norman west door – no doubt coeval with the brethren's arrival – and Perpendicular window above, still retaining fragments of its tracery; to the south a walled garden must represent the cloister court, with something of its south range, and a little of its west still standing. There is the fragment of a small tower, and other buildings, now part of the farmhouse. It is all a delightfully untidy, unselfconscious relic, with sheep grazing happily everywhere.

RIEVAULX ABBEY

Cistercian

A National Trust sign on the road from Stokesley to Helmsley announces 'Rievaulx Terrace'. A short woodland walk, and we shall reach an imposing rectangular temple with an Ionic portico surveying a stupendous view: below is the romantic ruin of Rievaulx Abbey, a scattering of cottages, the River Rye, and a distant prospect of hills and endless hills beyond. Ahead a wide green lawn stretches for half a mile in a serpentine arc, with a backing of noble beech trees to provide shelter. At the far end is a domed circular temple with a Doric colonnade. Walking the length of the terrace – and back – there are wondrous glimpses of the abbey below: now the east end and chancel, now the north transept, now the full length of the phantom nave, with ruined buildings all around, stone walls, empty arches, with only the walls of the refectory with its long lancet windows standing to any height.

In the eighteenth century every nobleman wanted a ruin in his park; sham ruins proliferated. It was all a part of the Romantic Movement. But here at Duncombe Park Thomas Duncombe needed no sham ruin: the real ruins of Rievaulx were ready waiting for him, and in 1758 he laid out this terrace, partly in emulation of his father's terrace close to the house. Sir Thomas Robinson was perhaps the architect of the two temples; the Ionic temple was designed to be a banqueting house, with grandly painted ceiling, and filled with superb furniture.

Descending the hill, the approach to the abbey itself is on the south side. Little remains of the cloister, and all the claustral buildings which surround it are but fragments – with the exception of the refectory, which still stands, a building of rare beauty and elegance, with its long lancet windows, built over an undercroft owing to the fall of the land. The chapter house, aisled and apsidal, must have been a wonderful room.

But it is the church which is the thing. The nave is almost all gone, but we know that it was a building of *c.* 1180 – Transitional in style, simple and austere. But *c.* 1235 a new great building campaign began. Under the great Abbot Aelred, the monastery had grown enormously, and no doubt more room was required for the monks in choir: first the transepts, and then the chancel were rebuilt. The style can be seen developing: earlier forms still appear in the transepts, with the old browner stone; then the chancel bursts upon us with its glistening white stone − purest and most elegant Early English, simple, austere, Cistercian in its otherworldly inspiration. The wall of the north aisle has collapsed, but two flying buttresses still stand to support triforium and clerestory: there is a delightful view from here across the chancel, with its clustered columns and lancet windows, all adorned with dog-tooth. This is one of the most beautiful Early English buildings anywhere.

Rievaulx was founded in 1132 by Walter l'Espec, Lord of Helmsley, the first Cistercian foundation in the north of England, and the daughter house of Clairvaux. At the height of its fortunes it numbered some 150 monks, and 500 lay brethren − but it is difficult to imagine how all these lay brothers can possibly have fitted into their modest quarters in the west range. Among its daughter houses were Melrose and Dundrennan. But its fortunes declined: at the time of the Dissolution there were but twenty-two monks left. To its declining fortunes can be ascribed the fact that little later work was done (except for the fifteenth-century building of the new abbot's lodging), and the church survived in its simple Early English beauty.

From Walter l'Espec the Helmsley lands descended to the Manners family of Belvoir, Earls of Rutland, and from them, by marriage, to George Villiers, Duke of Buckingham. On the death of the 2nd Duke the property was sold for the first and only time, to Sir Charles Duncombe, whose nephew built Duncombe Park, and whose great nephew Thomas Duncombe laid out the terrace, and built the temples − where our tour of these superlative ruins began.

ROSEDALE PRIORY

Cistercian Nuns

Gillamore, Kirkby Moorside, Lastingham, Rosedale − this is all magnificent countryside, magnificent moorland. Here, in this remote spot a Cistercian nunnery was founded *c.* 1158. It was a very small house, numbering usually about nine, and all that survives is a little buttressed turret − perhaps of the south transept − containing a few steps of the stairway.

SNAINTON PRECEPTORY

Templar

A mile and a half below the village, on the bank of the River Derwent, stands an eighteenth-century farmhouse (or so it appears), surrounded by a cluster of barns and buildings. It was known that in the Middle Ages a preceptory of the Templars and the Hospitallers stood here, and indeed the Great Hall of the Knights has in recent years been discovered inside the eighteenth-century farmhouse. It comprises the timber structure of a late thirteenth-century hall, three bays long, with a magnificent roof, all concealed within the extensive farmhouse. Dendrochronology provides a clue for the dating of the building: the timber is of *c.* 1288. The hall originally would have been aisled, and an inventory of 1308 lists five tables in the room, and two large chests and one small chest in the adjoining chamber. On the suppression of the Templars (1308–12), the place was handed on to the Hospitallers. Snainton, with its long-forgotten preceptory, makes an unusual and delightful contribution to the study of monastic ruins and remains.

WHITBY ABBEY

Benedictine

Fountains in its valley, Rievaulx in its valley – but Whitby stands on its cliff top, exposed to wind and storm, dominant and defiant across land and sea. We can approach it from the south along the cliff-top road, exposing ourselves to all the winds of heaven, where the gaunt ruin appears before us, ever more magnificent as we approach. Or we can come from the north, from the town, from the grand esplanade above the harbour, or through the labyrinth of tiny hilly streets, and visit Fortune's, where some of the best kippers in the world are smoked. We can climb the 199 steps up to that incredible parish church – and so across to the abbey.

The original abbey was founded by St Hilda in 657, but destroyed by the Danes in 867. It was refounded in 1078 by William de Percy as a Benedictine house, but of the eleventh-century building nothing survives – though the plan of the earlier, apsidal, church has been

excavated and marked out. What we see is the distinguished thir-
teenth- and fourteenth-century rebuilding. Work began at the east,
with that unforgettable east end, with its three tiers of lancet windows.

We enter by the fourteenth-century west doorway, all so deeply
eroded, with only a fragment of the west end of the north aisle to keep
it company. Virtually nothing is left of the nave itself, except for stumps
of some of the pillars, but the north aisle wall survives, with several
good fourteenth-century traceried windows. Past the crossing the
north transept remarkably survives, and the north quire aisle is still
almost completely vaulted. The quire is also unbelievably well preserved, and this is work of extraordinarily accomplished design – with
clustered columns, triforium profusely decorated with dogtooth, and
a clerestory composed of a single narrow lancet, with two blank arches
either side. Nothing survives of the south aisle, nothing of the south
transept, which collapsed in 1763. The central tower, incredibly, stood
till 1830. The visitor may be confused by the three mediaeval arches
standing against the wall, opposite the north transept: these are three
of the nave bays, re-erected here; the nave itself collapsed at much the
same time as the south aisle and transept. Whitby has the distinction of
being the only monastic ruin to have received several direct hits from
a German cruiser squadron, patrolling the North Sea in 1914.

Nothing survives of any monastic buildings. We know that the cloister lay to the south side of the church, but nothing is left. The
Cholmleys (of Howsham – a Yorkshire branch of the great Cheshire
family) were granted the property after the Dissolution, and built a
mansion to the southwest of the church, no doubt using monastic
stone; and the claustral buildings were close at hand. But the only
building of any importance to survive is the sad, silent, enigmatic
façade – its windows all blocked up, itself but a shell – of the Banqueting Hall, built by Sir Hugh Cholmley c. 1680. A wonderful frontispiece
to a house that has long since vanished, it stands with its long rows of
eleven windows and two storeys, glistening white, blind and beautiful.

Sir Hugh's Banqueting Hall makes a moving finale to the dramatic
splendour of the abbey. And the views are thrilling, across the town,
and out to sea.

WYKEHAM ABBEY

Cistercian Nuns

The village of Wykeham is architecturally rewarding with the late Georgian Downe Arms Hotel to grace the main street, and the delightful church, vicarage and school, all by Butterfield, *c.* 1853, nearby.

Wykeham Abbey is the seat of Viscount Downe; in fact Wykeham was never an abbey, merely a priory of Cistercian nuns, but 'abbey' sounded better to eighteenth-century ears, so (as we have met elsewhere) the eighteenth-century mansion was raised in rank. It is partly Palladian, and partly Edwardian (*c.* 1904), and probably occupies the site of the prioress's lodging and adjacent claustral buildings. A wall in the garden is the north wall of the church; with its two blocked twelfth-century arches, which seem to have led into the Lady Chapel, and a small round-headed doorway nearby, we can see that this was an aisleless church, which must have been built soon after the foundation (*c.* 1150). There were twenty nuns here in the thirteenth century, and still a dozen, with their Prioress, at the time of the suppression in 1539.

YEDINGHAM PRIORY

Benedictine Nuns

Standing on the north bank of the River Derwent, the priory is in the North Riding, while the village of Yedingham, on the south bank, is in the East. There is a stone farmhouse, called Abbey Farm (in fact, it never was an abbey), built on the site of part of a small Benedictine nunnery. Attached to it is a long stone wall, clearly mediaeval, the long wall of a shed. It was the south wall of the nave of the aisleless church, and its two blocked doors would have been the two doors into the cloister; beside one of them is a holy water stoup. The priory was founded *c.* 1160, and contained perhaps a dozen nuns, with their prioress.

YORK – ST MARY'S ABBEY

Benedictine

St Mary's Abbey was in its day one of the wealthiest religious houses in the Northern Province; founded before 1055, it moved to its present site in 1088, thanks to benefactions from William II.

Marygate leads to St Olave's Church, and adjoining the west tower of the church is the Norman gatehouse to the abbey; the path leads up to the west front, once magnificent, now but the jambs of the doorway, with the west wall of the north aisle adjoining. Inside there is very little surviving – only the outer wall of the north aisle, eight bays long, the arch that once led from the aisle into the north transept, and the lofty and elegant northwest crossing pier; there are the stumps of the others, and the base of one nave pier nearby; that is all. There is nothing to show of the grand chancel, only the markings in the grass of the original Norman apsidal east end. However, the wall of the north aisle is distinguished work, part of the grand rebuilding of the church by a great building abbot, Simon of Warwick (1270–80), the elegant windows all surviving, with fragments of geometrical tracery, and geometrical wall arcading below.

The cloisters stood on the south side, surrounded in the usual way by the claustral buildings; the abbot's house lay to the southeast. After the Dissolution this was converted into a palace for the Lord President of the Council of the North; it is now part of the University of York. In 1827 part of the cloister site was handed over to the York Philosophical Society, who here established the Yorkshire Museum (William Wilkins, architect). Extraordinarily, this incorporates in its basement gallery the vestibule to the early thirteenth-century chapter house, and a very important collection of mediaeval figures, many from the abbey itself, but some from the minster and elsewhere.

Yorkshire – West Riding

ECCLESFIELD PRIORY

Benedictine

Looking out across the Pennines is this unusual and interesting monastic relic, the former Benedictine alien priory of Ecclesfield, founded in the early twelfth century, and dependent on the Benedictine abbey of St Wandrille in Normandy. It is unusual in that it is more of a monastic manor house than the normal claustral building, being L-shaped, with the church (really no more than a chapel) standing above an undercroft in the east wing. The monks' domestic quarters would have been in the south wing – but this has been much rebuilt. The chapel wing retains many mediaeval features. This seems to have been one of the larger alien foundations, but in 1337 most of the brethren were recalled, leaving only a very small company here – when the spare accommodation was made available for guests and visitors. At the suppression in 1386 the endowments were granted to the Carthusians at Coventry.

FOUNTAINS ABBEY

Cistercian

Fountains in the snow – on a short December day: the stillness, the silence, not even a footprint on the great lawn before the west front. We can move back centuries in time, and imagine this rocky, steep-cliffed, desolate valley, watered by the River Skell, to which the monks came on 27 December 1132. Archbishop Thurstan had befriended these first thirteen, who had left St Mary's Abbey, York, dissatisfied with the laxity of life there, and had given them this solitary place. This is how Fountains Abbey began. In 1133 it became Cistercian, a daughter house of Clairvaux, and in course of time the most important Cistercian house in England.

Fountains in sunshine – on a long July day: the crowds of tourists, families with children, swarm across the lawn, many not knowing what they are looking at. The monks have come, and gone, and the place belongs to the National Trust, and is one of their great 'tourist attractions'.

The monks have come and gone; so have subsequent owners – the Proctors, who, using abbey stone, built Fountains Hall at the end of the sixteenth century; so have the Messengers, an old Roman Catholic family, who protected the abbey ruins with such reverence. So has William Aislabie, who bought the place in 1768, to add to Studley Royal, and who landscaped it all, and made it the paradise it is today; so have the Robinsons, Earls and Marquises of Ripon; so have the Vyners, the last private owners. But Fountains remains.

Standing on the lawn before the west front, we can admire the grand twelfth-century church, its austere late Norman façade, with its gaping Perpendicular window above the Norman door, the magnificent very unCistercian tower built in the early sixteenth century on the left, and to the right the long, long lay brothers' range, extending from the church across the river to the right. Here in this narrow valley the first monks established their house.

Entering the church, we shall be overwhelmed by the late Norman nave, the remarkable rhythm of round pillars supporting arches just pointed, the lack of triforium – a touch of Cistercian austerity – the round-headed windows in the clerestory above. Moving up the nave, to the transepts, we shall see the lofty arch in the north transept supporting the tower, that very unCistercian afterthought, and move into the quire, extended in the thirteenth century. Here the arcades have gone, but Early English lancets, Early English arcading, the shafts for Early English vaulting, are clear for us to see. At the east and the eastern transept was the chapel of nine altars – a prototype for Durham – and here the arcades, wonderfully lofty, still stand, and the windows are lancets, though a large Perpendicular east window was later inserted.

Passing through the south transept we emerge into the cloister: on the east side is very grand triple-arched entrance to the chapter house (c. 1170); on the south the refectory, a magnificent hall, with central arcade; warming house and kitchen lay on either side. So we return to the lay brothers' range, whose undercroft of no less than twenty-two bays, with its rib vault rising from low columns with no capitals, makes this the largest such building in Europe. Originally, of course, it would have been divided up into smaller rooms. The lay brothers' infirmary and guesthouses lay close to the river, or over the stream itself to the west – the monks' infirmary with its attendant offices and the abbot's house, to the southeast; and although little is left of them they can be easily identified. It was, in all, an enormous establishment.

As has been said, William Aislabie bought the place in 1768: it is to him that we owe the beauty of the abbey's setting, and the landscaping of its surroundings. His father, John, MP and later Chancellor of the Exchequer, had inherited the adjoining property of Studley Royal in 1699, and it was he who began the creation of the water garden there. He was involved in the scandal of the South Sea Bubble, and was obliged to resign from Parliament. So he returned to Yorkshire, and devoted himself to the creation of the garden. The more formal works are his – the Moon Pond, and the Crescent Ponds on either side, the Cascade, where the canalized Skell pours into the lake between the two Classical pavilions; all this is his work, as are the charming folly buildings. It was he who contrived the celebrated 'Surprise View' of Fountains from one of his follies – the ruins did not then belong to him. But the sense of the Romantic was very strong in him, as it was in his son William, and it was William who added Fountains to Studley in 1768, and landscaped the surroundings so romantically.

A last pleasure must be mentioned: the amazing Victorian church at Studley Royal, built by William Burges, 1871–8, for the 1st Marquis of Ripon, a former Viceroy of India and descendant of the Aislabies. It is one of the most remarkable, most lavish, and most beautiful of all Victorian churches, and with its sumptuous decoration and colour the extreme antithesis to the austere ideals of Cistercian Fountains.

The great house at Studley Royal was destroyed by fire in 1946, and never rebuilt. The stables survive, and have been converted into the house. They make a magnificent quadrangular courtyard house, with Palladian pavilions at the corners, and an open loggia on the east side. From the deer park here we can walk back to the lake, and so to the water gardens and the abbey. In winter snow or summer sunshine Fountains has no rivals among the ruined abbeys of England.

KIRKSTALL ABBEY

Cistercian

Kirkstall, the best preserved of all the Cistercian abbeys of Britain, stands grand, austere, forbidding, in the western suburbs of Leeds – an unlikely setting indeed, unlikely and unsympathetic. It is a mere two and a half miles from the centre of the city: Leeds suburbia has reached it, and passed on. Think of Rievaulx, think of Fountains, think of Tintern – still solitary in their beautiful valleys. But Kirkstall stands facing the long rows of smug suburban semis, a bitter fate.

The road from Leeds to Skipton, called Abbey Road, now the A65, was opened in 1827, and passes close to the ruins. Up to that time, unbelievably, the lane ran through the church itself from east to west, the east wall and the east window being removed for the purpose. The road now separates the abbey from the gatehouse, which stands at the corner of Abbey Walk opposite. Its old part is twelfth century, but it was greatly altered and added to when it became the Abbey Farmhouse after the Dissolution. It is now a museum.

Kirkstall was founded in 1147, originally at Barnoldswick (not far away), and moved to its present site five years later. Its history after the Dissolution has in many ways been fortunate: granted first to Archbishop Cranmer, it reverted after his martyrdom (1556) to the Crown. In 1583 it was sold to Sir Robert Savile, and later in the seventeenth century passed by marriage to the Brudenells, Earls of Cardigan. As absentee landlords, and at that time still a Roman Catholic family, they seem to have been disinclined to destroy the monastic church. Some of the outlying buildings were quarried away, but the chapter house and adjoining parts became cattle sheds, the lay brothers' quarters a barn, and the cloister court an orchard, while the farmer, as has been said, made himself a home in the gatehouse.

As the eighteenth century proceeded, under the influence of the Romantic Movement, the ruins of Kirkstall became increasingly admired; celebrated artists painted it – Girtin, Cotman, Turner; poets and writers found inspiration here, visitors came. What is more, repairs were begun, a caretaker was appointed, refreshments for visitors were provided, boats became available for hire on the river. In 1873 the redoubtable Countess of Cardigan (widow of the hero of the Charge of the Light Brigade) celebrated her third marriage (to the Portuguese Count de Lancastre) by including a visit to Kirkstall in their honeymoon festivities. She and her husband drove over from Harrogate in a chariot and four, with outriders, and were received at the abbey with a salute of fifteen guns from the local artillery.

In 1889 Lady Cardigan sold the abbey to Colonel John North, who presented it to the City of Leeds. Repairs were set in hand under the architect J. T. Micklethwaite, the vegetation of centuries was removed, and the place opened to the public in 1895. Since then the ruins have been beautifully maintained by the City: if suburban housing frowns on the north side, sweet water meadows smile on the south, along the banks of the River Aire.

Kirkstall was founded from Fountains, and the churches have much in common. It is only possible at present, for reasons of safety, to inspect the interior here through the open doorways: through the grand Norman west doorway the long nave is immediately reminiscent of the nave at Fountains. It is perhaps twenty years later than Fountains – there are clustered columns, with simple waterleaf capitals – but the impression is the same: great solid pillars with slightly pointed arches, no triforium, and round-headed windows in the clerestory and in the narrow aisles. The church is remarkably all of one date – only the large traceried Perpendicular windows at the east and west ends being later insertions, together with a few smaller Perpendicular windows elsewhere, and charming ornamental pinnacles added to the gable ends outside. The central tower, like the great tower at Fountains, was added in the sixteenth century, a sign of the relaxing of the Cistercian ideals of austerity and simplicity. The collapse of the western arch of the crossing in 1779 brought down its west and north sides; the south and half the east still stand perilously upright – an extraordinary sight. Equally amazingly the rib vaulting of the presbytery survives.

Much of the cloister court survives, too, if not the cloister arcades themselves: on the west side, the inner wall of the lay brothers' quarters; on the south, a substantial part of the refectory, and adjacent kitchen; the east side is remarkably complete. Next to the south transept, the library was converted, most amusingly, into a grotto or summerhouse in the early nineteenth century, its walls lined with iron slag, its floors paved with mediaeval tiles. Next to this the impressive double-arched doorway leads into the chapter house. The original chamber, with its rib vault on clustered columns, became later the vestibule to the grander and loftier thirteenth-century chapter house beyond. Next door is the parlour, still vaulted, and beyond that the day stairs to the dorter above.

A vaulted passage leads through to the infirmary, which survives only as foundations, but much more remains of the abbot's house, an important thirteenth-century three-storeyed building, with grand (later) fireplaces, and its own kitchen and chapel. Between this and the infirmary was the visiting abbots' lodging, with the remains of a fifteenth-century oriel window.

Little more than the foundations survive of the guesthouse, which stood opposite the west end of the church; but the lay brothers' reredorter, which extends to the west of the lay brothers' range, still stands – and has been converted into a café.

MONK BRETTON PRIORY

Benedictine

The industrial landscape so often to be found in the West Riding is perhaps an acquired taste: the drab hill-top towns, the blackened valleys, the mining villages, the terraces of mean houses, the chimneys, the pitheads, the mills, glum-looking churches and grim-looking chapels, railway lines and viaducts, power stations with all their accompanying litter – all this is not to everybody's taste. Monk Bretton stands on the outskirts of Barnsley; what was a beautiful site in a wide green valley is now surrounded on three sides by dreary housing, the landscape eaten up by industry. But the monastic gatehouse still stands erect, to admit us to what is still the secluded world of the priory.

Monk Bretton was founded *c.* 1154 for Cluniac monks. The first century and more of its existence was clouded with the most unedifying squabbles between Monk Bretton, its parent house at Pontefract, and Cluny itself, over the election of its priors. It will be remembered that the Cluniac Order, for all the nobility of its spiritual ideals, insisted on this curious administrative fad which made every house dependent on Cluny. This was more than Monk Bretton could stand, and in 1281 the monks here broke with Cluny, and Monk Bretton became an independent Benedictine house, recognizing only the jurisdiction of the Archbishop of York.

We were standing outside the gatehouse: what we see today is virtually an early fifteenth-century building, but it incorporates a much earlier, probably thirteenth-century gatehouse. It admits us to the outer courtyard, with the remains of church, cloisters and claustral buildings ahead; and to our left a puzzling building, still standing intact and roofed. It is a double-piled building, and must have been partially rebuilt, and adapted for some purpose after the Dissolution. Its interior is divided by a thirteenth- or fourteenth-century arcade; its original purpose is unknown.

Only the foundations of the church survive. It is of normal plan, with a narrow twelfth-century aisleless quire, and later, fourteenth-century aisled nave, and transepts with the usual square-ended chapels.

There is still the feeling of a courtyard in the cloister court. Little survives of the buildings on the east side: the chapter house stood next to the church, and we can imagine the scene on 4 January 1281, when Archbishop Wickwane here received the oath of canonical obedience to himself and his successors, and so Monk Bretton became the independent (and contented) Benedictine foundation which survived until the Dissolution.

A surprising amount of the refectory survives on the south side, with two elegant Decorated windows rising to their full height; still more of the west side, which was the prior's lodging. Some of this is, of course, post-Dissolution, when the prior's house was converted into a house, and the second gatehouse added to the west – but much monastic survives, including the wide-arched chamber downstairs, and the grand fireplace in the prior's hall above. Only low walling, or foundations, survive of the guesthouse to the south of the refectory, and of the infirmary to the southeast, but much attention should be paid to the splendid drain, which connected kitchen, reredorter, and guesthouse, and flowed off into the River Dearne. The monastic sanitary system was obviously very modern.

After the Dissolution (1538) Thomas Wentworth purchased the north aisle of the church, with its arcade, and rebuilt them at Wentworth, where they formed part of that church until 1877, when all but the Wentworth chapel was pulled down on the rebuilding of the church by J. L. Pearson in 1876. In 1589 the property was bought by the 6th Earl of Shrewsbury for his fourth son, Henry Talbot, and so descended through Armynes and Pierreponts, until bought by the Wombwells in 1785. Excavation took place in the 1920s, and after one or two changes of ownership, the place was put into the care of the Ministry of Works.

Spare a thought for the dispossessed priors and monks, who, when the axe fell at the Dissolution, were so cynically pensioned off by a cruel king. Here in 1538 the prior and thirteen monks signed the deed of surrender: the prior received a pension of £40 and a gift of £30: the monks a very much lower pension and gift. The prior and two of his brethren went to live in the nearby village of Worsborough, and actually *bought* no less than 148 books from the monastic library. Did they continue the life of prayer, the life of monastic scholarship at Worsborough? One likes to think that they did. But what happened to all those books, after that?

ROCHE ABBEY

Cistercian

Roche stands in its own beautiful, secluded, rocky limestone valley. Moreover this was all landscaped by Capability Brown in 1775 and the year following for the 4th Earl of Scarbrough, of Sandbeck adjoining – whose father had inherited the estate, here and in Lincolnshire, from his cousin James Saunderson, Earl of Castleton. Paine had already rebuilt Sandbeck Hall, *c.* 1760, using, it is said, stone from the abbey. Capability's landscaping was to complete the scheme.

An agreement was drawn up in 1774, whereby Capability was 'to finish all the valley of Roach Abbey in all its parts, according to the ideas fixed on with Lord S. (with Poets feeling and with Painters eye), beginning at the Head of the Hammer Pond, and continuing up the valley towards Loton in the Morn, as far as Lord Scarbrough's ground goes, and to continue the Water & Dress the Valley up by the Present Farm House, until it comes separation fixed for the boundary of the New Farm. N.B. The paths in the Wood are included in this Discription, and everything but the Buildings.' The scheme in fact embraced Lord Scarbrough's land from Laughton-en-le-Morthen to Sandbeck Hall, a mile from the abbey ruins. What Capability did was to turf over all the foundations which were in the way, and to divert the stream in such a way as to create little islands and cascades – with Poet's feeling and with Painter's eye indeed, but with little interest in the archaeology.

Roche Abbey was founded in 1147 by Richard de Bully of Tickhill and Richard FitzTurgis (whose lands adjoined), and was a daughter house of Newminster in Northumberland. The plan followed the normal Cistercian plan, with a spacious cruciform church, with straight east end, and transepts with chapels with straight east ends. The cloister was on the south, the lay brothers' range on the west side, sacristy, chapter house and parlour on the east, and refectory, built north to south in accordance with Cistercian practice, with kitchen on one side, warming house on the other. The dorter was on the first floor on the east side (with reredorter along the stream), while on the farther side of the stream stood lay brothers' infirmary, abbot's lodging, the infirmary and infirmarer's lodging.

Little remains of all this above the foundations – but these were all excavated earlier this century, after the 10th Lord Scarbrough had handed the ruins over to the Office of Works; it is the 12th Lord Scarbrough who lives at Sandbeck now. Of the church, all built towards the end of the twelfth century, only the east end stands to its full height, but these parts of the building are of immense interest and considerable beauty – the east walls of both transepts, with the transept chapels still largely vaulted. Less remains of the sanctuary, but here sedilia and piscina are later, fourteenth-century, additions. Clearly the church was a fascinating example of the transition from Romanesque to Gothic: the arches of the arcade are pointed, but stand on late Norman clustered columns; the arches of the blind triforium are pointed, the clerestory windows round-headed.

To the northwest of the church stands the grand late thirteenth-century gatehouse, with a wide entrance for carriages, and a narrow one alongside for pedestrians. And nearby is a charming little lodge with Gothick features, erected by Capability no doubt for the caretaker or gardener. Capability's work, and Lord Scarbrough's vision, are of great interest – proving the newly awakened interest in monastic remains under the influence of the Romantic Movement. Of almost equal interest is the fact that in the Official Guidebook to Roche no mention whatever is made of Capability or his work here: until quite recently the taste of the eighteenth century was beneath contempt.

SAWLEY ABBEY

Cistercian

On the very borders of Lancashire and Yorkshire, and set in magnificent country, Sawley (or Salley) was a Cistercian house founded in 1147 by William de Percy; it was never rich or famous, yet numbered several distinguished men among its brethren, including William of Symington, who became Chancellor of Oxford in 1372. Its end was glorious, but terrible.

There is not a great deal to see here, as its ruins have suffered appallingly; but it is a pleasure to walk among its low walls and rugged lumps of stone – against the backdrop of its dramatic hills. The nave appears to have been very short – either never completed, or half demolished when numbers dropped. The transepts were long, and the quire, originally aisleless, was later extended and given aisles. The cloisters lay on the south side of the church, and all the buildings were in their customary position – but again it is a case merely of low walls and foundations. Many carved stones are set out against the precinct walls, and elsewhere.

The abbey was suppressed in 1536, but the leaders of the Pilgrimage of Grace restored the abbot and his monks and reopened the house. Alas, this was short-lived, and the abbot, Thomas Bolton, was beheaded, and four of his brethren with him.

SYNINGTHWAITE PRIORY

Cistercian Nuns

This is the low undulating country of the York plain near Tadcaster: a single signpost announces 'Syningthwaite', and leads to a farmhouse, and a couple of cottages. The farmhouse is partly mediaeval and partly nineteenth century – and incorporates a richly carved twelfth-century doorway, and the remains of twelfth-century windows; this is probably the south cloister range, and represents the monastic refectory; moreover the two simple lower arches to the right of the Norman door must represent the lavatorium, where the nuns would have washed before entering the refectory.

The priory here was founded c. 1160 for Cistercian nuns; it is recorded that at the time of the suppression (in 1536) there were nine nuns in residence, together with the prioress, the ex-prioress, and two chaplains.

TEMPLE HIRST PRECEPTORY

Templar

Temple Hirst stands north of the River Aire, in quiet market-garden country. Across the flat fields between the mammoth power stations of Drax and Eggborough there suddenly appears a brick tower – a tall, polygonal, embattled staircase tower attached to what appears to be a Tudor house, seemingly the fragment of a much larger house. More puzzling and unexpected still is to find a Norman doorway which appears to have been reset in the Tudor brick porch. 'Temple Manor Nursing Home', declares a notice by the roadside. 'Temple', of course, is the clue word, and indeed a Templars' preceptory was founded here *c.* 1150. After the suppression of the Templars Hirst was not (as so often happened) transferred to the Hospitallers, but was secularized, and what remained was incorporated in a large fortified mansion for the Darcy family. It is the fragment of their house, with the Templars' Norman doorway, which survives to puzzle and please us today.

TICKHILL FRIARY

Austin Friars

It is difficult to decide whether Tickhill is a small town or a large village: whichever it is, it is full of interest, with its three wide streets meeting at the Market Cross – an eighteenth-century domed rotunda – and the most magnificent of churches, the mediaeval castle conspicuous on its mount, and a number of bigger or smaller houses everywhere. The remains of the friary stand on the far western outskirts, where, half-hidden in trees and gardens, a long range of mediaeval buildings – now two houses – stands, enchanting but puzzling. There are in fact two ranges, interconnected, and, over the years, so much cobbling of (probably) thirteenth- and fourteenth-century building has been done in converting these remains into a house after the Dissolution, and so little excavation has been attempted, that it is hard to determine what is what. There is the fragment of a fifteenth-century arcade in one house, but it cannot belong to the church as it is aligned north–south. There are many other mediaeval features, too, such as traceried windows and buttresses; the whole ensemble is romantic and beautiful. The friary was founded for Austin Friars *c.* 1260, and a century later there were twenty friars in residence: it remained important and influential to the end.

WALES

ABBEY CWMHIR

Cistercian

'Cwmhir' means 'the long valley'. It is not only long: it is exceedingly remote, lost in the Radnorshire hills, well wooded, romantic. A minor road leads up to the tiny village, presided over by a big Victorian house in what Geoffrey Grigson has described as 'coniferous architecture of the purest Victorian conifer age' – by the architects Poundley and Walker, 1867. The little church is in the same style, and by the same architects. The ruins of the abbey lie in the valley below, close to the little river.

Abbey Cwmhir was originally founded in 1143 at Ty Faenor (also in Radnorshire), and refounded here in 1176, for sixty monks, which would explain the extraordinary length of the nave – of fourteen bays: indeed in its day it was the largest monastic church in Wales. Only a few walls survive, together with the bases of a few piers. But, *mirabile dictu*, part of one of the arcades, five most beautiful bays with clustered columns and stiff-leaf capitals (*c.* 1190), was re-erected at Llanidloes in Montgomeryshire in 1542, giving us just a glimpse of what the great church at Cwmhir was like. One longs to know who first dreamt of the idea, and who carried out this remarkable feat. The claustral buildings lay below, closer to the river, but nothing whatever exists of these.

BASINGWERK ABBEY

Cistercian

Holywell and Flint sound romantic enough: in fact this coast of North Wales is industrialized and vulgarized. There may be a mediaeval castle at Flint, but the historic town is now dominated by three horrific blocks of high-rise flats.

Basingwerk Abbey is exceedingly difficult to find. Not only does it lie invisible on a ledge above the coast road, it is scarcely signposted. Instead there are endless signposts marked 'Heritage Park'. Apparently somebody thought out this plan to include among fragments of industrial ruins – a wool mill, a flannel mill, some old copper works – the ruins of the abbey, and call it a 'Heritage Park'. 'Heritage Park' indeed!

However, one single sign, at the corner of a suburban road, is allowed to point to the abbey, and if it is difficult to find, it is also difficult to reach: it is not easy to drive at all close to the abbey. But once there, it is a charming spot, with green lawns, old trees, old stone walls. We arrive in the cloister garth: little is left above ground, but with the church in its usual position to the north, it is possible to grasp the general plan. There are only bases of the nave piers, foundations of the north and south transepts and chancel – together with one arch from the south aisle into that transept. A little more survives of the west front. It was of the usual Cistercian plan, with short square-ended chancel, and two chapels apiece in each transept.

The best things to survive are the claustral buildings on the east side of the cloister: sacristy, chapter house – with two arches still standing – parlour, novices' room – they all form, as it were, an undercroft to the dorter. To the south of this is the warming room, with its fifteenth-century fireplace. The refectory adjoining must have been splendid: it is in a slightly odd position, at right angles to the south walk of the cloister in usual Cistercian fashion, but built adjoining the dorter. So its east wall is plain inside, but its west is adorned with elegant lancets, and there are traces of the pulpit and its staircase. The long range running east from the warming room may have been the infirmary: it was partially rebuilt for use as farm buildings after the Dissolution.

Basingwerk was founded as a Savigniac abbey *c.* 1132, and with all the rest of the Savigniac houses became Cistercian in 1147. The last abbot is said to have been the son of his predecessor.

CARDIFF – BLACKFRIARS

Dominican

It is extraordinary to think that Cardiff was only a country town and small port until the middle of the eighteenth century – and that only then the growth of the ironworks in South Wales resulted in the expansion of the port. It is equally extraordinary to think that the person behind the great early nineteenth-century development of town and port was not a self-made industrialist, but a Scottish nobleman, the 2nd Marquis of Bute, whose grandfather had married the Windsor heiress, and so acquired enormous property in and around Cardiff. His son, the 3rd Marquis, was a very different character, scholarly, unpractical, a passionate mediaevalist and convert to Rome, deeply imbued with a love of architecture. In his architect, William Burges, he had a great ally. It is Burges' brilliant, if scarcely orthodox restoration of Cardiff Castle which still surprises and (probably) delights us today – its incredible silhouette due to Burges' remarkable imagination.

In the great park behind the castle was the site of the Dominican Friary; the 3rd Marquis excavated this, and had the footings of the walls and the foundations neatly laid out in the grass, and where necessary rebuilt them, having the area of the church paved with copies of the original mediaeval tiles. It is all a great success – though perhaps more Victorian than thirteenth century.

CYMMER ABBEY

Cistercian

The name Cymmer means 'the meeting' – the meeting, that is, of the two rivers, the Mawddach and the Wnion, a mile or so northwest of Dolgelly. This is all most beautiful country, where mountain, wood, and water may all be enjoyed together. The little abbey of Cymmer lies in the very heart of it.

Cymmer was founded for Cistercian monks in 1198 – seventy years after the founding of Waverley. So it took a long time for the Cistercians to reach this remote part of Wales, and indeed Cymmer was always a small and poor foundation. But none the worse for that: Cymmer is an endearing and delightful place. To the west of the church stands a farmhouse, and next to that a cottage, both obviously mediaeval in origin, and both charming: the house is thought to be the monastic guesthouse. Standing here, we could almost fancy that this small church is a private ruin in a private garden, with the soft green grass and beech hedges all in place. The church, as it is, probably represents merely the nave of the much bigger church intended: a modest western tower, the fragment of the north arcade still standing, but the south arcade gone, three lancets of Cistercian simplicity at the east end – indeed this eastern gable is reminiscent of a similar gable in the monks' dorter at Waverley. There are no transepts, no chancel, and nothing to see of the cloister except foundations; farm buildings appear to have swallowed up chapter house and all. So this is all there is, yet in its quiet way Cymmer is perfection.

LLANTHONY PRIORY

Augustinian

J. M. W. Turner's watercolour of Llanthony, with the River Honddu in full spate in the foreground – a rushing, rocky, mountain river – is wonderfully atmospheric. There is the great church, with its three towers, long line of nave windows, ruined eastern parts, set in wild countryside, a single figure walking by the river bank, a solitary twisted tree. Behind the church, rising to a seemingly impossible height, stand the Black Mountains, with clouds, white swirling clouds, hanging low around them. There is something sombre about the Black Mountains, even on a fine day, and their tops are often half-invisible.

The date 1103 is generally given for the first settlement of hermits here, 1109 or a little later for the establishment of a full conventual life, but the fervour of the first brethren attracted others, and numbers grew. Towards the end of the century the church was built – the eastern half, quire, transepts, central tower coming first (1180–90); the aisled nave and western towers followed (*c.* 1210). It is all in the simplest, most austere version of Transitional–Early English, with round-headed windows, or lancets, all ornament eschewed, the arcades formed of the simplest, plainest arches.

But trouble was ahead. Welsh raids drove all but the bravest canons out, first to Hereford where they were befriended by the bishop, later to Gloucester, where they founded a daughter house, a second Llanthony. This soon became established, and flourished, and in time became the mother house (qv). In 1136 there were forty canons at Llantonia Prima: after the founding of Llantonia Secunda there were but thirteen at Prima, and by 1481 but a prior and four canons at Prima.

Llantonia Prima is, of course, a marvellous place, and with the church hauntingly beautiful. And yet it is forbidding, bleak, lonely in the extreme, intimidating, the ever-present awesome mountains sinister at times, the narrow valley grim. It is perhaps not surprising that it proved too much for all but the bravest. Little remains of claustral buildings: they must have been near-ruins at the time of the Dissolution. The little infirmary chapel, by the entrance to what is now the farmyard – though once the cloister court – is now the parish church.

Llanthony casts its spell, and must always have done so: under the influence of the Romantic Movement cultivated visitors began to discover this, one of the most romantic of all ruins. Colt Hoare (of Stourhead) was here in 1803, and saw the windows of the west front collapse. A few years later Walter Savage Landor fell for the place and bought it, intending to rebuild the church, but being of a quarrelsome disposition fell out with everybody – and departed; he had only just begun to build a house for himself on the hillside overlooking the priory. Later in the century Father Ignatius (Joseph Leicester Lyne), who felt called to revive Benedictine monasticism in the Church of England, came here, and tried to buy the ruins, but had to be content with founding his monastery at Capel-y-Ffin, three miles away. Father Ignatius died in 1908. In the early 1920s Eric Gill had his eye on Llanthony, and spoke of acquiring it, and rebuilding it. But in the end he settled for Father Ignatius' monastery at Capel-y-Ffin, where he stayed for some years; but it was too isolated for him, and he moved.

There is, however, one legacy of Landor: he lived for a time at the prior's house, adjoining the west front of the church. His predecessor had begun forming guest rooms in the adjoining tower, and Landor continued this. So was established the hotel, which flourishes here today, partly in the southwest tower, partly in the prior's house.

NEATH ABBEY

Cistercian

To the Glory of God and in affectionate memory of
GLEN ARTHUR TAYLOR F.S.A.,
Leader of the Neath Abbey Research Party 1923–1935.
During this period some 4,000 tons of debris were
removed from this church, revealing the beautiful stonework carved over 600 years ago. This tablet is erected by
Lord Dynevor and the members of the Research Party
who laboured with him in this work, as a lasting memorial
to an inspirer, scholar and friend.

The history of Neath Abbey since the Dissolution is more extraordinary and bizarre than that of any other monastic house – as the tablet
in the south transept to Glen Arthur Taylor testifies. A grand Tudor
mansion was formed out of the abbot's house at the end of the sixteenth
century by Sir John Herbert – a common enough fate for abbots'
houses and other claustral buildings. But here in the early eighteenth

century, after the departure of the Herberts, industry moved in. The industrialization of the neighbourhood had already begun with the introduction of copper smelting at the end of the sixteenth century: in the early eighteenth century the ruins of the abbey began to be used for smelting. Neath, after all, was ideal for the industry, with its ample supply of wood, coal and water – and navigation at hand. So every space, every spare piece of land, was made use of, and, after all, what could be more useful than old monastic buildings? They were ready-made workshops. Two furnaces were installed in the lay brothers' quarters – and the work spread into the church and everywhere, and the Herberts' mansion became a block of tenements for the workers and their families. Hence the 4,000 tons of debris which had to be removed from the ruins between 1923 and 1935.

Neath Abbey was founded for Savigniac monks in 1111: in 1147 the Savigniac Order was absorbed into the Cistercian (the two Orders had much in common). The lay brothers' range dates from the late twelfth century (but the two chimneys on the east wall are those of the eighteenth-century furnaces). Building proceeded from there, the church being rebuilt in the late thirteenth and early fourteenth centuries. A substantial part of the west front survives, much of the aisle walls in the nave, and there are fragments of the transepts with their chapels. In the south transept the remains of the night stair are clearly visible. Here is the memorial to Glen Arthur Taylor, and on the opposite wall a red tile marks the height to which the mountains of debris rose – some 17 feet. There is another round the corner in the south choir aisle, and in the ground, surviving almost by a miracle, are considerable remains of beautiful mediaeval tiles. There is enough to show that this was a grand and spacious Decorated church.

Little remains of the cloister, but its plan is laid out: entrances to chapter house and refectory are in their usual places, but little survives of either. The superfluous monastic buildings were destroyed as the Tudor mansion rose, and they supplied invaluable building material. The house stands to the southeast, and with its large mullioned windows looks every inch a Tudor house – from the outside. But within is preserved the finest fragment of the whole abbey.

This is the undercroft of the dorter – a quite splendid and beautiful room, with a quadripartite vault rising from elegant round columns; there is an original fireplace of great size, but the large windows are, of course, Tudor. A novices' room when it was first built, it became the servants' hall in the time of the Herberts. The family rooms were all then on the first floor, and a long gallery ran across the 'bridge' –

the otherwise puzzling open arcade which connected the dorter with the reredorter.

In all there is much to see, and great efforts have been made in recent years to provide a setting worthy of the ruins. There is one last fragment to see. On the main road, close to the Hope and Anchor Inn, stand forlorn and shamefaced the remains of the gatehouse, a section of thirteenth-century walling close to the pavement. All else was hacked away when the road was made. Thus mercilessly have the ruins of Neath been treated.

ST DOGMAELS

Tironensian

Little is known of St Dogmael, who does not seem to have been widely venerated outside this part of Wales. The village of St Dogmaels adjoins Cardigan, and the abbey ruins are easily found, hard by the parish church. A short walk across the meadow – then into the abbey precinct: there is little above ground, except for the north transept of the church, and the infirmary. The transept reveals a most unexpected fragment of fan vaulting; it was the burial place of the Lords of Cemaes. A portion of the north nave wall still stands upright, as does the west wall of the nave, with its gaping window. There is a crypt to the chancel, and the south transept chapel is apsidal.

St Dogmaels was founded *c.* 1115 by Robert FitzMartin for Tironensian monks – one of the few such foundations in Britain. Much of the building evidently belongs to the twelfth century. After the Dissolution the church continued to be used as the parish kirk, and the rector occupied part of the claustral buildings. Then all went to decay: a new church and rectory were built nearby. But it is a pleasure to walk round the whole precinct. The ground rises towards the west, so there is a good view across the low foundations of the cloister and its attendant buildings, most of which seem to have been in their normal places, with the exception of the chapter house, which seems very oddly placed, half-attached to the south transept. A last pleasure is a visit to the infirmary, to see the collection of effigies and crossslabs, carved capitals and bosses, salvaged from the wreck.

STRATA FLORIDA ABBEY

Cistercian

A glorious remote spot in a beautiful Cardiganshire valley: a charming little village church in a churchyard studded with beech trees, a large farm and its capacious barns and buildings, a cottage or two, a letter box, and the abbey. This was founded for Cistercian monks in 1164, originally two miles away, but was then moved here, twenty years later. There is not very much to see, but what there is is worth coming a long way for. First, there is the very unusual west doorway, where the five shafts continue all the way round the head of the arch, tied as it were by the narrow rings to hold the shafts together. Its date is thirteenth century, and it is a round arch. Walking up the nave we shall see the curious arrangement whereby the aisles were walled off from the nave, where the pillars of the arcade only start on the nave side some five feet up from the floor. Reaching the transepts, the walls stand to some little height – and here is the second great pleasure of Strata Florida, for in these slaty walls, the deep crevices in spring and early summer are filled with wild flowers. A third great pleasure is the chapels of the transepts, all for protection roofed over, where there is a memorial slab of 1951 to the Welsh mediaeval post Dafydd ap Gwilym, and a colourful display of many old floor tiles adorning the sanctuaries. Here one can come close to the Cistercians who once worshipped at these altars. Little survives of the cloister and claustral buildings – for the farmhouse has completely taken over the south side. But here, as everywhere, through gaping wall or open archway, the sweeping Cardiganshire landscape reaches our very feet, and we can sense to the full the peace and seclusion which brought the monks to this lovely valley.

TALLEY ABBEY

Premonstratensian

A wonderful sight: the east and north walls of the central tower, perilously poised on their two crossing arches, against the background of the steep Carmarthenshire hills. 'Talley' or more properly 'Talyllychau' means 'two lakes', and these glorious lakes lie to the east, green fields beyond and around, and closer to the ruins, farm buildings, a farmhouse and cottages. Not much is left of the church, except this gaunt fragment. It was cruciform, of course, and the bases of the piers of the nave are there, together with walls of the transepts and their chapels. It seems that the westernmost bays may never have been completed. The cloister lay on the south side, but not much of this or the claustral buildings survives, and the buildings and barns of the farm have triumphed. Talley was founded *c.* 1185. It was the only Premonstratensian house in Wales.

TINTERN ABBEY

Cistercian

Tintern: the very name is beautiful, the very name romantic.

> Five years have past; five summers, with the length
> Of five long winters! and again I hear
> These waters, rolling from their mountain-springs
> With a soft inland murmur. – Once again
> Do I behold these steep and lofty cliffs,
> That on a wild secluded scene impress
> Thoughts of more deep seclusion; and connect
> The landscape with the quiet of the sky.

So wrote Wordsworth, in 'Lines Composed a Few Miles above Tintern Abbey, July 13, 1798'. Tintern has become synonymous with all that is thought beautiful, all that is thought romantic about a ruined abbey. Pictures flood the mind – of the bend in the river, the steep wooded hills descending to its banks, the great church set in its valley.

Tintern has been almost miraculously preserved; so, perhaps more than in any other great ruined church, a very great deal survives. This is largely due to the Dukes of Beaufort, who owned the ruins, were its most beneficent guardians, and in the later eighteenth century, the days of the Romantic Movement, began to repair the ruins, and cut back the vegetation. 'Nature', wrote Archdeacon Coxe (Archdeacon of Wiltshire) at this time, 'has added her ornaments to the decoration of art; some of the windows are wholly obscured, others partially shaded with tufts of ivy, or edged with lighter foliage; the tendrils

creep along the walls, wind round the pillars, wreathe the capitals . . .
or hanging down in clusters obscure the space beneath . . .'

Now all is tidied up, the grass cut, the edges trimmed, and we are
admitted through a ticket office, a souvenir shop, a museum, into the
north transept.

But leave all this behind, enter the great church by the west door:
apart from the north arcade, apart from the roof, it is intact: even the
fourteenth-century tracery in the west window is intact; and we can
gaze past the crossing to the choir and sanctuary, and wonder at the
wooded hillside, which augments the more scanty tracery at the east
end, or stand in the south transept and look across to the tracery
surviving in the north transept window, the night stairs below, clustered columns everywhere. There is no more beautiful ruined monastic
church in the country.

Tintern was founded for Cistercian monks in 1131 by Walter Fitz-
Richard. Little is left of the original twelfth-century work: rebuilding
began in 1270, and was completed in the early fourteenth century.
We can walk through the north door in the nave, into the cloister; the
chapter house, of course, stood on the east side, warming room, refectory and kitchen on the north. Both the warming room and the little
pantry alongside are still vaulted; the lay brothers' quarters were on
the west. Tintern was a great establishment: the infirmary cloister lay
to the northeast of the main cloister court, the infirmary itself beyond,
with the abbot's house beyond that, to the north. Little remains of all
this, but the foundations are all marked out, and we can walk all over
this labyrinth of monastic buildings.

Before taking our leave we should go down to the bank of the river,
and watch the great Wye, its waters 'rolling from their mountain-
spring'. So we depart, leaving noble church, noble river, behind us,
and can understand how Wordsworth wrote:

> How oft, in spirit, have I turned to thee,
> O sylvan Wye! thou wanderer thro' the woods,
> How often has my spirit turned to thee!

VALLE CRUCIS ABBEY

Cistercian

In most beautiful countryside, not far from Llangollen – the Valley of
the Cross: the first sight of the Cistercian abbey cannot be forgotten,

Cymmer: Cistercian fragment, near Dolgelly. The name means 'meeting place' – the meeting of the Rivers Mawddach and Wnion.

Neath Abbey: the Tudor mansion formed by Sir John Herbert in the Cistercian abbot's house.

Right: Strata Florida: a detail of the unusual west doorway of the Cistercian abbey in Cardiganshire, where the five shafts continue all round the head of the arch, tied as it were by narrow rings.
Below: a colourful display of 14th-century tiles still adorns the transept chapels.

Talley: a wonderful sight – the east and north sides of the central tower poised on the crossing arches, against the steep Carmarthenshire hills *(photograph by Edward Piper)*.

Tintern: almost miraculously preserved in the valley of the Wye – its waters 'rolling from their mountain stream'.

Valle Crucis: 13th-century tracery survives in the west windows – the green hills descending all around are like outside walls encircling the buildings.

Arbroath: the west end of the ruined nave, with Victorian gravestones, in true Scottish fashion, pressing on the foundations of the north transept.

Right: Scottish thistle – 15th-century carving now in the Abbot's House (Museum) at Arbroath.

Crossraguel: the 14th-century gatehouse at Crossraguel in Ayrshire, a symbol of the considerable secular power of the abbey in the Middle Ages.

Dryburgh: the cloister – only the west wall of the refectory stands upright, with its 14th-century wheel window.

Dunkeld: Cathedral Street, with magnificent 18th-century gates leading into the cathedral churchyard.

Dundrennan: the crossing and transepts, reminiscent of Rievaulx, its mother house, no doubt built by Yorkshire masons.

Elgin: the west doorway, part of the rebuilding after the fire of 1390, glorious with carved foliage and angels.

standing against the steep hills, all green and brown, the high gables
of the east end, and of the west, lancet windows, traceried windows,
and the ancillary buildings adjoining the transept on the south.

Valle Crucis was founded for Cistercian monks by Madog ap Gruff-
ydd in 1201, and the church must have been begun almost at once
– the east end with its simple lancets, later work towards the west,
where the west front has three two-light traceried windows, and a little
wheel window above. Only the bases of the nave pillars survive, not
much of the north transept or aisles, but more of the south aisles,
and much more of the south transept, where the chapels are still
vaulted.

After the Dissolution this south range was converted into a house
– sacristy and chapter house below, dorter above, divided into smaller
rooms, with even a pretty eighteenth-century hob grate or two still in
position. All this was still in use as a farmhouse when Sir George
Gilbert Scott began his restoration in the middle of the nineteenth
century. Much credit is due to him for his sympathetic preservation
of the building. The chapter house is a lovely room, with its rib vault
rising from four columns without capitals. Close to its door is an
elaborately traceried recess opening into the cloister: a book cupboard.

The setting, of course, is divine: we can sit in the cloister court and
enjoy the view of the countryside – the south and west ranges having
almost disappeared – and then go round to the east end, where there
is still a little eighteenth-century farm building, and then on to the
fishpond beyond. This is an idyllic spot. Here we can look up at the
east gable of the church, where the lancet windows are beautifully
framed in unusual flat buttressing. The green hills descending around
are like outer walls, encircling all the buildings.

SCOTLAND

INTRODUCTION

There is no need to say that the religious history of Scotland is quite different from the religious history of England. Despite that early lighting of the monastic lamp on Iona by St Columba in the sixth century, and the still earlier presence of St Ninian in Galloway a century before, despite the labours of other early saints, St Serf, St Kentigern and others, Scotland was so far removed from European civilization that in the eleventh century, which saw the establishment of some forty Benedictine houses in England, no Benedictine house was founded in Scotland – until, at the very end of the century, Queen Margaret (St Margaret) persuaded some Benedictines from Canterbury to come to Dumfermline. It is to her son, David I, that is due the monastic revival that followed. He visited the reformed Benedictine abbey at Tiron near Chartres: he was so moved by what he found that he persuaded the abbot to send a colony to found a Tironensian abbey in Scotland. This was at Selkirk, which eventually became the great abbey of Kelso. It was thanks to him, too, that Augustinians were established at Holyrood and at St Andrews, Augustinians from Arrouaise at Cambuskenneth, and Cistercians at Melrose and Dundrennan. It was his influence that led to the founding of Dryburgh for Premonstratensians.

So the brief Scottish summer opened, brilliantly, and all the great monastic orders were represented. Unique to Scotland is an order which by-passed England completely: the Valliscaulians, the monks of the Cabbage Valley in Burgundy. An austere offshoot of Cluny, they established themselves at Ardchattan, Beauly and Pluscarden: Ardchattan is tiny, Beauly small, but Pluscarden magnificent. Moreover, as we shall see, life has returned here in recent years, and monks are once more walking its courts.

When the end came, it must be remembered that there was no Henry VIII, no suppression, no Dissolution – nor was there any single date at which the monasteries cased to exist. They all, more or less, in their own way bled to death. The all-overpowering wave of Protestantism drained that vital religious impulse, that sense of vocation, which is the *sine qua non* of any monastic community; so no new postulants appeared, there were no novices, and diminishing numbers meant diminishing funds; so by degrees the lay commendators, or lay abbots, who had perhaps bought the reversion of the property – or on whom it had been conferred – took over. But the monks were not driven out, and in some places they remained, almost alone, in a large decaying building, still held in some regard by the commendators. Sometimes the commendators would keep parts of the buildings in repair, and use them as burial places for their families; Dryburgh is a case in point, but there is hardly a major abbey which is not favoured by a ducal tomb or two. This is all rather different from the conventional picture of John Knox mob-violence and Jenny Geddes stool-hurling in the scenery of the Scottish Reformation. Thus the Scottish monasteries died out.

As for the ruins, there is much to see: the Border abbeys are an incomparable clutch – Jedburgh, Kelso, Melrose, Dryburgh. In Galloway, Dundrennan, Sweetheart and Glenluce are superb, and the two island monasteries of Inchcolm and Inchmahome are specially beautiful for their setting and their architecture. Iona must be visited for its ruined nunnery and for its erstwhile ruined cathedral, and perhaps even more for its associations with St Columba and his Celtic monastery.

And then, finally, there is Pluscarden. Set in glorious, sweeping Morayshire countryside, this great Valliscaulian priory, now Benedictine abbey, is once again humming with life. The last monk of the old order died at the very end of the sixteenth century, still at Pluscarden, more than half a century after his opposite number in any English monastery. Then silence descended, but for the occasional fall of timber or masonry, the occasional visit from an enquiring pilgrim. Then unexpectedly the tide turned: the 3rd Marquis of Bute bought the place in 1897, and in 1943 his son Lord Colum Crichton-Stuart gave it to the Benedictine abbey of Prinknash in Gloucestershire. A community of Benedictines from Prinknash settled here in 1948, and rebuilding began. The domestic east claustral range had been made habitable as a shooting lodge by the Duke of Fife in the mid-nineteenth century. The church was largely sound and required little more than reroofing: the transepts and tower were completed by 1960, the quire by 1983, and the windows were filled with outstanding modern glass, some of it made on the spot. It is, besides, a noble Early English building with its beautiful lancet windows and its steep-pitched roofs. The place is permeated with that sense of stability and peace, so emphasized by the Benedictines. Three bells have been hung in the low tower – so once again the valley echoes with their music: *In loco isto pacem dabo* – 'In this place I shall give peace'.

ARBROATH ABBEY

Tironensian

Arbroath is a dour little town on the rocky coast of Angus, famous for Arbroath 'smokies'. The grim-looking fragments of the abbey deserve attention, too.

Arbroath Abbey was founded for Tironensian monks in 1176 by William the Lion, and the first monks came from Kelso. The abbey gatehouse stands on the right as we approach the church and leads to the abbot's house, an imposing early sixteenth-century rebuilding of an earlier, smaller lodging. This alone survives intact of all the monastic buildings. It not only gives us some idea of how later mediaeval abbots lived: it also now serves as an admirable monastic museum. The abbot's house originally was attached to the south range of the cloister, but today the lines of the cloister are merely marked in the neatly mown grass, as are the foundations of all the claustral buildings: hardly a stone stands upon another.

We must return to the church, and stand before the west front. Here we are confronted by the shattered twin western towers, the deeply recessed late Norman doorway, the three little gabled Gothic windows above, and the remains of a large round window above these. All this prepares us for the tragedy of the abbey: there is very little left. The nave of nine bays must have been tremendous, but of the arcade only a fragment remains, close to the northwest tower. There is the wall of the south aisle with its single lancet windows, but no crossing, no chancel, the east wall half destroyed. One curiosity there is, above and behind us: the tribune, or gallery, above the west door. This is open to the nave on the inside, and looks out through the three little gabled windows on the outside, and connects the two western towers. No doubt it would have been used for musicians and choir inside, and for trumpeters outside.

Moving up the nave we can imagine the central tower, rood screen and pulpitum, the chancel beyond. But on reaching the sanctuary we can actually see the setting of the high altar, with the stone bench surrounding the east end, the elegant blind Early English arcading above it, three lancets in the east wall, and the remains of three more above. This was, as usual, the first part of the church to be built: it must have been completed by 1214, the year of the death of William, the founder, who was buried in accordance with his express wish before the altar. Here in 1814 was discovered what may indeed be the royal tomb – with a splendid, though headless, figure upon it, dressed as a king might be, with long tunic, girdle, purse and mantle, his feet supported on a lion. The figure is now in the abbot's house.

The gable end of the south transept stands tall and magnificent, with its long lancet windows, a round window above them, and three tiers of blind arcading below, one with round-headed arches, two with pointed. This is all a beautiful composition, and tells us much of the glorious church which we have lost. On the east side of the transept is the early fifteenth-century sacristy, which is still vaulted. The room above it, connected by a spiral staircase, was probably the treasury. Virtually nothing remains of the north transept. Pressing hard upon the low foundation wall are the graves of the enormous cemetery which clings to the entire length of the north side of the church. Here they stand, in truly Scots fashion, row upon row, row upon row, of ponderous gravestones, commemorating the worthies of Arbroath, in polished marble, granite, stone.

ARDCHATTAN PRIORY

Valliscaulian

The Connel Bridge, bearing a certain family resemblance to its older and bigger cousin, the Forth Bridge, stands guarding the seaward end of Loch Etive. It was built by the Caledonian Railway, and opened in 1903, carrying the line to Ballachulish: it was of such ingenious design that despite its rails it could carry road traffic, even horse-drawn traffic, too – which is all it does now, since the demise of the line to Ballachulish. The road north from Oban has already passed through spectacular scenery, and the Connel Bridge is a dramatic introduction to the even more spectacular scenery which awaits us, under the bridge, along the minor road which runs along the northern shore of the loch, and leads to Ardchattan.

The house, grey, solemn, romantic Victorian Gothic, does not at first appear monastic, even specially ancient; its secrets it keeps to itself. On the right, as we approach, a lawn sweeps down to the loch: from here there is a glimpse of the ruined choir of the church – but the approach for visitors is on the north side. Here outbuildings occupy the site of the cloister, and of the nave of the church, and a path leads round the east end of the church – to the entrance to quire and crossing.

The Valliscaulian priory of Ardchattan was founded *c.* 1230 by Duncan Macdougal. The earlier buildings date from the mid-thirteenth century, but a larger choir and crossing were built in the fifteenth century, together with a new refectory. The Valliscaulians, an austere Order, who owed much to Cistercians and Carthusians, took their name from the Val des Choux – cabbage valley – in Burgundy, and had only three houses in Britain, all in Scotland. Since the Reformation Ardchattan has belonged to the Campbell and Campbell-Preston family, and it is their home now.

Until the early eighteenth century the monastic quire was used as the parish kirk; a new kirk was built in 1722. The ruined church is in the care of the Secretary of State for Scotland, and open to the public. Few architectural details survive, but the texture of the walls, of slate and larger stones, is very attractive, and the sense of antiquity is deeply moving. Of special interest are tomb slabs of the seventeenth- and eighteenth-centuries and some earlier crosses, with beautifully carved inscriptions, lying in the grass; some are enclosed in wooden covers, but these can be lifted up. Attached to the south side of the church is the Campbell of Ardchattan aisle; to the north, the burial aisle of the Campbells of Lochnell.

But the most interesting feature of Ardchattan is the refectory, which occupied – and indeed still occupies – the south range of the cloister despite much alteration. All the claustral buildings were soon converted into a house for the Campbells after the Reformation. The nineteenth century bestowed upon the house a chaste Gothic skin, but there are delightful earlier rooms behind. The Campbells' dining room occupies the eastern end of the refectory, and here is still the vaulted pulpit of the monks' frater – a delightful and unexpected mediaeval feature in what otherwise might pass for an eighteenth-century room. In the attic above, despite all later alterations, the impressive fifteenth-century timber roof survives. But the house is not open to the public.

The gardens, however, are, stretching from the house to the side of the loch – indeed, glimpses of the glittering water from the windows of the house, or from the ruined church, are a special pleasure of Ardchattan. Here from spring till autumn visitors may enjoy the wonderful display of old roses and herbaceous borders and shrubs which Colonel Campbell-Preston cultivates in this remote and romantic place.

BALMERINO ABBEY

Cistercian

In a glorious position on the Fife coast of the Firth of Tay – where the Firth is at its widest and its best, and there are views eastwards to the two Tay Bridges, and the great city of Dundee across the water: a beautiful, sequestered spot. The scanty remains of mediaeval buildings give little hint of the important abbey which once stood here.

Balmerino Abbey was founded for Cistercian monks *c.* 1226 by Queen Ermengarde, widow of William the Lion, and in his memory. It is possible to make out the plan of the cruciform church from these scanty remains: there was a nave, and south aisle, and chancel, with north and south transepts. Cloisters abutted the north side of the church, and next to the transept was, and still is, the vaulted sacristy. Next to this is the chapter house, also still vaulted: four low piers uphold the rib vault.

All this is precious and delightful; but perhaps the best thing at Balmerino is the ancient sweet chestnut tree, which still stands, propped up, the most remarkable living survivor of this foundation. It is said to have been planted by Queen Ermengarde herself: it is certainly very ancient.

Balmerino is in the care of the National Trust for Scotland.

BEAULY PRIORY

Valliscaulian

One of the most remote and least-known religious houses in Scotland – its Order also little known – the Valliscaulians. They took their name from the Val des Choux – the Valley of Cabbages – in Burgundy, and were an austere offshoot of Cluny. Here at the end of the village street at Beauly, stands their roofless, aisleless, cruciform little church. The Order was founded in 1205, and reached Scotland in 1230, when Beauly Priory was founded – an astounding achievement. The brethren were protected by the Frasers, Lords Lovat, of Beaufort nearby – and Simon Fraser, 15th Lord Lovat, lives at Beaufort today; and by the Mackenzies of Kintail – the tomb of Kenneth Mackenzie is in the north transept (1491), and the transept was restored to receive the tomb of another Kenneth Mackenzie (1901). In the south transept is the tomb of Prior Mackenzie (1479). The trefoil windows on the south side of the nave are above the corbels – outside – which once held the cloister roof; elsewhere there are lancets.

Like Beaulieu, Beauly means 'beautiful place'; it is certainly romantic, and there are wonderful views over Invernesshire from the churchyard.

CAMBUSKENNETH ABBEY

Augustinian

The tower of Cambuskenneth stands grand, solitary and unexpected, close to the suburban roads of a suburb of Stirling – the town itself and its castle a mile away on its hill, on one side – the River Forth flowing fast, smooth and magnificent, on the other. Cambuskenneth was in its day one of the most important abbeys in Scotland, founded by a king, David I, in 1147, and close to Stirling Castle, the royal residence of its founder. Yet nothing now remains except the tower, and the foundations of church and claustral buildings to accompany it: all else has vanished. For us it is but to walk on the greenest and most beautifully mown grass, and to imagine what once stood here.

There was nothing unusual – except the tower. It was a cruciform church, with chapter house and refectory built in the usual way around the cloister, and the tower itself, that rare thing – a detached campanile standing on the north side of the nave. In 1326 Robert Bruce held an important parliament here; in 1488 James III was buried here, by the side of his wife, Queen Margaret.

The tower is late thirteenth or early fourteenth century in date, with lancet windows in the lower stages, paired lancets above, and a staircase turret in its northeast corner. The ground floor is vaulted, and it is possible to climb up to what would have been the ringing chamber, and to the room above that, where many mediaeval carved stones are on display.

Excavations were carried out in 1864–5, when the coffins of James III and his Queen were discovered, and much restoration work was carried out on the tower. The royal remains were reinterred close to the site of the high altar, under a new memorial stone. 'This restoration of the tomb of her ancestors was executed by command of Her Majesty Queen Victoria AD 1865', reads the inscription.

CROSSRAGUEL ABBEY

Cluniac

An imposing sight, close to the road from Maybole to Girvan: the lonely ruins of Crossraguel Abbey – and puzzling, too, because the existence of an impressive castellated gatehouse, and the tower of the abbot's house, give the impression almost of a castle, certainly a fortified manor house. There is something in all this, in fact – because the monks of Crossraguel possessed considerable secular power, minting their own money, and administering local law and order.

This Cluniac house was founded in 1244 by Duncan, Earl of Carrick, a daughter house of Paisley. The church is long and aisleless, and was extended to the east in the fifteenth century with an apsidal chancel, an unusual and distinguished piece of work; the sedilia and piscina here are remarkably well preserved. The nave at this time was separated from the chancel, and became the Lady Chapel, with the cloisters to the south. Here sacristy and chapter house survive, both still vaulted, with less of the refectory. Beyond is another court – the south court – with another unusual feature: the ruins of the five little houses for corrodiers, or pensioners, which line the south side. The gatehouse presides magnificently, remarkably well preserved. A spiral staircase ascends to rooms on first and second floors (with the floors recently restored), which were the monastic guest rooms, and by no means uncomfortable. The abbot's court was to the east of the cloisters, with his house and his kitchen – but, above all, with his tower, which so much impressed us on arrival, and of which much still stands. But a special pleasure of Crossraguel, in the far corner of the enclosure, is the abbot's dovecote, with the view of the sweeping Ayrshire countryside beyond.

CULROSS ABBEY

Cistercian

Culross is one of those delightful little fishing towns that adorn the coast of Fife, where many small houses and cottages near the harbour, or in the narrow streets which climb the hill, have been restored by the National Trust for Scotland. Culross Palace, a very modest palace, but a captivating house, built at the end of the sixteenth century by Sir George Bruce, now in the care of the Secretary of State for Scotland, is open to the public. Climbing the hill, there are views over the Firth of Forth across pantiled roofs and crow-stepped gables presided over by the tower of the eighteenth-century Tolbooth. The abbey stands at the top: from here the views are even better.

Culross Abbey was founded in 1217 for Cistercian monks. It stands on a very steeply sloping site, the church at the top, the cloisters below, and the undercroft of the refectory below that; so a great deal of descending and ascending must be done. The nave of the church, which was the lay brothers' quire, has disappeared, indeed was dismantled c. 1500 when the lay brothers faded away: the tower was built then to provide a new west front close to the crossing. What was the monastic quire became the parish church in 1633. Although attractive enough, it has been so much rebuilt, and is so unrepentantly Presbyterian that there is very little monastic, let alone Cistercian, about it.

The abbey manse, a beautiful eighteenth-century L-shaped house, stands abutting what was the south wall of the nave of the monastic church, and the west wall of the cloisters. This was the lay brothers' range, and a fragment of their refectory survives, bordering the garden of the manse. This, of course, is private: the entrance for visitors is lower down. It is possible to see the undercroft of the lay brothers' refectory, and what was the undercroft of the monks' refectory, which was in unCistercian fashion parallel with the cloister. Foundations of the undercroft of the dorter and of the chapter house adjoin the south transept – but, owing to the steepness of the hillside, these are below the cloister garth. Enough survives of broken arches and fragments of vaulting to show that much rebuilding was done in the fourteenth century.

The position of Culross Abbey is superb: the remains may be fragmentary, but to explore them on this dramatic hillside overlooking the Firth of Forth, is unforgettable.

DEER ABBEY

Cistercian

Northeast Aberdeenshire can be bleak and cold near the coast – try Peterhead on a wet, gloomy day. But Old Deer is inland, and altogether different. There is the village called Old Deer, with its Episcopal church – but the ruins of the abbey are almost a mile to the west, and the roving eye will pick them out across the fields, half concealing themselves among the stone walls and hedges. And then a most unexpected sight: a small, but imposing, indeed captivating, Doric portico greets the visitor, like the front of a miniature Greek temple. What is this? In the nineteenth century the monastic precinct was adopted as a burial place by the Fergusons of Pitfour, the local lairds, who enjoyed adorning the demesne with unusual Classical gateways; this delightful portico made a solemn and appropriate entrance to their mausoleum. This has disappeared, but it makes a solemn introduction to the ruins. We approach from the north.

Virtually nothing survives of the church – merely foundations or slight stone walls. The cloister beyond is better preserved, and we can identify chapter house, slype and parlour in their rightful positions in the eastern range; in the southern a little more stands upright of the refectory, with cellars beneath, and kitchen alongside – though the refectory lies parallel with the walk in unCistercian fashion. There were the usual stores along the west range. Infirmary and abbot's house lay in a little courtyard of their own to the east.

There is nothing in the least bit dramatic or unusual in any of this – but it is all a delightful place, with its soft grass and fruit trees. The abbey was founded in 1219, and much credit is due to the Ferguson family for preserving it.

DRYBURGH ABBEY

Premonstratensian

The signpost in St Boswells points to Dryburgh Abbey: a delightful road it is, across the green in St Boswells, with its lime trees, then on and up – and another signpost points to Scott's View. The road climbs, past the gates of Bemersyde, to a point where a low wall commands the prospect. It is 593 feet above sea level. Below winds the Tweed through its deep valley: the Eildon Hills are a compelling presence beyond, and with the aid of the metal chart fixed to the wall it is possible to descry (or imagine) Abbotsford, and Melrose, and New-town St Boswells in the middle distance, other landmarks beyond. Here Sir Walter Scott would come from Abbotsford, and here the horses rested on their way to his funeral at Dryburgh in 1832.

Returning, the gates of Bemersyde remind us of the Haigs, Lairds of Bemersyde since the twelfth century:

> Tyde what may, whate'er betyde
> Haig shall be Haig of Bemersyde.

Here the peel tower, the centre of the house, was built in 1535 with stones from the ruins of Dryburgh Abbey. In 1928 Field Marshal Earl Haig was buried within the abbey ruins.

So we descend and follow the signpost to Dryburgh once more; there is a charming post office, with tweed shop next door, on the road side, and the glimpse of a pretty village street down the lane to the side, and we are at the entrance to the Dryburgh Abbey Hotel. Built as Dryburgh House in 1845, it was subsequently much enlarged and became an hotel in 1929. It is the ideal place to stay, absorb the beauties of the abbey – and fish.

The gate to the abbey is at the end of the avenue leading to the hotel. Dryburgh was founded, the first Premonstratensian house in Scotland, in 1130. Its situation is as beautiful as that of any monastic ruin anywhere: not only does the Tweed here make a horseshoe bend – but the parklands which surround the ruins were landscaped at the end of the eighteenth century by David Erskine, 11th Earl of Buchan: his are the plantings of splendid beech trees and cedars of Lebanon which make the place. Across the park may be glimpsed the Abbey House (seventeenth century and later), which was the seat of Lord Buchan as hereditary Commendator of Dryburgh Abbey.

Not very much survives of the church, but the monastic buildings are some of the most complete in Scotland. Entering by the west door, part of the fifteenth-century rebuilding after severe damage wrought by the English in 1385, we see the foundations of the nave arcades and aisle walls, and, beyond the crossing, the beautiful fragment of the north transept and quire arcade – purest Early English: clustered columns below, lancets in the clerestory above. The east end, empty now, frames a majestic cedar; little remains of the south transept, except for the high gable end of the south wall, with its simple traceried window, and the night stairs leading up to the canons' dorter.

A twelfth-century doorway of considerable splendour leads down into the cloisters, and here, under the dormitory are the wonderfully preserved sacristy, parlour and chapter house; and beyond the day stairs steps lead down to the warming house, and the Novices' Day Room. Only foundations survive of the refectory, which occupied the south side of the cloister, but its high west gable still stands, pierced by an elaborate fourteenth-century wheel window.

To the southwest stands the gatehouse, also ruined, which was built after the Reformation when the claustral buildings were converted into a house for the Commendator, and beyond that is the curious and amusing obelisk, erected by the 11th Earl, as a memorial to his ancestors, James I and James II of Scotland, showing them oddly dressed as Tudor or seventeenth-century warriors.

It is a pleasure just to walk round the buildings in their wonderful setting. But the most moving thing of all is to walk back to the north transept, and to gaze on the tombs under the Early English vault of the aisle:

SIR WALTER SCOTT BARONET
died September 21st AD 1832

reads the inscription on one; and

HERE AT THE FEET OF WALTER SCOTT
lie the mortal remains
of
JOHN GIBSON LOCKHART
His son-in-law, biographer and friend
born 14th June 1794
died 25th November 1854

reads another. Nearby, in the roofless transept itself are two headstones:

DOUGLAS HAIG
born in Edinburgh June 19 1861
departed out of this world
January 29 1928
He trusted in God and tried to do the right

and alongside it, another:

DOROTHY MAUD
his wife
born 9th July 1879
died 17th October 1939
God never changeth

DUNBAR FRIARY

Trinitarian

The tiny relic of the Dunbar Friary has today as curious a setting for a monastic ruin as any in the land: it stands in the car park of a supermarket, in the centre of Dunbar. The Dunbar Friary was always very small, with rarely more than a single friar in residence, and the church was like many other friary churches, with nave and chancel and, in between, a narrow tower. This tower, with its (now) saddleback roof, of fifteenth-century date, has only survived through having been converted into a dovecote after the Reformation. It stands now, surrounded during the daytime by a sea of cars, in the car park of William Lowe's Supermarket, an odd reminder of a long-forgotten monastic foundation. The Trinitarians, or Red Friars, were under the rule of St Augustine, and had much in common with the Augustinian Canons. The Dunbar Friary was founded in 1218 by the 5th Earl of Dunbar.

DUNDRENNAN ABBEY

Cistercian

'Monument closed. Custodian on holiday' announced the notice on the gate. But the gate is open! 'I'm only the dogsbody,' says the man sweeping the leaves in the car park. 'I can't give you postcards or guidebook, but do come in.' A welcome indeed.

Dundrennan was founded in 1142 by King David I, and the first monks came from Rievaulx. They must have brought their Yorkshire masons with them, because this beautiful ruin much resembles Rievaulx. Nothing remains of the nave except low walls and bases of the piers – but a substantial part of the transepts is still standing, with lofty pointed arches, blind arcading for the triforium, and round-headed windows in the clerestory – it is, in fact, accomplished Transitional–Early English work. The cloisters lay on the south side, and here are the remains of the chapter house, with triple openings from the east walk – a little later in date than the church itself. Rectangular in plan, only the bases of the pillars which once supported the vault survive, but it is possible to imagine the beauty of the building when it was complete.

The Cistercians always chose remote and delectable places for their houses. Dundrennan is no exception. It is wonderful to look through the empty arcades, and absorb the rolling countryside beyond.

DUNKELD CATHEDRAL

Collegiate Church

Thomas Telford built Dunkeld Bridge across the Tay in 1809: it makes a magnificent introduction to Dunkeld. The Atholl Arms is on the right as we cross the river, and the main street goes on ahead, pleasant indeed, and full of all the usual useful shops. But not far along, on the left, is another street – Cathedral Street, which leads to the cathedral.

Dunkeld is the Southwell of Scotland – a little town with a great cathedral. At Southwell the existence of a grand mediaeval church is always a surprise: it is the same at Dunkeld. 'The village cathedral of the Midlands', Southwell has been described: 'the village cathedral of the Highlands', Dunkeld might be dubbed – a great half-ruined mediaeval cathedral set against a glorious Highland backdrop. There were two Bishops of Dunkeld in the ninth century: the see as we know it was founded in 1114.

Cathedral Street is enchanting – a small street lined on either side with little Georgian houses – stuccoed walls, sash windows, doorcases: the rhythm is continuous. And at the end stand magnificent eighteenth-century wrought-iron gates, as though to a nobleman's seat, or an Oxford or Cambridge college. No, this is the entrance to the cathedral, and the gates display the coronet and cypher of the Dukes of Atholl.

The chancel of the cathedral is in origin thirteenth century, but has been rebuilt and restored, not only in the seventeenth century after the Civil War, but also in the nineteenth; it is now the Church of Scotland parish kirk. The chapter house, on the north side, is the mausoleum of the Dukes of Atholl.

The nave is a ruin, and has been so since the Reformation – but although roofless is still an impressive example of fifteenth-century Scottish Gothic. There are long arcades of clustered columns, with the curious triforium above with its wide, low, round arches enclosing unusual Gothic tracery, the small windows of the clerestory perched precariously above. There is a bold buttressed northwest tower, built on to the west end of the north aisle towards the end of the century.

But the great thing is the setting – with the cathedral in its incomparable churchyard. There are but a few headstones, and those mostly near the church, but many magnificent trees to adorn the spreading lawns. And a few yards away the Tay moves majestically by.

ELGIN CATHEDRAL

Collegiate Church

Elgin must have been the most beautiful cathedral in Scotland. With its three towers, its octagonal chapter house, its exquisite architecture of both the Early English and the Decorated periods, its setting on the edge of a delightful country town, the precinct watered by the River Lossie, the Moray coast but a few miles away – no cathedral in Scotland could surpass it. The diocese of Moray was founded in 1107; Birnie, Kinnedar, Spynie were all in turn briefly the seat of the bishopric and the cathedral – though none of them of any size. In the early thirteenth century it was determined to make the Church of the Holy Trinity the cathedral, and to enlarge, rebuild and glorify it, to be worthy of its new status. Spynie remained the episcopal palace, and with its fifteenth-century keep was the grandest non-royal residence in the kingdom; its magnificent ruin still stands.

At Elgin a great consecration took place in 1224: we do not know much of the Church of 'Holy Trinity juxta Elgin' before its elevation to cathedral rank, but we can be sure that for some years work had been in progress to enlarge and glorify it for its new status. By the middle of the thirteenth century the cathedral comprised chancel and sanctuary, crossing and central tower, and aisled nave with two western towers – in fact, already a considerable church. But in 1270 a serious fire broke out; its causes are not known, but it resulted in great building works, and the cathedral was extended to its present dimensions. Double aisles were added to the nave on both sides – each extra bay being a chapel – the chancel and sanctuary were doubled in size, aisles were added to the chancel, and the chapter house was built. So, at the end of the thirteenth century, a great cathedral, a great work of art, had been completed in distant Moray.

Then in 1390 disaster occurred again: Alexander Stewart, Earl of

Buchan, 'the Wolf of Badenoch', who had been excommunicated by the Bishop, determined to get his own back: with his 'wyld wykked Heland-men he burned the town of Forres, the Choir of the Church of St Laurence there also the manse of the Archdeacon . . . and the whole town of Elgin, 18 noble and beautiful manses of canons and chaplains, and what was still more cursed and lamentable the noble and highly adored Church of Moray with all the books charters and other valuable things of the country therein kept.'

The Wolf did public penance, and contributed to the rebuilding, as did the King and the Bishop. An even grander rebuilding was the result – the west front gloriously rebuilt as we see it today, the sanctuary repaired, the chapter house rebuilt, the central tower rebuilt. Bishop succeeded bishop, and all vowed annually to contribute a third of their income to the rebuilding of the cathedral. All was completed, and then came the Reformation.

Boswell and Johnson came to visit Elgin in 1773. 'Thursday, 26 August. We dined at Elgin, and saw the noble ruins of the Cathedral. Though it rained much, Mr Johnson examined them with a most patient attention . . .' So can we: the most noble west front, the Early English twin towers, and the new and magnificent Decorated doorway set within the older context. With its glorious carved foliage, despite much carving hacked away, it cannot but recall the chapter house of Southwell. Only a fragment remains of the nave chapels – but here an example of Morayshire Decorated tracery may be enjoyed. The transepts are clearly the earliest part of the building, with round-headed 'Norman' windows to match early Early English lancets. The great central tower fell on Easter Day, 1711.

Thereafter the cathedral became little more than an easy quarry for the town, and a refuse dump. But in the early nineteenth century, opinion changed. What had been built to the Glory of God, and had become regarded as the work of the devil, began to be appreciated again. The Crown assumed ownership, and in 1825 a custodian was appointed, one John Shanks, an erstwhile cobbler. To him is due the remarkable work of clearing the ruins of debris: his small, almost hunchback figure appears in two or three illustrations in *A series of views . . . of Elgin Cathedral* (1826).

So we can complete our tour. The nave does not survive: we can but envisage it. But the chancel does – and this and the sanctuary are without doubt the great glory of the building. Survey it inside and out. Outside, the east end, with its two tiers of five lancet windows, with its wheel window above, and the bold, pinnacled buttresses on either side, must constitute a work of the greatest beauty. Inside it is the same, and with the long line of lancets forming the clerestory on the north and south sides it must again recall (rather earlier) work at Southwell. The chapter house, approached by its little lobby-way, again on the north side of the chancel, may recall Southwell, too. All this is work of supreme beauty.

'My church was the ornament of the realm, the glory of the kingdom, the delight of foreigners and stranger guests; an object of praise and glorification in foreign realms by reason of the multitude of those serving and the beauty of its ornament and in which we believe God was rightly worshipped; not to speak of its high belfries, its ancient furniture and its innumerable jewels'. So wrote Alexander Bur, Bishop of Moray (1362–97) to King Robert III, after the onslaught of the Wolf of Badenoch.

As we walk round the Chanonrie, we can only think: What would he say now?

FORTROSE CATHEDRAL

Collegiate Church

Despite its name the Black Isle is not an isle at all – though the Cromarty Firth to the north, and the Moray Firth and the Beauly Firth to the south for centuries rendered it almost so. Now the new bridge carries the A9 from Inverness across: Fortrose is a small town to the east, not far from the coast, of little consequence but for its ruined cathedral, once the cathedral of the Diocese of Ross. The original cathedral was at Rosemarkie (a few miles to the northeast), but Bishop Robert (1214–49) moved the see town to Fortrose, and began the building of the cathedral. Only the thirteenth-century chapter house survives of this period, standing with its vaulted undercroft on its own, to the north of the remaining south aisle: it has been used for various purposes in the past four centuries. Chancel and nave stood adjoining, but these disappeared after the Reformation. From the foundations marked out in the grass this formed a long oblong building, with a tower standing at the west end.

The south aisle, however, survives, and this is of considerable beauty, though open to the elements on its north side. The Regent Moray gave permission for the lead roof of the cathedral to be removed in 1572, and nave and chancel soon disappeared; the south aisle survived, protected by its stone vaulting.

The western half of this aisle, the nave aisle, must be late fourteenth century – the slightly wider chancel aisle, early fifteenth, and was probably built as the chantry chapel for the Earls of Ross. Here there are three canopied table tombs – one to Bishop Fraser (1507), one to Bishop Cairncross (1545), and one to Euphemia, Countess of Ross (1398). Countess in her own right, after the death of two husbands (the second the notorious Wolf of Badenoch) she died as Abbess of Elcho. There are many later memorials – the portentous Adamesque monument to the Mackenzie family, with its obelisks and pilasters framing a doorway to their vault, being of special interest.

But the greatest pleasure is the building itself – the elegant rib vaulting, so wonderfully preserved, and the rhythm of the fourteenth-century arches, with their clustered columns standing open to the weather so unexpectedly after four centuries of chilling northern winds. The little octagonal bell turret still contains the bell preserved by Bishop Tulloch in 1449, dedicated to St Mary and St Boniface, which still tolls the passing hours.

GLENLUCE ABBEY

Cistercian

A beautiful, remote, Cistercian setting – not far from Luce Bay on the Wigtownshire coast: Glenluce Abbey was founded in 1190, by Roland, Earl of Galloway; but of the church only a little of the south aisle and of the south transept survive. These fragments are thirteenth century. What makes Glenluce memorable is the chapter house, and this was rebuilt as late as the early sixteenth century, and miraculously survives. Square, with a central pillar, and so vaulted in four smaller squares, it is a most enchanting little building. The traceried windows are glazed, the stone seat for the brethren still surrounds the room, and there are mediaeval tiles on the floor.

HOLYROOD ABBEY

Augustinian

The castle dominates Princes Street, and Princes Street dominates Edinburgh – Princes Street, the busy thoroughfare which divides the New Town from the Old, which leads from the Scott Monument and Waverley Station at one end to St Mary's Cathedral with its three spires at the other. The castle on its rock is in origin mediaeval, but much is seventeenth century or later. One building, however, is earlier: the little Norman Chapel of St Margaret of Scotland, the heart of the castle. Queen Margaret of Scotland – later St Margaret – died in the castle in 1093; a deeply religious woman, she venerated a relic (as she believed it to be) of the true cross, the Holy Rood: this she kept in a golden casket. Her son David became King in succession to his elder brother, Alexander I, in 1124, and in 1128 founded the Augustinian Abbey of Holyrood, a mile to the east of Edinburgh Castle. It is always a thrill to walk, or drive, from the castle down the Royal Mile, that dramatic cobbled street lined with the grand, if faded, mansions of the great ones of the past, to its majestic end – where the Palace of Holyroodhouse stands against the tremendous backdrop of the great craggy rock of Arthur's Seat.

Holyrood stands serene, grand but domestic; classical pillars, sash windows, round fortified towers, all somehow add up to an authentic Scottish royal palace. Only on walking round to the north side does the ruined abbey church reveal itself.

The abbey was a daughter house of St Andrews; one doorway (into the cloister) survives from this period. Otherwise, the nave is a rebuilding of the mid-thirteenth century, beautiful and accomplished work, with tall clustered columns and stiff-leaf capitals. Transepts and quire followed, with the cloisters on the south side, and twin towers – of which only one survives – at the west end. Close to this west end stood the guesthouse, and this, increasingly during the mediaeval period, became used as a royal residence. James IV (who married Margaret Tudor, daughter of Henry VII) built the northwest tower which greeted us on our arrival. So Holyrood developed into a royal residence.

The transepts and quire of the church were demolished in 1569, and the nave was for a time used as the parish church of the Canongate. However, in 1633, it was grandly refurnished as the Chapel Royal for the Scottish Coronation of Charles I. It was at this time that the traceried east window was inserted in the blocked-up crossing arch, and the west front restored – when the charming 'angel lintel' was inserted to support the tympanum in the beautiful but sadly defaced west doorway.

In 1685 James II, with his usual tactlessness, declared the church a Roman Catholic Chapel Royal, and established a Jesuit college in the palace. This was too much for the protestant-minded people of Edinburgh, and at the news of the landing of William of Orange at Torbay in 1688, the mob closed in on Holyrood, ransacked the church, and burned all the popish furnishings. An engraving exists in *Vitruvius Scoticus* of the Chapel Royal in 1688, filled with Baroque fittings, as the Chapel of the Order of the Thistle. The roof collapsed in 1768, and was never rebuilt.

The palace itself was rebuilt for Charles II in 1671, by Sir William Bruce, 'the Inigo Jones of Scotland', who retained, on the King's insistence, the historic northwest tower, and reproduced it at the south-west corner. To link the twin towers he built the two-storeyed frontis-piece, with its long sash windows and pillared entrance gate which leads into the inner court. This delightful courtyard with its Doric pilasters setting off the arched colonnade on the ground floor, and Ionic and Corinthian ones between the sash windows on the two floors above, is adorned in its central pediment with the arms of Charles II. On the first floor are the State Rooms, with their sumptuous plaster ceilings and elaborate carved woodwork: perhaps the most interesting is the Picture Gallery, which runs the length of the north side, and contains the portraits of eighty-nine Scottish kings painted for Charles II by Jacob de Wett in 1684–6.

Holyrood is for ever associated with tragedy and romance. It was in the northwest tower that Rizzio, French secretary to Mary, Queen of Scots, was murdered by Darnley in the presence of the Queen in 1566; and if no king ever visited the palace between Charles I and George IV, the house had a brilliant taste of royal glory in 1745, when the Young Pretender held court here from 21 September to 31 October, before setting out on his ill-fated march to Derby. There-after Holyrood slumbered, being used for various official functions, but not seeing a king till George IV, in Highland costume, visited it in 1822. Queen Victoria first came here in 1842, and was much moved by its romance and its melancholy. Since 1850 Holyrood has been regularly used by the British monarch. It was the Prince Consort who laid out the garden round the ruined abbey.

INCHCOLM ABBEY

Augustinian

Things shut down early in Scotland: on 1 September winter times set in, ancient monuments close at 4 p.m. and the ferry to Inchcolm from South Queensferry ceases altogether for the winter. But there is compensation in this: the only means of access to Inchcolm then is by a little motor boat from Aberdour, quite an exciting introduction to one of the most romantic of Scottish abbeys, and one of the most complete. Aberdour is a small town on the coast of Fife, with a partly ruined castle overlooking the harbour, and a most unexpected and delightful Italian restaurant in one of the narrow streets which descend to the shore.

Inchcolm Abbey looks perfect on the little green island in the Firth of Forth, as we speed across in the open motor boat – an enchanting little group of stone walls and stone roofs, the square tower of the church, the conical roof of the chapter house. Inchcolm was founded for Augustinian Canons in 1123 by Alexander I. The King had been driven ashore here in a gale, and took shelter in a hermit's chapel, which may indeed be the little stone chapel still standing to the west of the abbey. The original twelfth-century church stood on the north side of the little cloister court. It was gradually extended, and eventually entirely rebuilt to the east during the thirteenth and fourteenth centuries, the thirteenth-century tower being built over what was the chancel. The Norman church was divided horizontally in the late thirteenth century, the upper part becoming the abbot's lodging. Little survives of the later cruciform church, which was separated from the earlier building by a small open corner, leading up to the dorter, which occupied the upper floor of the east cloister range.

It is the use of the upper floors of the cloister court which makes Inchcolm so unusual, and indeed their preservation seems almost miraculous. There are the usual cloister walks below, with a doorway on the east side leading into the chapter house, one of only two octagonal chapter houses in Scotland, and, of course, still vaulted. Above are the really splendid vaulted rooms – dorter, frater, guest hall –

occupying the three sides, lofty, empty and echoing; above the chapter house is the warming room.

South of the cloisters a gateway leads into a green court, which is only separated by a low stone wall from the shore, and the infirmary wing, largely ruined, continues to the very shore itself. Of course the very inaccessibility of the place has helped to preserve its buildings.

The setting of Inchcolm on its little island, with its walls washed by the waves, is quite wonderful; so are the amazingly preserved claustral buildings, unusual, evocative and atmospheric; so are the views from the island – to the coastline of Fife to the north, to Edinburgh to the south, up the Firth westwards towards the Forth Bridge, and eastwards to the open sea.

INCHMAHOME PRIORY

Augustinian

ANCIENT MONUMENT
INCHMAHOME PRIORY
SAIL FROM PIER

So reads the signpost on the road which skirts the Lake of Menteith. The wording is thrilling, intriguing, inviting: how many hours' sailing will it be? How big a ship? Do not be disappointed. This is not a long sea trip, like the journey to Oronsay. It is a gentle afternoon's jaunt – ten minutes across the lake, in a little motor boat. Yet to sail like this, to the largest of the lake's three islands, and visit Inchmahome, is one of the most enjoyable pilgrimages that any of us can make.

Inchmahome was founded as a priory for Augustinian Canons in 1138 by Walter Comyn, Earl of Menteith. The island was thus set apart as an island of prayer in this gloriously beautiful lake, from which the canons could go ashore to serve the needs of the Church here in Perthshire. And much remains for us to enjoy today.

The little motor boat sets forth from the pier – no more than a diminutive jetty – and soon the island with its ruined church comes in sight. The priory stands close to the shore, and, on landing, a few paces take us to the west front of the church. The doorway is of great beauty, an Early English archway with clustered columns, and, on either side, a blind arcade of paired arches. Within the church two bays of the north nave arcade are still standing, as are the walls of the choir, with its five-lancet east window, lancets on either side, piscina and sedilia in the south wall. It must have been an intimate, charming church. The tower – a later addition – sits perhaps a little awkwardly at the northwest corner of the nave, opposite a doorway which leads out into the cloister.

Here, on the east side, the barrel-vaulted chapter house is remarkably intact, with its stone bench, and later effigies brought in for protection from the roofless church. Little remains of the adjoining slype, or warming house, above which would have been the dorter – and the refectory on the south side can only be envisaged from its foundations. Even less remains of the west range.

Few monastic sites are so evocative of the ideals of religious life – its seclusion and its peace. The setting is perfection – the island with its mature trees, the hills of Perthshire on the mainland all around, the gentle waves of the lake lapping the island shores.

INVERKEITHING – GREYFRIARS

Franciscan

Almost under the shadow of the Forth Bridge, there stands in the High Street of Inverkeithing a mediaeval building: the Greyfriars. It is attractive with its crow-stepped gables, Gothic doors and windows and other, blocked-up, openings. It was probably the guesthouse of the Franciscan Friary, founded here in 1268. There is a small public garden behind, and the fragment of a vaulted undercroft beyond, but nothing is known of church or other buildings. The ground floor of the guesthouse is used as a pensioners' club, and, approached by the external stone staircase, the upper floor is the local museum. Surrounded as it is by the bustle of daily life, it is just the site that the Franciscans would choose for their friary.

IONA

Augustinian Nunnery, Benedictine Abbey and Cathedral

The ferry from Oban to Mull, and the long drive across Mull, big, bleak and barren, to the landing stage at Fionnphort – all this is enough to fire the imagination, and raise the spirits: Iona seems very remote, and there is still the final sea trip to Iona itself, goal of every pilgrim.

From the little ferry boat the eye will be searching for landmarks: the houses in the village, the terrace of cottages near the landing stage, the cathedral, square and squat with its surrounding buildings – exciting indeed.

It is a brisk walk up the gentle slope from the quay – turn right, and the ruins of the priory are upon us. This was founded for Augustinian nuns in the early thirteenth century, and of the church enough survives for us to get a good impression of it. Of the north aisle the east chapel still stands, vaulted. It is interesting to see that the arches of the nave arcade are still round, though the capitals have later been made octagonal. The clerestory windows are round-headed, too, as are those in the west wall. Little survives of the cloister, which lay on the south side, but the plan is marked out, and foundations of chapter house and parlour are there on the east side, and a good deal stands of the refectory.

Nearby, to the north, stands the little church of St Ronan, the former parish kirk, now restored as a museum for the priory, containing an impressive collection of stone crosses and other carved fragments, the greatest treasure being St Oran's Cross, possibly the earliest of all the wonderful crosses in which the island abounds (eighth century).

Iona Abbey (or Cathedral) really has no part in this volume, having been so wonderfully restored and rebuilt in recent years. But something must be said. It was here that St Columba founded his little monastery in 563. It was refounded in the twelfth century, and again in the thirteenth as a Benedictine house, and became mitred in 1247. In the sixteenth century it became the Cathedral of the Isles.

After the Reformation both church and monastic buildings decayed, but in the eighteenth century interest in their history and architecture developed, fanned by the Romantic Movement. In October 1773 Dr Johnson and James Boswell came here on their tour to the Hebrides. Boswell describes in his *Journal* how they landed in the evening of the 19th, saw lights burning in the village, and were met by their friend Sir Allan Maclean, 6th Baronet and Chief of the Clan Maclean; they supped on cuddies and oysters boiled in butter, and spent the night in a barn prepared for them. There was a fire, hay had been laid on the floor, and sheets provided by Miss Maclean – 'and some very good blankets from the village'. Next morning, before breakfast, they went to see the ruins. Boswell was much shocked by the state of the nuns' church, used as a cow house, its whole floor covered in dung; they went on to visit the cathedral. After breakfast Boswell returned to the cathedral 'to perform some pleasing serious acts of piety', and was much moved by St Martin's Cross, where he knelt to say a prayer. Later he returned to the cathedral 'which is really grand enough when one thinks of its antiquity and of the remoteness of the place, and at the end, I offered up my adoration to God.' Boswell was obviously moved, and added a prayer to St Columba. 'That man is little to be envied,' remarked Johnson, 'whose patriotism could not gain force upon the plain of Marathon, or whose piety would not grow warmer among the ruins of Iona.'

Later visitors included Walter Scott, Keats and Wordsworth. During the nineteenth century the 8th Duke of Argyll instigated some restoration of cathedral and priory, and in 1899 transferred both to trustees, known as the Iona Cathedral Trust, for the rebuilding and restoration of the cathedral. This began in the early twentieth century, under the architects Thomas Ross and John Honeyman for choir and transepts, and later for the nave under P. MacGregor Chalmers.

In 1938 the Iona Community was founded by Dr George MacLeod (later the Very Revd Lord MacLeod of Fuinary) as a Church of Scotland community, based on Iona, but dedicated to the work of the Church throughout Scotland and beyond. It is due to him that the rebuilding of the cloister and community buildings has been undertaken – so attractively – under the architect Ian Lindsay. All this can be visited and enjoyed.

There is much else to enjoy, too: the delightful hotel near the cathedral, with its commanding view of the Sound of Mull, and the little ferry boat plying its way – and its secondhand bookshop nearby. Bishop's House, not far away, is the Episcopalian retreat house and guesthouse, with its beautiful chapel (by Alexander Ross, 1894), belonging to the Bishops of Argyll and the Isles – and, of course, at all times the wild flowers, the birds, the fishing, the rocky landscape, and the views everywhere, across the water to Mull and the world beyond.

JEDBURGH ABBEY

Augustinian

One of the best ways to Scotland is by the A68 – which passes through miles of empty countryside in Northumberland before reaching the rolling hills of the Border; and Jedburgh is only eleven miles from Carter Bar. It is always a thrill to reach Jedburgh: the great roofless abbey dominates the town. Although it lacks the romantic setting of Dryburgh or Melrose, it is undoubtedly the finest church to survive of the Border abbeys; indeed, although roofless, the building is almost intact. Like an enormous ship, it towers above the streets of the town.

Jedburgh was founded *c.* 1138 as an Augustinian priory by David I, before he became King, and it became an abbey in 1147. The approach to the church now is through the ticket office and shop, across the river, and past the foundations of the claustral buildings. There is not much to make of all these, but from the layout of the cloisters we can recognize everything, more or less; and there is a very fine view of the south side of the church. The claustral buildings became a useful stone quarry after the Reformation.

But the mighty church makes up for all, and we enter from the cloister through the south door into the nave, a very early Early English nave of considerable splendour, nine bays long, with clustered columns surmounted by beautiful waterleaf capitals, a triforium of great elegance, with pairs of pointed arches under a round-headed arch, lancets in the clerestory. The west window is round-headed, but above this is an elaborate wheel window, a later insertion of perhaps the late fourteenth century; outside, the grand Norman west doorway is worth looking at, together with (rather surprisingly) narrow pointed arches on either side of the west window.

Round arches at the crossing support the tower, completed early in the sixteenth century, and lead into the chancel, which is Norman: as usual, building began from the east end. The arcades here are unusual, and of great interest, for the triforium is fitted within the grand arches of the arcade – with lesser arches below leading into the aisle, an arrangement reminiscent of Christ Church, Oxford, and of Romsey. The east end of the choir and the south transept have collapsed. The north transept is the mausoleum of the Kerr family, Marquises of Lothian, to whom much is due for the remarkable preservation of this wonderful building.

KELSO ABBEY

Tironensian

Kelso, with its streets of Georgian houses, and its grand market place dominated by its equally grand town hall, is a delightful and distin-guished town. The River Tweed sweeps by, Floors Castle, seat of the

Duke of Roxburghe, overlooks it to the north, and Ednam House, the former Dower House and now most excellent hotel, overlooks it by the bridge. The towering, broken fragment of the abbey presides over all.

Kelso Abbey was founded by King David I in 1128 for Tironensian monks. Although but a fragment, it is a particularly imposing fragment, and the plan of the church is unusual, indeed unique in Scotland, with western as well as eastern transepts, and a tower over both crossings – as at Ely, the only other comparable example in Britain. Is it too fanciful to see a family resemblance in the two west towers of Ely and Kelso? The plan, it seems, is derived from the Carolingian minsters in Germany. What remains at Kelso is the western transept and crossing, with part of the tower, and part of the narthex or diminutive nave. It is all in the severest Norman or Transitional style, with tier upon tier of round-headed windows, or blind arcading, breaking out into tiny lancets in the upper stages of the tower. There are round, almost castellated turrets at the corners of the transepts – again reminiscent of Ely – and everywhere the sense of immense strength and towering height. Virtually nothing remains of the rest of the church, or of the claustral buildings: some of the arches of the cloister have been reconstructed to provide a burial ground for the Dukes of Roxburghe – and a civil war memorial.

KILWINNING ABBEY

Tironensian

Kilwinning is an unremarkable little town, with a pedestrianized main street, and all the usual shop fronts. But a stone's throw from the street stand the fragmentary remains of a once-great abbey, standing in the churchyard of the present parish kirk.

The abbey was founded *c.* 1162 by Hugh de Morville – and the first monks came from Kelso. The high gable of the south transept survives, dating from the late twelfth or the early thirteenth century, and with its long lancets is almost complete. Parts of the southwest tower and the south wall of the nave must be contemporary with these, and there is one beautiful Early English doorway in what was the northeast corner of the cloister. The northwest tower survived until 1805, when it was struck by lightning, and was replaced by the present nineteenth-century tower. The quire was used as the parish kirk till

1775, but was demolished when the present parish kirk was built –
more comfortable, no doubt, for good Presbyterians, than a draughty
monastic chancel.

KINLOSS ABBEY

Cistercian

The Cistercian Abbey of Kinloss was founded in 1150 by King David
I, and was a daughter house of Melrose. It had a grand cruciform
church, with a central tower added in the fifteenth century, cloisters
on the south side, and a commodious abbot's house free-standing
beyond that. Moreover it became mitred in 1395, so was a house of
some importance. Now there are but a few ivy-covered ruins set in
an enormous public cemetery. It is hard to imagine anything more
unCistercian or more cheerless.

Approaching the site of the church, it is possible to make out the
general plan, though little remains above ground. Most of the stone
was carted away in 1650 to build a fort for Cromwell's army at Inverness. Only against the south transept does the sacristy, with library
over, stand upright, with a fragment of a transept chapel adjoining.
The sacristy is locked, being used as a family mausoleum, and the
whole building is smothered in ivy. Two more mausolea have been
contrived in the cloister. The abbot's house became the residence of
the commendator after the Reformation, and has been much altered.

So there is very little to see, but graves, graves, graves. But the
setting, raised up and commanding distant views across the Moray
coast, is exhilarating.

LINCLUDEN

Benedictine Nunnery : Collegiate Church

To plough through the outer suburbs of Dumfries, and discover one
of the most beautiful ruined churches in Scotland, is a rewarding
experience. Lincluden was originally founded in 1164 as a Benedictine
nunnery, but this was suppressed in 1389 by Archibald the Grim,
third Earl of Douglas, and refounded as a collegiate church for a
provost and eight canons. The ruined south transept survives, together

Fortrose: in the Black Isle – the south aisle is still vaulted, but the 14th-century arcade is exposed to the ravages of the north wind.

Inchcolm: on its little green island in the Firth of Forth, its ruined buildings reaching to the shore itself.

Above: Inchmahome: the priory stands close to the shore of its little island in the lake of Menteith, surrounded by the hills of Perthshire.

Right: Jedburgh: best preserved of the Border abbeys, like an enormous ship towers above the streets of the town.

Lincluden: an exquisite 14th-century building, probably the work of
Jean Moreau, the French mason who also worked at Melrose.

Melrose: the east window is English – the work of York masons,
whereas the earlier south transept is French – the work of Jean Moreau.

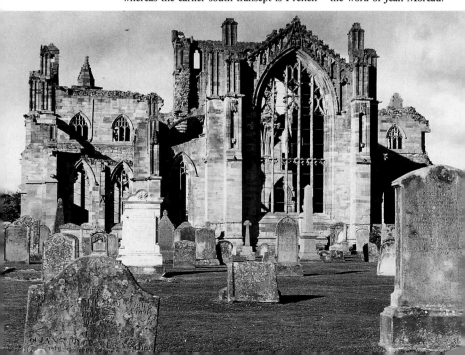

Peebles: the Cross Kirk, founded in the 13th century, in honour of the Holy Cross and St Nicolas, later taken over by the Red Friars.

Restenneth: in remote and beautiful countryside near Forfar, the priory across the cottage garden by the gate.

St Andrews: the ideal way to arrive here is by sea, to tie up in the little harbour dominated by the cathedral ruins, and St Rule's tower.

Opposite above: Sweetheart Abbey: remarkably well preserved, even the 14th-century tracery still surviving in the east window.
Below: Torphichen: the grand transepts and tower of the Hospitallers' Preceptory, to which an 18th-century nave was added as the parish kirk.

Whithorn: a Norman doorway in the tiny nave of the priory – a place for ever associated with St Ninian.

with much of the south wall of the nave, with two of its traceried windows, mutilated but still evocative.

This is only a preparation: the pulpitum leads into the chancel, which even in its roofless state is an exquisite building, in all probability the work of Jean Moreau (or John Morrow), the French mason who worked at Melrose, where his inscription in the south transept refers to work in 'Nyddysdayll' – where but Lincluden? It is a chancel of three bays: gaping windows with fragments of Decorated tracery, buttresses to support a vaulted roof, it is all most accomplished work. Close to the sanctuary is the tomb of Princess Margaret, wife of Archibald, 4th Earl of Douglas, an elaborate and impressive work, with the Princess' effigy still in place, and much carved heraldic decoration.

A doorway next to the tomb, carved with foliage and two little monkeys, led into the sacristy – and so to the long domestic wing beyond, which housed the canons, probably on the site of the east range of the nuns' cloister. After the Reformation this was converted into a house, and the church, as usual, became a stone quarry. To the southeast is the castle mound, or motte, which marks the site of the castle which preceded the nuns. This was later terraced, and in the sixteenth century became a formal garden for the mansion house. This is the final surprise and pleasure of Lincluden.

'Do you get many visitors here?' 'No,' replied the custodian, 'but when the channel tunnel opens . . .'

LINDORES ABBEY

Tironensian

To drive along the North Fife coast, overlooking the Firth of Tay, and to discover in a quiet road the overgrown remains of Lindores Abbey is a most unexpected pleasure. A sudden mediaeval arch on the roadside – a fragment of a monastic gatehouse – a glimpse of ancient walls, old trees, a comfortable farmhouse, horses – it is all unselfconscious, half-forgotten. With permission from the house we can go in and explore.

Lindores was a Tironensian house, the daughter of Kelso, and founded in 1191. It became mitred in 1395, so was evidently of some importance in its day. Now it is fallen, overgrown, sad but beautiful. It is in fact a pleasure (for once) to forgo the neatly mown grass, the guidebook, the notices, the turnstyle of an official 'ancient monument', and visit Lindores.

The cloister and its claustral buildings stood close to the gate: a little low walling, a heap of stones – it is just possible to envisage the layout. There is actually a little vaulting left in the parlour, next to the chapter house, a broken arch or two, a little walling of the refectory. Of the church beyond, fragments of chapels in the transepts can be made out, an aumbry here, a piscina there, at the west end the base of the tower. To imagine the bustle of mediaeval monastic life, here among the long grass and thistles, is difficult indeed. But it is a moving spot.

MELROSE ABBEY

Cistercian

Gorgeous Border countryside, a little town of charm, and a ruin of incomparable beauty: Melrose Abbey was founded by King David I in 1136, but Melrose has been a holy place for far longer than that. At Old Melrose, nearby, was a monastery founded by St Aidan in the seventh century; the first prior was St Boisil (St Boswell), who was succeeded by St Cuthbert – until his call to be prior of Lindisfarne in 664. The new Cistercian house was founded at a place called Little Fordell, a short distance to the west, but the name Melrose was transferred to it.

Very little survives of the earliest church here, or its monastic buildings, sacked by the English in the very earliest years of the fourteenth century, again in 1322, and yet again in 1385. The abbey we see today is a rebuilding of the early fifteenth century, and represents the finest work in Scotland of the period when Decorated was merging into Perpendicular.

Walking round the outside, the surviving fragment of the tower will be observed, then a section of the nave, apparently still roofed, then five more bays of the south aisle, with its buttresses and traceried windows. Beyond this to the east is the south transept – which by any count will be admired as a building of outstanding beauty. The short sanctuary follows, and east end, which almost miraculously, it seems, still retains its vault, and the tracery in its east window. The north transept is simpler; and all around are the foundations of the claustral buildings. In the angle of the north transept and the nave is arcading

– on the transept wall highly ornamental, the arches and frieze carved with leaves and flowers and berries; on the nave wall simpler, but also of great beauty.

The rebuilding of the west front was never completed: we enter through the foundations of the earlier west wall. It will be observed at once that the plan of the nave was not symmetrical – the north aisle was narrow: the south was wider, and led into a second aisle with chapels in every bay, some of which retain their vaulting, and their traceried windows. Passing through the pulpitum, we are confronted with an extraordinary spectacle – of a curious arcade built in front of the original fifteenth-century arcade, with a strange barrel vault above. This is seventeenth-century work: after the Reformation what had been the monks' choir was for a time used as a Presbyterian parish kirk, and fitted out accordingly.

But when we reach the crossing it is possible to appreciate the splendour of the original interior. Although the north transept was ruined by the fall of the larger half of the tower, much of the wonderful vaulting in the south transept and sanctuary survives – that in the sanctuary, with its carved figures of eight of the apostles being specially notable. The east window retains most of its Perpendicular tracery, but the great window of the south transept is quite different, being filled with remarkable flamboyant Decorated tracery. The sanctuary and east window are English, the work of Yorkshire masons, whereas the transept is the work of a Frenchman, Jean Moreau (or John Morrow), and two inscriptions in the transept record his name and work. The south transept is the 'show front' of the church, and emerging here we can survey the full glory of Jean Moreau's design.

Melrose is specially rich in its sculpture. Above the east window is the Coronation of the Virgin; on the westernmost buttress of the nave a figure of the Virgin and Child; in the north transept one of St Peter with his key (high up, west wall), and so on.

As will have been noted, cloisters and claustral buildings here were on the north side of the church: only foundations survive, but from these it can be seen how great the scale of everything was. Beyond the north boundary wall is the sixteenth- and early seventeenth-century commendator's house, partially built from abbey stone, which now houses an excellent museum. A charming garden has been planted against the boundary wall, and beyond the house the Mill Lade flows by.

NEWBATTLE ABBEY

Cistercian

South of Dalkeith the road (B703) leads down into the wooded valley of the Esk, and before long follows a long wall on the left-hand side, which leads to a stately entrance with lodges and magnificent Baroque gate piers. At the end of a long avenue there is a glimpse of a plain, battlemented, stone mansion: Newbattle Abbey.

Newbattle was founded for Cistercian monks in 1140, by King David I, and was the daughter house of Melrose. The abbey prospered under royal patronage, and became one of the richest in Scotland. After the Reformation, Mark Kerr became the first Commendator in 1560. In the words of Scot of Scotstarvet, 'he so metamorphosed the building that it cannot be known that ever it did belong to the Church, by reason of the fair new fabrick and stately edifices thereon.' The church was pulled down, and in the usual way the domestic buildings were converted into the Kerrs' great house. Much rebuilding took place in the seventeenth and eighteenth centuries, and there are still very fine state rooms with good plasterwork and carvings, as well as grand Victorian rooms. The Commendator's son became Lord Newbattle, then in 1606 Earl of Lothian; the marquisate was conferred in 1701.

The 11th Marquis, who was Ambassador in Washington at the beginning of the Second World War, presented Newbattle to the Scottish Universities in 1936 (it was he, too, who gave Blickling to the National Trust at this time). It has since been used as an adult residential college. New extensions have been added (1968) on the site of the north-cloister walk; the site of the church is marked out, but in fact it is only the mediaeval undercrofts which survive of the Cistercian building.

NORTH BERWICK PRIORY

Cistercian Nuns

The priory of North Berwick was a Cistercian nunnery, founded in 1150 by Duncan, Earl of Fife, in 1150. After the Reformation it was acquired by the Home family, who converted part of the conventual buildings into a house. This became ruinous in the eighteenth century. Early in this century a new house was built nearby, called (of course) The Abbey – which it never was – and the priory ruins became merely a romantic feature in the garden.

It is not easy to make much of this ruin, but it represents probably the north side of the cloister; various features, such as fireplaces, are obviously post-Reformation and domestic. The church probably stood roughly where the present house stands. The house now is an old people's home, and permission to inspect the ruins should be sought here.

ORONSAY PRIORY

Augustinian

Oronsay is the most remote and the most inaccessible of all the monastic houses in Britain. The tiny island of Oronsay lies to the south of the much larger island of Colonsay. But Colonsay is itself small, and can only be approached from Oban by boat three times a week – so it is necessary to spend two nights in the island. Oronsay can only be reached from Colonsay on foot, across the sands at low tide. Oronsay is so remote that (it is rumoured) a Roman Catholic Order of monks actually established themselves in the priory there, years after the Reformation, and remained there for several years before their presence was detected.

It is a two-and-a-half-hour trip by the boat from Oban: we are met at the landing stage by a motor from the hotel, one of the very few cars in the island. The village is small, and very scattered: the post office, the kirk, the hotel, all at a nodding distance from each other. The hotel is delightful, the perfect place to stay for a few nights or longer.

But to reach Oronsay! It is a longer drive to the end of the road, and Oronsay lies beyond – a walk of a mile or two across rocky land to the shore, with just one cottage for company on the way: then across the sand to set foot on Oronsay. After that there is another mile or so to walk along the track, and so to the farm, and the priory itself.

Oronsay Priory was founded, or perhaps refounded, *c.* 1340 for Augustinian Canons. Its origins may be much more ancient – but the building which we see is fourteenth century. It is not only remote: it is tiny – a little aisleless nave and chancel, a south chapel, tiny also, being the MacDuffie Aisle, the burial place of the family; there is the base of a tower at the west end. A little door on the north side leads into the cloister, which, of course, is tiny also – but although roofless is remarkably well preserved, with much of the very delicate arcading standing erect, some of it very careful nineteenth-century rebuilding. The refectory occupied the north side, the chapter house the east – all in the usual way, but on a miniature scale.

Beyond the north range stands the prior's house. This has been reroofed, and now contains a splendid collection of mediaeval cross slabs. There they lie, like beds in a school dormitory – among them the magnificent canopied figure of Prior Sir David MacDuffie (*c.* 1555), which was once in the MacDuffie Aisle. Outside, on the east side, is a standing cross, reassembled; the head does not belong to the shaft, but it is of considerable charm and interest. But at the southwest corner, close to the doorway, is Oronsay's greatest treasure, the Oronsay Cross, complete with carved crucifix on its west side, its shaft all carved and perfect, as though the Reformation had never occurred, and the monks were still here. An inscription tells us that it is in memory of Prior Colin, who died in 1510.

All this has taken time: the tide is coming in, and we must take off shoes and socks and *paddle* our way back to Colonsay. But we have reached Oronsay, and the end of the world.

PEEBLES FRIARY

Trinitarian

Peebles is an attractive town, with its glorious setting and its grand Victorian hotels. A little to the north of the town centre stands the Cross Kirk, as it is usually known, or the Church of the Red Friars. The Trinitarian Friary was founded in the middle of the fifteenth century, though the church is in origin much older. Alexander III built a church here in 1261, in honour of the Holy Cross, following the discovery here of relics (it was believed) of the Holy Cross, and associated with St Nicolas. The aisleless nave is certainly thirteenth century, but the Friars built the tower, and their conventual buildings round the cloister on the north side of the church: little more than foundations survive. The small round-headed arch into the chancel is obviously old, denoting the antiquity of the church; little is left of the sanctuary. After the Reformation the church was used for over two hundred years as the parish kirk, after which it became ruinous. It is a romantic ruin.

PITTENWEEM PRIORY

Benedictine

Pittenweem has great charm. The sight of the harbour, with small boats tied up, and the stone houses along the quayside, with the ground rising steeply behind, the rugged stone houses that comprise the priory on the top, with the blunt but delightful spire of the parish kirk nearby – all this is one not lightly to be forgotten. From the quayside a precipitous footpath leads up, with handrail to assist the decrepit, to the entrance to St Fillan's Cave, and so on to the steps to the priory above. St Fillan was the local saint, the eighth-century hermit who inhabited the cave, and who later, somewhat unwillingly, became abbot of the earliest religious house here, a relic of whose arm Robert the Bruce took with him to the Battle of Bannockburn.

Pittenweem Priory (as we know it) was founded for Benedictine monks by King David I in the twelfth century – on the Island of May in the Firth of Forth. Insecurity drove them onto the mainland, where there already existed a manor house belonging to the prior. Part of this survives, in the fifteenth-century, heavily corbelled, gatehouse, restored and used as a meeting place by the local Episcopal congregation; in the Great House, formerly the monks' dormitory; and the prior's lodging, now the seat of a secular feudal baron. The Great House has sixteenth-century oriel windows, similar to those of Cardinal Bethune's ruined archiepiscopal castle at St Andrews, and was renovated by Sir Robert Lorimer; it is now a retreat for retired episcopalian clergy and mature ordinands. The prior's lodging, or manor house, dates mostly from the seventeenth and eighteenth centuries, built on a much older vaulted basement, from which a passage ran under the prior's garden, to St Fillan's Cave. This can also be reached (as we have said) from the harbour. The cave has been reconsecrated, and the chapel is served by the Episcopal church. The key may be obtained from the Gingerbread Horse, in the High Street.

RESTENNETH PRIORY

Augustinian

Remote and beautiful countryside, to the northeast of Forfar: a cottage stands beside the gate, and a footpath leads across a field of flax to the priory – a romantic sight. The high cloister walls – almost defensive in their appearance – stand in front, the tall broach spire of the church behind; a broach spire, unusual in Scotland, as though we were in the limestone belt of Lincolnshire and Rutland. This spire crowns a much more ancient tower; indeed its base is said to have been built by King Nectan of the Picts, as a thankoffering for his baptism by St Boniface in the eighth century – though nothing else of his very early church survives. The upper part of the tower is said to be pre-Conquest. In any case, it was round this ancient tower that the Augustinians built their church and cloister in the twelfth and thirteenth centuries. There are very early doorways in the base of the tower, some mediaeval tombs and other features of interest – but very little to remind us that anything existed within the cloisters. Nothing seems to have happened here since the sixteenth century. It is a matchless spot.

The priory was founded by King Malcolm IV *c.* 1153.

SADDELL ABBEY

Cistercian

The incredible remoteness of Kintyre: how many realize that the shortest crossing from Britain to Ireland is from the Mull of Kintyre, a mere twelve miles? Saddell is some eight miles north of Campbelltown, along the Carradale road, and from here there are splendid views across to Arran.

Saddell Abbey was founded for Cistercian monks *c.* 1160 by Somerled, Lord of the Isles, and his son Reginald, and was the daughter house of Mellifont in County Louth. It is a most romantic spot, but very little survives of any of its buildings.

However, close to the entrance stands what is known as the 'bus shelter' – built to protect no less than eleven very fine mediaeval grave slabs. They stand there, as Mr Anthony New has described them, 'like a petrified bus queue'. They are magnificent. There is a monk in his habit holding a book, his head, alas, missing; a priest in his chasuble with a chalice; a number of slabs carved with decorative emblems, and, at the end of the queue, there are three colossal knights; one has the tiny figure of a priest for company – with another tiny figure at his feet to unbuckle his spurs. Under the patronage of the Lords of the Isles there were established several schools of stone carvers in the neighbourhood, *c.* 1350–1500; one must have been at Saddell.

A small fragment of the north transept of the church, a small fragment of the quire: no more survives of the aisleless building. It is just possible to make out the site of the cloister, with the remains of the refectory undercroft on the south side. The community, never large, seems to have dwindled in the fifteenth century, and to have died out in the early sixteenth. The abbey with its endowments was then annexed to the Bishopric of Argyll; Bishop Hamilton used much of the monastic stone to build Saddell Castle early in the sixteenth century. This is still a delightful feature of Saddell Bay, and adds to the romance of the place.

ST ANDREWS – BLACKFRIARS

Dominican

A delightful fragment of the Dominican church stands in South Street, in the forecourt of Madras College (with its handsome nineteenth-century Jacobean front). Apsidal, and facing north into the street, it must represent a chapel of the church. There are beautiful traceried windows, still retaining their simple tracery, and apart from the apse itself the building retains its sexpartite vault and piscina. The friary was founded in 1274, but the church was largely rebuilt in the early sixteenth century. Although the buildings were burned by the Reformers in 1547, the friars remained here till 1559.

ST ANDREWS CATHEDRAL

Augustinian

We ought to arrive at St Andrews by sea: the coast of Fife, with its many small fishing villages, each with its little harbour, is one of the pleasures of Scotland, and, unsuspected by many visitors who know only the fashionable town with its elegant shops, the great university and the celebrated golf course, St Andrews has its little harbour, too. Little visited, and little known, it is just below the east end of the cathedral, within a stone's throw of the high precinct wall; we should arrive here, walk slowly along the harbour wall, and absorb the view. We shall see St Rule's tower, the lofty pinnacles of the east end of the cathedral, the solitary pinnacle of the west end, a little farther round the spire of St Salvator's College, the precinct wall fortified by its projecting round towers, and, to right and left, the houses of the city grouped all around, all solid stone and pantiles. If it is morning, the sun from the east will perhaps illuminate the buildings with brilliant light; if it is evening, they will stand out stark, silhouetted against the western sky.

But we shall probably arrive by road – and this has its rewards, too: the West Port, the sixteenth-century city gate, leads into South Street. Here are the fine shops, the mediaeval parish kirk. Market Street is parallel and, beyond, North Street is parallel again. Here are university buildings, and St Salvator's College, many charming houses, and, just behind the street in its little secluded courtyard, All Saints' Episcopal Church, with its beautiful, numinous interior. Parallel again is The Scores, which at one end leads to the Royal and Ancient Clubhouse, at the other to the ruins of the castle. The Scores, North Street and South Street all converge at the east end of the town, at the west front of the cathedral.

St Rule (alias St Regulus) is said to have brought a relic of St Andrew back from Greece in the eighth century, and to have founded a monastery to guard it. The Bishopric, originally founded at Abernethy in Perthshire, was transferred to St Andrews in 908, and the Augustinian priory was founded in 1133. St Rule's Church, with its remarkable lofty tower (108 feet high) probably dates from the late eleventh or early twelfth century, and was the original cathedral, the original priory church. Tower and surviving roofless choir are the original church; in the twelfth century a nave to the west and a sanctuary to the east were added, but these have disappeared. This precious little church with its wondrous tower stands to the southeast of the cathedral.

The cathedral was in its day the largest church in Scotland, as befitted the Metropolitan see – St Andrews was raised to an Archbishopric in 1472. It is tragic to stand at the west front today and survey what is left: the east gable with its lofty twin pinnacles and east window bereft of its tracery, the solitary lofty pinnacle of the west front, the wall of the south aisle of the nave, the west wall of the south transept – otherwise but a few stumps of pillars; all else is gone. Adjoining south aisle and south transept the line of the cloister court can be seen, but there is so little left of claustral buildings: only on the east side the Early English triple-arched entry to the chapter house, and the somewhat earlier entrance to the slype stand in an empty wall. A museum occupies what is called the Prior's House, and this contains some wonderful early carved crosses, and the very important and intriguing sarcophagus, dating from the late eighth or early ninth century. Its provenance is mysterious, as is its purpose; it could have been used as a reliquary for the relic of St Andrew.

The reformers and the looters have so successfully destroyed so much of the once-great church that there are all too few architectural features on which to comment. We know that building went on apace during the second half of the twelfth century: there are round-headed windows at the east end, and late Norman interlacing in the south transept. There are Early English windows in the south wall, and we know that a great storm in 1275 destroyed the west end of the nave. A fragment of the rebuilt west front is still standing – the sumptuous doorway with its elegant blind arcading above, and one flying buttress. From this we may get some idea of the Early English work here.

But all is laid low, and rows and rows and rows of gravestones occupy much of the monastic site. There is something forbidding in this Scottish passion for gravestones; but they have their pathos, and sometimes their humour. 'In memory of Allan Robertson,' reads one, 'who died 1st September 1857 aged 44 years. He was greatly esteemed for his personal worth, and for many years was distinguished as the Champion Golfer of Scotland.'

SWEETHEART ABBEY

Cistercian

'Monument closed. Custodian away on holiday. Reopening Wednesday 29th October.' There is a wonderful remoteness, an inconsequential elusiveness about this delightful part of Scotland. In fact there was no Wednesday, 29 October in 1987, when the author visited Sweetheart. Nearby, the small tea shop had a notice: 'Season ends Sunday October 27.' Bad luck again: there was no Sunday, 27 October in

1987 either. Tea or no tea, custodian or no custodian, it was possible to climb over the low wall which surrounds the abbey, and absorb its splendour.

Sweetheart is one of the most complete monastic churches to survive in Scotland, thanks to the enterprise of local worthies in the eighteenth century. But all the monastic buildings have disappeared. Only the incredible precinct wall, built of granite boulders four feet in diameter, still stands upright and surrounds much of the monastic precinct.

Sweetheart Abbey was founded in 1273 by the Lady Devorgilla, widow of John, Lord Balliol (founder of Balliol College, Oxford) who died in 1269. His heart she kept in a casket, and it was buried with her body in Sweetheart Abbey on her death in 1289. Sweetheart was a daughter of Dundrennan. The church with its lofty tower dominates the little village of New Abbey, and is built of warm red stone. It is of special interest architecturally as having been built in the early fourteenth century, a barren time for church building in Scotland; Sweetheart was the last Cistercian house to be founded in the country. It is a pleasure to stand in its nave, so remarkably complete with its arcades and clerestory, gaze up at the central tower, still poised upon its crossing arches, and enjoy the varied and elegant tracery which so amazingly survives in many windows.

TORPHICHEN PRECEPTORY

Hospitaller

This was the preceptory of the Knights of St John of Jerusalem, the Knights Hospitallers, and was founded in 1153. It was the mother house of the Order in Scotland, the equivalent of the Priory Church of the Order at Clerkenwell in London. It has lost its choir, its nave was rebuilt as a Church of Scotland parish kirk in the eighteenth century, but the transepts and tower survive – indeed, with its fortified tower and exceedingly high transepts the building looks more like a castle than a church. Perhaps this is appropriate for an Order of Knights.

What survives at Torphichen is impressive and unusual: tower and transepts are early thirteenth century, spacious and vaulted; and commodious upper rooms were added in the early sixteenth century. A circular stone staircase in the tower leads up to the rooms above, in tower and transepts, where an exhibition is on display to illustrate the work of the Hospitallers.

As in any other monastic foundation, there was a cloister court, surrounded by the usual claustral buildings here on the north side of the church, where the foundations are marked out, but little survives, and nothing at all of the chancel. The survival of the preceptorial crossing, however, is of great interest and importance in the religious and monastic history of Scotland – just as its silhouette of immense saddleback tower and awe-inspiring, lofty transepts is so memorable architecturally.

WHITHORN PRIORY

Premonstratensian

Whithorn is a small town in Galloway. Its main street is wide and descends gently: its houses and shops, though forming an agreeable ensemble, seem of no particular interest – but then, at the bottom, there appears an arched entrance, modest enough, but somehow important, clearly mediaeval for all the sash windows and stucco. Above the arch is a heraldic cartouche of the Royal Arms of Scotland.

The archway leads into an enclosed churchyard. On the left stands what appears to be small roofless mediaeval chapel, and ahead the much grander parish kirk, a typical somewhat forbidding building of 1822; on the right is a museum. A notice at the gate announces 'Church of Scotland – Whithorn Priory': the list of the services, and the name of the minister follow. How can this be – this inconsequential roofless chapel? Whithorn Priory?

But not only is this all that remains of a Premonstratensian priory, this was also the mediaeval cathedral of the Bishop of Galloway. What we see is merely the very ancient aisleless nave, with a couple of Norman doorways, a Gothic window or so. There is, it seems, little to see. But it is an historic spot – the very cradle of Scottish Christianity. The priory was founded *c.* 1175, on the site of a monastic house founded by St Ninian *c.* 400. The little aisleless church was extended in the thirteenth century: aisled transepts, an aisled chancel, a large Lady Chapel on the south side of the chancel; but only the crypt of some of this survives, and the crypt key must (normally) be obtained from the museum (where, incidentally, there is a wonderful display of ancient crosses).

COLLINS GUIDE TO RUINS

This still is not all: three miles to the southeast is the Isle of Whithorn – so called; it is, in fact, a peninsula, the southernmost village in Scotland. Along the quayside, where small boats and fishing craft tie up, there is a path leading to a gate; through this, and a swift walk over the grassy headland leads to St Ninian's Chapel, where pilgrims to his shrine at Whithorn would turn in to pray on landing here. It is a very early building on the site of his *Candida Casa*, the little white house built here towards the end of the fourth century. Nearby, a mile or so to the west, on the rocky seashore, is St Ninian's Cave, where Ninian the solitary first established himself in quiet seclusion to pray and wait. Ninian was born nearby, himself a Celt of royal blood. He journeyed to Rome, was consecrated bishop, and returned to his native land, the first apostle of Scotland.

This is a very remote part of Scotland. As we stand on the headland we can look across to the west and see the misty outline of the Isle of Man – and, perhaps a boat speeding thereto. It is full of shoppers. For the inhabitants of Galloway Douglas provides the best shops nearby, and, incidentally, the nearest branch of Marks and Spencer.

GLOSSARY

Abbey — Monastic church ruled by an abbot or abbess.

Alien — Abbey or priory dependent on mother house overseas.

Ambulatory — Processional walk round apsidal or square east end, behind the high altar.

Anchorite — Solitary religious person.

Apse — Semi-circular or polygonal east end of church or chapel.

Ashlar — Masonry of finely finished even blocks.

Aumbry — Cupboard, usually in north wall of sanctuary, to hold the Blessed Sacrament, or sacred vessels.

Augustinian — *see* Introduction.

Baldacchino — Canopy over altar, supported on columns.

Ballflower — Petalled globelike ornament, used as decoration in early 14th century.

Baroque — Large-scale, forceful and original treatment of Renaissance architecture, associated with Vanbrugh, Hawksmoor and Archer.

Benedictine — *see* Introduction.

Boss — Carved stone at intersection of the ribs of a vault.

Box pew — Enclosed pew with door and high partitions, much favoured in 18th century.

Broach spire — Earliest type of spire, where the tower rises direct into the spire without parapet or pinnacles; the 'broach' is the sloping triangular piece of masonry connecting the angle of the square tower with the adjacent face of the octagonal spire.

Calefactorium — Warming house – only room where fire was provided.

Campanile — Free-standing bell tower.

Canons — Augustinian, Secular: *see* Introduction.

Capital — The crown of a column.

Carmelite — *see* Introduction.

Carthusian — *see* Introduction.

Cartouche — Decorative tablet for inscription or coat of arms.

Cell — Small dependent community.

Cellarer — Monk in charge of housekeeping.

Cellarium — Housekeeper's department.

Chancel — The eastern limb of a church.

Chanonrie	Canonry.
Chantry chapel	Chapel endowed for the saying of Mass for the soul of a particular person or family.
Chapter	Governing body of cathedral (Dean and Chapter) or monastery.
Chapter House	The council chamber for the Chapter.
Chevet	French term denoting the radiating chapels and ambulatory of an apsidal east end.
Chevron	Inverted 'V' ornament.
Cinquefoil	Five-leafed decoration in tracery.
Cistercian	*see* Introduction.
Clerestory	Top stage of nave or chancel, lit by windows.
Cluniac	*see* Introduction.
Coade stone	Artificial stone manufactured in the late 18th and early 19th century by the Coade family in Lambeth.
Collegiate church	Church served by college of Canons or Prebendaries.
Commandery	House of Knights Templars.
Commendator	Lay Abbot (Scotland).
Corbel	A block, usually of stone projecting from a wall to support an arch or vault.
Corinthian	*see* Orders.
Cornice	Horizontal projection at the top of a wall.
Crocket	Small carved ornament on the side of a spire or pinnacle.

Crossing	The intersection of nave, choir and transepts in a cruciform church.
Crypt	Vaulted chamber below church.
Curvilinear	Later Dec tracery of flowing pattern.
Cusp	Connecting point between the arcs in Gothic tracery, constituting trefoils, quatrefoils, etc. (q.v.)
'Dec'	The Decorated style: first half of 14th century.
Diapering	Decoration of wall surface in patterned brick or stone.
Dog-tooth	Small pyramidal carved ornament in late Norman and E.E. architecture.
Dominican	*see* Introduction.
Doric	*see* Orders.
Dorter	Monastic dormitory.
'E.E.'	The Early English style: the earliest English Gothic (13th century).
Easter Sepulchre	Carved and usually elaborately decorated recess on the north side of a sanctuary where the Blessed Sacrament was placed on Good Friday.
Fan vault	*see* Vault.
Feretory	Space (usually behind high altar) for the shrine of a saint.
Fleche	Small timber or lead-covered spire.
Flushwork	Decorative use of dressed stone in flint walling to provide (often elaborate) patterns.
Flying buttress	Buttress in the form

of an arch or demi-arch to support the thrust of a high vault.

Franciscan — *see* Introduction.

Frater — Monastic refectory.

Friar, Friary — *see* Introduction.

Frontal — Embroidered drapery to cover an altar.

Galilee — a porch, often at west end.

Geometrical — Earliest form of Dec tracery, composed of geometrical patterns.

Gilbertine — *see* Introduction.

Gothick — Fanciful 18th-century version of Gothic.

Grand montine — *see* Introduction.

Groined vault — *see* Vault.

Grisaille — Grey-white monochrome glass, adorned with enamelled patterning.

Hatchment — Corruption of 'achievement': painted board depicting a deceased person's coat of arms, displayed first on his house, then removed to a church.

Hospitaller — *see* Introduction.

Hospiticem — Guest house.

Infirmarium — Infirmary.

Ionic — *see* Orders.

Lancet — Narrow pointed arched window, characteristic of E.E. architecture.

Lavabo — Washing place.

Lierne — *see* Vault.

Minster — Loosely-used term for a major church: the cathedral at York is always known as York Minster.

Misericord — Projecting ledge on underneath of hinged seat of stall, to support the occupant standing; also a room where meat was served for aged or infirm monks.

Mitred Abbey — Abbey ruled by abbot on whom had been conferred the privilege of wearing a mitre.

Narthex — Entrance vestibule.

Nave — Western limb of a church.

Newel — Retaining pillar in circular staircase; newel staircase.

Norman — Norman architecture, the English version of Romanesque.

Novice — New member preparing to take vows – member of Novitiate.

Ogee — Design of an arch or window incorporating both convex and concave curves.

Orders — The classical orders in Greek or Roman architecture. Doric – Greek Doric: solid, often fluted, column with simple cushion capital and no base; Roman Doric: narrower column, sometimes fluted, with base and cushion capital; Tuscan Doric: a later, plain and severely designed version of Roman Doric. Ionic: elegant column, sometimes fluted, with ram's horn capital. Corinthian: graceful column, with base and elaborately carved capital of acanthus leaves.

Palladian	Architecture based on the principles of Andrea Palladio (1518–80).
Parlatorium	Parlour.
Pediment	Classical low-pitched version of the Gothic gable.
'Perp'	The Perpendicular style, the latest phase of Gothic architecture in England (c. 1350–1550).
Pilaster	Pier or pillar attached to wall.
Piscina	Recess with basin and drain, usually in south wall of sanctuary, for washing the sacred vessels.
Prebendary	Canon (q.v.); adjective, prebendal.
Preceptory	House of Knights Hospitallers.
Premonstratensian	*see* Introduction.
Presbytery	Sanctuary of church, or priest's house.
Priory	Monastic church ruled by prior or prioress; subordinate to an abbey.
Pulpitum	Stone screen dividing chancel from nave in major church.
Quatrefoil	Four-leafed decoration in tracery.
Quire	Alternative name for chancel (or choir).
Quoin	Dressed corner stone.
Refectory	Dining hall.
Reredorter	Lavatory.
Reredos	Carved or decorative screen behind altar; altarpiece.
Retrochoir	Eastern space behind high altar.

Rib vault	*see* Vault.
Rococo	Exotic, extravagant flowering of Continental Baroque – a style rarely employed in England.
Romanesque	In England usually termed 'Norman'.
Rood	Crucifix; rood loft, rood screen – loft, screen, supporting a rood.
Rotunda	Round Church.
Rustication	Large blocks of ashlar, or of rough-faced stone, with sunk joints, used in classical architecture to emphasize the base of a building or other wall space.
Sacrarium	Sacristy.
Sacrist	Monk in charge of sacristy.
Sacristy	Room for sacred vessels and vestments.
Sanctuary	Space surrounding the altar.
Saxon	Pre-Conquest English architecture.
Scriptorium	Monastic library.
Sedilia	Stone or wooden seats for the officiating priests on south side of sanctuary.
Shaft	Small column attached to pier or wall.
Slype	Narrow passage room in a monastery, usually between the transept and chapter house of the church, used as a common room by the monks (or nuns), where the rule of silence was relaxed and guests could be received.

Spandrel	The triangular space between two arches, or between an arch and an adjoining pilaster.
Springers	The base stems of a vault, springing from a pillar or wall.
Stiff-leaf	Carved foliage, typical of the E.E. style.
String course	Projecting horizontal band of masonry.
Tabernacle	Receptacle for housing Blessed Sacrament.
Tabernacle-work	Traceried decoration of wall.
Templar	*see* Introduction.
Tester	Canopy for altar or pulpit.
Three-decker	Three-tiered pulpit, with reading desk, stall and pulpit above one another.
Tierceron	*see* Vault.
Tironensian	*see* Introduction.
Tracery	Intersecting decoration of a window; *see* Curvilinear; Geometrical; Perpendicular.
Transept	The north and south extending limbs of a cruciform church.
Transitional	'Transitional Norman' – the transition from Norman to Gothic.
Trefoil	Three-leafed decoration in tracery.
Triforium	Arcaded storey above the arches and below the clerestory in a major church, often containing a gallery.
Tympanum	Space between the lintel arch in a Saxon or Norman doorway, often containing elaborate carving.
Undercroft	Crypt.
Vault	Arched covering of space in stone (or brick or wood); *barrel vault*: a vault built in one continuous arch; *groined vault*: the intersection of such vaults (Norman); *rib vault*: the simplest form of cross-vaulting – quadripartite, employing two diagonal and two transverse ribs; sexpartite, employing an extra rib springing from the centre of the wall on each side (late Norman and E.E.); *tierceron vault*: employing secondary ribs, from wall to central boss (E.E.); *lierne vault*: the use of small decorative ribs, introduced for ornamental rather than structural purposes (Dec); *fan vault*: the latest phase of Gothic vaulting, where fan-shaped panelled ribs extend in equal lengths from wall to centre of roof (Perp).
Venetian window	Palladian triple window, the central opening arched.
Vesica window	Oval window, with pointed head and foot.
Voussoirs	Wedge-shaped stones used in the construction of an arch.

INDEX